Viewing Islam: From Text to Context

Edited by
Peter Riddell

Occasional Papers in the Study of Islam
and Other Faiths Nos. 1 & 2 (2009 & 2010)

The Centre for the Study of Islam
and Other Faiths

Occasional Papers in the Study of Islam and Other Faiths
Nos. 1&2 (2009 & 2010)
ISSN 1836-9782   ISBN 978-0-9876154-0-4
© 2009, 2010 Melbourne School of Theology Press.
All rights reserved. 2016 Reprint.

Series Editor
Peter Riddell

Editor
Peter Riddell

Assistant Editor
Kathryn Simon

Production and Cover Design
Ho-yuin Chan

Publishing Services
Published by Melbourne School of Theology Press.
Thank you to Richard Shumack for his publishing services.

Centre for the Study of Islam and Other Faiths
Melbourne School of Theology
5 Burwood Highway, Wantirna, Victoria 3152, Australia.
Ph: +61 3 9881 7800, Fax: +61 3 9800 0121
csiof@mst.edu.au
www.mst.edu.au

People involved in the field of Muslim-Christian relations are welcome to submit related items to the Editor for consideration for publishing in the CSIOF Occasional Papers.

Opinions and conclusions published in the CSIOF Occasional Papers are those of the authors and do not necessarily represent the views of the Editor or the CSIOF. The Occasional Papers is purely an information medium, to inform interested parties of religious trends, discussions and debates. The Occasional Papers do not intend in any way to actively promote hatred of any religion or its followers.

CONTENTS

INTRODUCTION
Peter Riddell   5

PART ONE: TEXT

THE DEVELOPMENT OF EARLY ISLAM
ACCORDING TO THE NEO-REVISIONISTS
Daniel Janosik   15

JIHAD: WHAT DOES THE QUR'AN REALLY SAY?
Bernie Power   33

FIGHTING THE UNBELIEVERS: VARIOUS
PERSPECTIVES ON QUR'AN 9:29 BY MUSLIM
THEOLOGIANS
Denis Savelyev   47

THE KHARIJITES
John Kingsbury   65

GREATER AND LESSER JIHAD: COMPETING
OR COMPLEMENTARY PERSPECTIVES?
Peter Francis   81

PART TWO: CONTEXT
THE VISION FOR PAKISTAN: MUSLIM STATE OR
ISLAMIC STATE?
John Bales   99

A NEW DAY FOR ISLAMIST POLITICS IN
MODERN TURKEY
Richard Duncalfe   111

ISSUES AFFECTING THE RELATIONSHIP
BETWEEN ISLAM AND THE STATE IN AUSTRALIA
Richard Bath   133

IS ISLAM COMPATIBLE WITH 21ST CENTURY
WESTERN VALUES AND IDEALS?
Theo Kalmbach   157

ISLAMIC FINANCE: A POISONED CHALICE?
Peter Riddell   175

MUSLIM WOMEN IN PRAYER
Moyra Dale   183

Notes to Contributors   201

Introduction

Peter Riddell

Melbourne School of Theology

The volume of works published about Islam has greatly multiplied since the terrorist attacks on US targets in September 2001. At first view there may appear to be an over-abundance of such studies, with the vast number of such works representing dramatically different points on an ideological spectrum.

Scholarly red lines

Nevertheless, there are gaps in this vast literature. In the latter years of the first decade of the 21st century, major academic publishers have been increasingly reluctant to publish works that present critical views of Islam as core arguments. The more common output from academic publishers are the kinds of works that, while extremely valuable in many ways, tread very carefully in their portrayal of core dogmas of Islam, especially relating to scripture and prophet.

Evidence of this trend is found in Jytte Klausen's *The Cartoons That Shook the World* (Yale University Press, 2009), a study of the controversial 2005 Danish cartoons of Muhammad that aroused a violent backlash in many Muslim communities around the world. Although this work includes an excellent analysis of the cartoons controversy, showing how radical Islamic orchestration of events was key in triggering the mass demonstrations, this work also illustrates the problem: the cartoons appeared nowhere in visual form in the very publication that was dedicated to them. Eloquent justifications for their omission by the Director of Yale University Press[1] beg more questions than they answer.

Another glaring example of this problem relates to a completed and much praised PhD thesis that shall remain unidentified. It was rejected by one leading western publishing house on the grounds of

---

[1] http://yalepress.yale.edu/book.asp?isbn=9780300124729, accessed 17 January 2011.

it being "too polemical". In fact, the work is in no way polemical. It is a very rigorous academic study of a particular aspect of Islam. But it reached conclusions that were at odds with core elements of standard Islamic dogma. Clearly, the publishing house concerned was not willing to run the gauntlet of cries of protest and possible threats of litigation.

This caution on the part of academic publishing houses does not spring from a vacuum. One need look no further than J M Burr's and R O Collins' *Alms for Jihad*, initially published by Cambridge University Press in 2006 but subsequently withdrawn from circulation, with accompanying requests from the publishers to distributors and libraries to discard their copies, because of "a potential libel suit in England by Sheikh Khalid bin Mahfouz, whose charitable activities have reportedly been linked to terrorist activities, as conveyed in the book."[2] Fortunately, some libraries demonstrated their commitment to values of freedom of speech and expression by continuing to stock the work in their collections. But such legal action would inevitably take a toll on publishing houses that need to be financially viable to survive.

There are exceptions, of course, such as Ephraim Karsh's excellent *Islamic Imperialism* (Yale University Press, 2006), a rigorous study that asks some very hard questions of Islamic empires down the ages, challenging the increasingly-heard dogma that Islam did not expand by the sword, but rather brought enlightenment wherever it went. Also deserving of mention is Rodney Stark's outstanding *God's Battalions: The Case for the Crusades* (HarperOne, 2009), which has severely dented the dominant politically correct culture among recent western academia that the West should attribute all blame for Crusader history upon the Crusaders themselves, ignoring the view of the Crusades as a response to preceding centuries of Islamic imperial expansion.

Hopefully this present volume will also contribute to filling the above-mentioned gap. The aim here is both to achieve a high level of scholarly rigour and to be willing to discuss any question, regardless of potential sensitivities. The Western scholarly tradition demands no less.

---

[2] Andrew Albanese & Jennifer Pinkowski, "ALA to Libraries: Keep Alms for Jihad, Pulped in the UK", *Library Journal*, 08/23/2007,
http://www.libraryjournal.com/lj/communitylegislation/851425-270/story.csp

Contents

This volume is a reprint of Numbers 1 & 2 of the CSIOF Occasional Papers, first published in the years 2009 & 2010. The papers in this volume fall into two parts. Part One papers consider the primary Islamic textual materials with particular reference to the much-discussed topic of jihad, providing various angles on this thorny question.

Dr Daniel Janosik draws our attention initially to the findings from a relatively new stream of Islamic scholarship, that he terms Neo-Revisionists, which argues for a slow development of the text of the Qur'an from non-Muslim sources, primarily Syriac, that were adopted and incorporated into an intermediate monotheism that was neither Christian nor Jewish, but which was influenced by beliefs from both. At first it was the religion of the elite, argues Janosik, but as the Arabs became more successful and began to settle in their conquered cities, the leaders recognized that they would need to fortify their hegemony by establishing their religious beliefs, authorizing their own scriptures and supporting their own prophet. For many Christians at that time, like John of Damascus, this new religion was understood as just a heresy of Christianity with anti-Christian beliefs and a false prophet. As time went on, however, written Arabic, as well as the scripture written in Arabic, became standardized and Muhammad became established in a religion that would soon rival Christendom.

Janosik's paper seeks to reconstruct the rise of Islam, the promotion of the prophet of Islam and the development of the scripture of Islam through the use of philological tools in conjunction with historical, archaeological, numismatic, and epigraphical accounts. The conclusion may reveal a very different story for the beginnings of the Muslim faith.

In the next article, Dr Bernie Power reviews the Qur'an's teaching about *jihad*. Although the word *jihad* occurs only four times in the Qur'an, the concept is widespread, and a full list of war-terminology is given. All of the more than 160 Qur'anic verses relating to *jihad* are cited in this article. A four-stage chronology is outlined. During his time in Mecca, Muhammad had no political or military powerbase, so the Meccan verses enjoin non-violence, tolerance and forgiveness. When invited to take power in Medina, Muhammad shifted ideologically as well as geographically, and the Medinan verses reflect this. Initially Muslims were told to fight only in self-defence or when attacked. The next phase allowed attacks without provocation but under certain limits. The final stage was unconditional war against the unbelievers. This stage receives the most attention in the Qur'an. It describes the incentives given to Muslims to encourage them to fight, the methodology for *jihad*, including specific strategies for war, along with the goals and results of *jihad*. Most commentators claim that these verses abrogate or cancel out the earlier more peaceful verses. This four-phase concept is critically analysed, and an alternative is suggested. The spurious 'greater jihad, lesser jihad' saying which is widely quoted in the West is also discussed.

Denis Savelyev proceeds by conducting a survey of Muslim scholarly writings, both classical and modern, with particular reference to the controversial verse 29 of Qur'an chapter 9, which calls on believers to fight against unbelievers. In this skilful analysis, Savelyev identifies that the Muslim commentators are ultimately more concerned with the details of the *jizya* tax to be paid by non-Muslims than they are with articulating a justification for fighting the non-believers. Savelyev also reflects some of the debates among Muslim scholars regarding how to interpret key verses such as Q9:29.

The sense of the diachronic, spanning past to present, is also captured in Dr John Kingsbury's paper on the Kharijites, an early radical sect, and their legacy down the centuries culminating in today's jihadist groups. Kingsbury expertly traces the transmission of radical thinking even where there is no seeming organic link between groups across time. He also persuasively debunks the often-heard claim that radical militants are not true Muslims, concluding that they "must be considered as a legitimate expression of a multi-faceted faith."

While the Kharijites had no doubt about the meaning of *jihad*, other Muslims have debated the core meaning of the term down the ages. In the third paper, Dr Peter Francis considers the tension between so-called Greater Jihad and Lesser Jihad, exploring diverse Muslim understanding across the centuries, right up to Shaykh Tahir ul-Qadri's March 2010 London *fatwa* condemning terrorism. That particular personality is as clear as the Kharijites on the meaning of *jihad*; however, their understandings are diametrically opposed.

Such is the state of Muslim discourse on this key term in the modern world.

In Part Two the papers focus upon particular themes, countries and cultures. Nevertheless, the theme of intra-Islamic debate reflected in Part One papers continues to be prominent.

John Bales addresses the context of Pakistan, considering struggles to define the shape and identity of the nation since it came into being in 1947. Debates between liberals and Islamists are complicated by various shades and hues from other less clearly defined groups and individuals. Yet within the discourse of figures such as Maududi and Jinnah one can hear echoes of, respectively, the more literalist approaches of some of the more militant groups discussed in earlier papers and the more rationalistic approaches of anti-militant voices. Pakistan is an important country to watch for those attempting to predict the future path of the world of Islam.

Like Pakistan, Turkey struggled during most of the 20th century to define its religious, cultural and political identity following the formation of the secular republic in 1924. Richard Duncalfe combines excellent research skills and considerable lived experience in Turkey to present a very thoughtful paper on the modern nation. He gives particular attention to the emergence of new Islamist actors on the Turkish political and social stage at the turn of the 21st century. At the same time he cautions readers against interpreting Turkish expressions of Islamism as identical with those found in other parts of the Muslim world. Turkey is a special case, he argues, and one which defies stereotypical methods of analysis.[3]

After the two studies of Pakistan and Turkey, where Islam is in the majority (97% and 99% respectively), the next two papers consider specific issues relating to Islam and the West. Richard Bath surveys a broad range of events and debates that have impacted the Muslim community in Australia. The connections between the successive papers on Islam in Turkey and Australia may seem remote, yet in fact Islam is an immigrant religion to both countries – though it has a 1000-year history in Turkey and barely a 50-year history in Australia – and Turkish Islam plays a prominent role in terms of

---

[3] Duncalfe's article predates the momentous political upheavals that took place in Turkey from 2014 onwards.

Australian Islam, with the Turkish community one of the most prominent and active in Australia. A question exercising the minds of some Australians is whether the taking root of Islam in the country in present times may lead to a future time where it comes to define the nation, as is the case in present day Islamic (but formerly Greek/Armenian Christian) Turkey/Asia Minor.

Theo Kalmbach's thoughtful paper poses the much-asked question regarding the compatibility between Western and Islamic values and ideals. He is at pains to underscore the diversity of Islam – a popular mantra among scholars of varied political leanings – while at the same time reminding his readers that there are elements of unity that hold Islam together, elements that cry out for dedicated attention and analysis. Kalmbach helpfully identifies flash points and fault-lines between Islam and the West, and affirms that they "are undergirded by two radically different worldviews." But this need not necessarily lead to negative outcomes, argues Kalmbach.

In his paper on Shari'a finance, Professor Peter Riddell considers one of the most dynamic elements in Muslim *da'wa* (mission) in the modern world. Shari'a finance and Islamic banking is exploding around the world, both in Muslim-majority countries and in the West as well. Some Western Governments (such as that of the UK) promote Islamic finance as a way of attracting much-needed cash in times of economic recession. But while some Western political leaders are lured by the Islamic dollar, some scholars are warning that Islamic finance is merely a step on a journey of creeping Shari'a. They caution Western governments against seeing Islamic finance as a quick fix as they face periods of economic decline.

Dr Moyra Dale devotes the concluding article to the formal *salat* prayers of Islam that the faithful Muslim prays five times daily and that serve as the basis of Muslim life and practice. This article explores how women interact with the requirements of *salat*. It also looks further at the other parts of the prayer life of the believing Muslim - the *du'a'* prayers of supplication, and the *dhikr* prayers that bring the worshipper into meditation on God and His nature. Attention is given to how the three kinds of prayer interact, the place given to each kind of prayer, and how people experience them. The article concludes by asking how these prayers and expressions of heart-longing may be a bridge between the Muslim and Christian understandings of who God is and how He may be approached.

We hope that readers enjoy this reprint of the 2009 and 2010 issues of the CSIOF Occasional Papers. We do not expect all readers to agree with everything in these papers. But we do hope that where readers disagree, they will nevertheless allow that alternative views should be aired publicly and frankly; debates should also be encouraged. Such values represent a key part of the greatness of the modern West. A drift towards silencing of debate in recent years, with increasing militancy by "thought police", represents a trend that must be vigorously resisted for the benefit of future generations.

Melbourne, 2010 [updated 2016]

CSIOF Occasional Papers No. 1 & 2 (2009 & 2010)

PART ONE

TEXT

The Development of Early Islam According to the Neo-Revisionists

Dr Daniel Janosik

Columbia, South Carolina

The evidence emerging from a new group of scholars of Islam, whom I have termed Neo-Revisionists, seems to reveal a slow development of the Qur'an from non-Muslim sources, primarily Syriac, that were adopted and incorporated into an intermediate monotheism that was neither Christian nor Jewish, but which was influenced by beliefs from both. At first it was the religion of the elite, but as the Arabs became more successful and began to settle in their conquered cities, the leaders recognized that they would need to fortify their hegemony by establishing their religious beliefs, authorizing their own scriptures and supporting their own prophet. For many Christians at that time, like John of Damascus, this new religion was considered as a heresy of Christianity with anti-Christian beliefs and a false prophet. As time went on, however, written Arabic, as well as the scripture written in Arabic, became standardized and Muhammad became established in a religion that would soon rival Christendom.

In light of the scarcity of primary sources for the 7th century, and therefore piecing together the events according to the "media" available to us from that time, Jonathan Berkey concludes that Islam emerged slowly and probably did not begin as anything more than a monotheistic religion of the Arabs shaped through a process of dialogue with Judaism and Christianity.[1] Patricia Crone also argues for a gradual evolution of Islamic institutions as the early

---

[1] *Jonathan P. Berkey, The Formation of Islam: Religion and Society in the Near East, 600-1800* (Cambridge: Cambridge University Press, 2003) pp.7, 57.

Arab community carried out an "exodus" (*hijra*) from their homeland to the newly established garrison cities in the conquered lands.[2] This *hijra* may have been fueled by the promise of a new Arab state based on "conquest, rape and pillage",[3] or it may have been a people movement aided by the withdrawal of the Byzantine forces and the discontinuation of subsidies to the *foederati* for guarding the borders.[4] Hoyland notes that papyri and inscriptions refer to a certain date given for the *hijra*, AD 622, but they do not explain the nature of the inauguration of this movement.[5] Crone believes that this *hijra* was an exodus taken by the "muhajirun", or those who were on the exodus to a promised land, but she also concludes that this *hijra* was not from Mecca to Medina, as in the Traditional Account, but rather from Medina to the promised land of Israel.[6] She bases her conclusions on the fact that the term "muhajirun" corresponds to the Syriac term "Mahgraye", or those who take part in a hijra, or exodus. The corresponding Greek term, "Magaritai" appears in a papyrus as early as 642, and the Syriac term, "Mahgraye", also appears around that time. Crone writes that there are two notions involved in the use of the term, one linking the Arabs to the "Mahgraye" as descendents of Abraham and Hagar, and therefore also called "Hagarenes", but also ascribing to these same Arabs a term describing their participation in an "exodus" or "hijra", and therefore known as the "muhajirun", or those who take part in the hijra.[7] The significance of this use of the

---

[2] see Patricia Crone and Michael Cook, *Hagarism: The Making of the Islamic World* (Cambridge: Cambridge University Press, 1977), p. 9, and Robert Hoyland, *Seeing Islam as Others Saw it: a Survey and Evaluation of Christianity Jewish, and Zoroastrian Writings on Early Islam* (Princeton, N.J: Darwin Press, 1997) pp. 547-8.

[3] Martin Bright, "The Great Koran Con Trick", *The New Statesman*, December 10, 2001p. 3, referring to Patricia Crone's assessment in *Meccan Trade and the Rise of Islam*.

[4] Yehuda Nevo and Judith Koren, *Crossroads to Islam: The Origins of the Arab Religion and the Arab State* (Amherst, New York: Prometheus, 2003), pp. 89-98. The *foederati* were Arab allies of the Byzantine forces who were paid a subsidy to guard the border lands. When the subsidies were paid, they acted as protectors of the empire. However, when the subsidies stopped, the disgruntled soldiers often took out their frustrations by attacking their former employers.

[5] Hoyland, *Seeing Islam as Others Saw it*, pp. 547-548. In fact, the attachment of the hijra to Muhammad and his escape to Medina is part of the late 8th century traditional literary account.

[6] Crone, *Hagarism*, p. 9.

[7] Crone, *Hagarism*, pp. 8-9. Also see Ibn Warraq, "Introduction", in *The Origins of the Koran: Classic Essays on Islam's Holy Book*, Saadi, Abdul-Massih. "Nascent Islam in the Seventh Century Syriac Sources." Chap. in *The Qur'an in Its Historical Context*(New York: Prometheus Books, 1998), pp. 29-30, and Abdul-Massih Saadi, "Nascent Islam in the Seventh Century

term is to demonstrate that the Islamic religion did not rise "full blown" until much later, perhaps in the time of Abd al-Malik. Therefore, the use of the terms "Muslim", "Islamic", or "Islam" would be inappropriate in the mid-7th century. Indeed, the first recorded use of the term "Islam" is the inscription in the Dome of the Rock, dated around 691-692,[8] while the first recorded use of the term "Muslim" by a believer is AD 741,[9] and AD 775 for a non-Muslim.[10] The preferred term used by the early Muslims was *"mu'minun"*, or believer, and is found 32 times in the Constitution of Medina,[11] though most of the 7th century non-Muslim witnesses of the Arabic conquests would not attribute any religious appellations to the "godless Saracens" that they encountered.[12] At this point some may want to point out that the term "Moslem" is used 98 times in the chronicle of John of Nikiu, for example, which is said to have been written around 690. However, the earliest copy of John's chronicle is from a 1602 Ethiopic translation of an earlier Arabic translation which, like the original Greek and Coptic manuscript, is lost.[13] Therefore, it would have been very easy to have replaced the original terms like "Ishmaelite", or "Saracen", or "Mahgraye" with the term "Muslim", even though the latter term probably had not come into common usage until the late 8th

---

Syriac Sources", chap. in *The Qur'an in Its Historical Context*, Routledge Studies in the Qur'an (London: Routledge, 2008), p. 218. Saadi even says, "The unprecedented name, Mhaggraye, is provocative because it provides the greatest evidence for their self-identification as immigrants (muhajirun in Arabic). In other words, the name Immigrants (muhajirun) implies that the Arabs had arrived to stake a claim on, occupy, and then inherit the land. The Syriac writers, reporting and repeating what they were hearing rather than inventing a historical event, merely Syriacized this native Arabic name."

[8] Crone, *Hagarism*, pp. 8-9.

[9] Hoyland, "The Content and Context of Early Arabic", p. 78.

[10] Nevo, Crossroads to Islam, p. 235, n.82. Also Hoyland, *Seeing Islam as Others Saw it*, p. 156. John of Damascus only used the terms "Ishmaelite", "Hagarene", or "Saracen", and this was in the middle of the 8th century.

[11] Hoyland, *Seeing Islam as Others Saw it*, p. 548. It should be noted that the existence of the Constitution of Medina cannot be verified until the 9th century, since it is first mentioned in Ibn Ishaq's *Sirat*.

[12] Hoyland, *Seeing Islam as Others Saw it*, p. 71. This quote is from Sophronius, who wrote around AD 634.

[13] Hoyland, *Seeing Islam as Others Saw it*, p. 152.

century.[14] This practice of substitution was apparently often used,[15] and is quite natural, for we also tend to refer to the "Muslims" in the time of Muhammad when the historical data tells us that the term was probably not used until 140 years later.

The Early Formation of Islam according to the Neo-Revisionists

What can we say, then, about the early development of Islam? On the one hand, the earlier skeptics led by Wansbrough and Crone, want to postulate, in the absence of documentary evidence, that "Mecca was not Muhammad's birthplace or the Hijaz Islam's home, that the Quran was not compiled in the seventh century or written in Arabic, and even that Muhammad and the Arab conquests were a later invention."[16] On the other hand, Hoyland argues that Islamic practices, which can be traced through the early non-Muslim sources and documentary evidence, are present early on. There is a new calendar dated from AD 622, the Muhajirun appear, written Arabic is used and their ruler is called the commander of the believers and serves a god named "Allah."[17] Jeremy Johns adds that coins, building inscriptions, tombstones and traveller's graffiti can be used to trace out the early growth and development of a new religious community.[18] Hoyland concludes that there is enough evidence to "infer that the newcomers did possess a distinctive cult."[19] Indeed, it is significant that the Christians in the 7th and early 8th century did not consider the religious beliefs of the Arabs to be a different religion altogether, but rather they viewed it as more of a cult or a heresy of Christianity. This is exactly what John of Damascus (c.675-c.750) concludes in

---

[14] see Nevo, *Crossroads to Islam*, p. 134, especially note 118, where Nevo says that "Hoyland (1997) consistently translates mhaggare as "Muslim" in order to differentiate it from tayyaye, which he translates "Arab."

[15] Nevo, *Crossroads to Islam*, p. 7.

[16] Robert Hoyland, "New Documentary Texts and the Early Islamic State", *Bulletin of SOAS*, 3 vols., 69, 395-416 (UK: School of Oriental and African Studies, 2006), pp. 403-4.

[17] Hoyland, "New Documentary Texts and the Early Islamic State", p. 396.

[18] Jeremy Johns, "Archaeology and the History of Early Islam: The First Seventy Years", *Journal of the Economic and Social History of the Orient* (Brill Academic Publishers) 46, 4 (2003), p. 414.

[19] Hoyland, "New Documentary Texts and the Early Islamic State", p. 404.

the middle of the 8th century.[20] His portrayal of Islam is that of an outgrowth of the pernicious Christian heresy, Arianism, and his apologetic approach is designed to help Christians deal with Muhammad as a "false prophet" and the false beliefs of the Ishmaelites whom he says will usher in the "anti-Christ."[21]

Muhammad and the "Full Light of History"

Was knowledge of the prophet Muhammad (570-632) present from the mid-7th century, or did it gradually evolve along with the religion? A British Muslim writer, Ziauddin Sardar, proudly pronounced that "The Life of Mohammad is known as the Sira and was lived in the full light of history."[22] Even in John's time, however, the first *sira* by Ibn Ishaq had not yet been written. It is possible, since Ibn Ishaq died in 767, that some other written stories were already circulating about Muhammad during John's life time. These were later collected by writers like Ibn Hisham (d. 833), who states that he incorporated a recension of Ibn Ishaq's biography in his own book. These are, however, all over 130 years after the death of Muhammad. Also, if Muhammad lived in the "full light of history", why do we have virtually nothing from Muslim sources pertaining to Muhammad before the time of Caliph Abd al-Malik (r. 685-705), nearly 70 years after the death of Muhammad? This is one of the central problem areas raised by the Neo-Revisionists.

Some Neo-Revisionists, like Yehuda Nevo, even doubt whether Muhammad was an actual historic figure, for he can only be traced back historically to around 72/691 when his name appears on a coin minted by Abd al-Malik.[23] Nevo also believes that the "very

---

[20] Jonathan P. Berkey, *The Formation of Islam*, pp. 74, 93.

[21] Daniel Sahas, *John of Damascus on Islam* (Leiden: E.J. Brill, 1972), p. 133.

[22] Bright, "The Great Koran Con Trick", pp. 1-2.

[23] Nevo, as well as Hoyland, believe the earlier numismatic reference to a Muhammad as prophet, in 687, probably refers to the governor of Azerbaijan, Muhammad ibn Marwan, or to a religious prophet at that time, Muhammad Ibn al-Hanafiyyah, who was also known as the *"mahdi."* Nevo also points out that Basheer argues that "many events in the life of the Prophet reported in the Muslim sources are in fact retrojections into the past of later incidents, e.g., some from the life of the mid -to late 7th century "prophet" Muhammad ibn al-

few passing references to him in earlier literary sources should be regarded as later interpolations by copiers who knew the Traditional Account."[24] In other words, it is difficult to explain how the central figure in a wildly successful religious conquest could avoid the "full light of history" until the time he is needed as a focal point in a religion that is also the basis for the government.

On the other hand, Michael Cook concludes that the non-Muslim sources give enough of a picture of the first 70 years to indicate that Muhammad not only existed, but that he was a leader in a movement that started around AD 622.[25] Even Patricia Crone, who once said that Muhammad did not exist as an historical figure, has changed her mind enough to say that "Mohammad is clearly an individual who changed the course of history", but she also points out that "we do not know how much of the Islamic tradition about him is true."[26] Part of the problem is that the biographies, as well as the other literary material written about Muhammad by Muslims in the late 8th and 9th centuries, were mostly constructed from the only literary source that may have existed, at least in part, before the end of the 7th century, which was the Qur'an. In the next section we will consider the development of the Qur'an, but suffice it to say at this point, that if the earliest biographical literature on Muhammad were derived from exegetical explanations of the obscure narratives in the Qur'an, and then parts of the Qur'an were written in order to give a "history" to a new religious movement, then how do we get at any "kernel of truth", much less an understanding of which events were played out under the "full light of history"?

Hoyland also finds it very curious that, aside from the early non-Muslim sources, "before AH 72 the archaeological record is strangely silent about Islam", as well as Muhammad and the Qur'an.[27] In fact, it really is not until 691 that we have a firm archaeological attestation to Muhammad on a coin minted by Abd

---

Hanafiyyah." See Nevo, *Crossroads to Islam*, p. 6 and Hoyland, *Seeing Islam as others saw it*, p. 550, n. 24.

[24] Nevo, *Crossroads to Islam*, pp. 10-11.

[25] Warraq, "Introduction", p. 27.

[26] Francis Robinson and Ira Lapidus, *The Cambridge Illustrated History of the Islamic World* (London: Cambridge University Press, 1996), p. 10. See also Patricia Crone, "What do we actually know about Muhammad?" published on Open Democracy News Analysis (http://www.opendemocracy.net), June 10, 2008 (first published August 31, 2006).

[27] Hoyland, *Seeing Islam as others saw it*, pp. 549-550.

al-Malik, as well as the inscription bearing Muhammad's name in the Dome of the Rock. Hoyland offers that "it is of course true that only with the passage of time does a man become a hero and a book authoritative",[28] but that does not account for the abrupt way that Muhammad suddenly "appears" on the Arab scene. Is it possible, then, that Abd al-Malik utilized Muhammad as a "propaganda weapon"[29] in his bid to make his new government more legitimate through an appeal to a religion, a prophet and a scripture?

John of Damascus considered Muhammad to be an historical figure when he was writing about him in the 730's,[30] but how much of his image of Muhammad had been created by the narratives that were probably circulating at that time[31] as well as the strong propaganda that had been in place at least from the time of Abd al-Malik? John called Muhammad a "false prophet" and he called the religion of his followers a "heresy." He also ridiculed the so-called writings that came down to Muhammad from heaven, which were later called the Qur'an. It is to these documents that we now turn.

The Development of the Qur'an

What if the Qur'an is not divine? R. Stephen Humphreys emphasizes that the Qur'an is the document that gives Islam its *raison d'etre*. If the Qur'an is not directly from God, then it is a human document; and since it claims a perfect, divine source, human authorship would undercut its authority. In fact, Humphreys states boldly that "if the Qur'an is a historical

---

[28] Hoyland, *Seeing Islam as others saw it*, pp. 549-550.

[29] Hoyland, "New Documentary Texts and the Early Islamic State", pp. 396-7.

[30] Ibn Warraq, "Koranic Criticism: 700 C.E. to 825 C.E.", *New English Review* (World Encounter Institute, Nashvillle, TN) http://www.newenglishreview.org/custpage.cfm/frm/11036/sec_id/11036 (October 2007).

[31] Hoyland mentions a papyrus from the late Umayyad period that contains some biographical material on the prophet. See Hoyland, *Seeing Islam as others saw it*, p. 545. He also says that the earliest theological writing is not documented before AD 718 (p. 546).

document, then the whole Islamic struggle of fourteen centuries is effectively meaningless."[32]

The Traditional Account says that the oral revelation given to Muhammad over a 23 year period was crystallized in the written Qur'an in the time of Uthman, 20 years after Muhammad's death. The early Revisionists and later Neo-Revisionists,[33] however, interpret the development very differently. Andrew Rippin, in the preface to Wansbrough's book, *Quranic Studies*, argues that "the emergence of a fixed and explicit script for the Arabic language suggests a considerably longer time frame than the community's account, on its surface, seems to allow."[34] In other words, the development of the Arabic script itself was still too indeterminate for a fixed text to be present in the time of Uthman, barely 20 years after Muhammad's death. Rippin contends that there is far too much evidence showing that, while Arabic as a written language was in limited use in the 7th century, as a consonantal language it was still too much in flux with too many variant readings for it to be considered fixed and authoritative until later in the 8th century after vowels and diacritical marks used to identify otherwise identical letters came into existence. By the end of the 8th century, with the standardization of Classical Arabic, the collection of material could finally be put together in a cohesive whole with a fixed text. However, some of the Neo-Revisionists contend that by that time a number of the original words, some of them possibly transliterations from Syriac words, were no longer understood by those compiling the Qur'an.[35] In other words, if the Qur'an could not have been

---

[32] Toby Lester, "What is the Koran?", chap. in *What the Koran Really Says: Language, Text, and Commentary* (New York: Prometheus Books, 2002), p. 110.

[33] Revisionists, like John Wansbrough, Patricia Crone, Michael Cook, Andrew Rippin and G.W. Hawting, were prominent in the 1970s and 1980s and tried to construct a more feasible understanding of early Islam through a textual-critical approach which viewed history as something that could be "scientifically" studied. Those whom I call Neo-Revisionists, like Robert Hoyland, Yehuda Nevo, Jeremy Johns, Sidney Griffith, Reuven Firestone, Christoph Luxenberg, Gerd-R Puin, Karl-Heinz Ohlig, and Kevin Van Bladel, have corrected some of the shortcomings of the Revisionists and bring to bear a much more scientifically accurate interpretation of the first two centuries of Islam based on a higher level of investigative research using a type of historical forensics, which involves the study of archaeological sites, epigraphic and numismatic material and 7th century non-Muslim eyewitness written accounts.

[34] John Wansbrough, *Quranic Studies: Sources and Methods of Scriptural Interpretation* (New York: Prometheus Books, 2004), p. xv.

[35] Toby Lester, "What Is the Koran?", chap. in *What the Koran Really Says: Language, Text, and Commentary* (New York: Prometheus Books, 2002), p. 110. Rippin even contends that to this

written in Arabic in the 7th century, and indeed, if some of it came from other religious sources, then it could not have been divine, or God's perfect book from heaven.

Rippin goes on to point out that even in the traditions of the Muslims there are "elements such as the fixing of the Arabic script, the establishment of written formats of manuscripts, and the codification of the variant readings."[36] However, the Traditional Account compresses all of these things within the time frame of Muhammad's death to the finalization of the Qur'an under Uthman's direction twenty years later. Rippin regards this compressed time scale as "quite anachronistic" since it would not account for the steps that would be necessary for a "full meaning" of the "Qur'an" to be fulfilled. In other words, the creation of a written text under Uthman is considered an "anachronistic element" because, for one thing, the "form of the Arabic script in early manuscripts is far too ambiguous to have accomplished the purpose of unifying the reading of the text."[37] Among other things, this would indicate that the fragments or "Qur'anic material" dated to the end of the 7th century and into the first half of the 8th century may simply be religious passages that later made their way into the final Qur'an. After all, a number of these fragmentary writings and inscriptions left on rocks merely give testimony to a monotheistic faith, which could easily fit a Jewish or Christian framework. It was not until the time of Abd al-Malik that an intentional pattern of scriptural material appears which distinguishes the beliefs as being neither Jewish nor Christian, yet somehow related to the two.[38]

Like many Revisionists and Neo-Revisionists,[39] Yehuda Nevo concludes that the Qur'an is a late compilation of a number of

---

day about 20% of the Qur'an is still considered "unreadable", even by Muslim scholars themselves. Christoph Luxenberg also comes to the same conclusion: "In spite of all these efforts one would not be far from the truth if one were to estimate the proportion of the Koran that is still considered unexplained today at about a quarter of the text." See Christoph Luxenberg, *The Syro-Aramaic Reading of the Koran: A Contribution to the Decoding of the Language of the Koran* (Berlin: Verlag Hans Schiler, 2007, p. 108).

[36] Wansbrough, *Quranic Studies*, p. xv.

[37] Wansbrough, *Quranic Studies*, p. xv.

[38] Wansbrough, *Quranic Studies*, p. xv.

[39] Nevo mentions Schacht and Wansbrough specifically, but Crone, Cook, Mingana, Rippin, Hawting and others could be added to the list.

assorted literary and scriptural sources, and therefore the canonization could not have taken place before the end of the 2nd century AH or early in the 3rd. "This conclusion", he says, "is supported by an analysis of extant rock inscriptions and an examination of the references to the Arab religion in the works of the peoples with whom they came in contact."[40] John Wansbrough also believes that the Qur'an and supporting literature seems to have grown out of sectarian controversies in the late 8th to early 9th centuries, almost 200 years after the fact, and then "projected back" onto an invented Arabian point of origin.[41] He indicates that the process may have been more "educative rather than merely communicative" and concludes that

> a concomitant homogeneity of subject-matter is reflected in the overlapping of genres: poetry placed within a narrative frame, prose relieved by poetic insertions both as exegesis and ornatus, juridical and lexical problems solved by reference to scripture, scriptural problems solved by reference to jurisprudence and lexicography, all with approximately the same end in view: historical description of a situation two centuries earlier.[42]

In other words, according to Wansbrough, the Qur'an is used to explain the sira literature and the hadith, and the sira literature and the hadith are used in order to make sense of the Qur'an. This close correlation indicates that both genres developed at the same time. Wansbrough also seems to indicate that the earlier chancery language, used for communication, politics and business, was quite different from what became Classical Arabic in the late 8th century. Thus, he concludes that the chancery Arabic developed first and got its real boost under Abd al-Malik when he promoted Arabic as the language of the empire. In time it would be developed poetically and scripturally, with the culmination being the Qur'an at the end of the 8th century or early 9th century.[43] Toby Lester, in his article called "What is the Koran?" writes that Wansbrough's conclusion

---

[40] Nevo, *Crossroads to Islam*, p. 11.

[41] see Warraq, "Introduction", p. 24. Ibn Warraq also states that Wansbrough argued that "Islam emerged only when it came into contact with and under the influence of Rabbinic Judaism."

[42] Wansbrough, *Quranic Studies*, p. 90.

[43] Wansbrough, *Quranic Studies*, pp. 85-91.

as to why no Islamic source material from the first century survived is that "it never existed."[44]

Patricia Crone also says that there is no hard evidence for the existence of the Qur'an "in any form before the last decade of the seventh century."[45] Even the verses found inscribed in the Dome of the Rock in Jerusalem (AD 691) attest only to the presence of material similar to verses found in the Qur'an. However, they display minor variations from the standard text, and Crone says that the existence of these verses "does not of course give any indication of the literary form in which these materials normally appeared at the time."[46] In other words, the inscriptions could very well be indications of an early attempt to express the developing beliefs of the Ishmaelites. After all, as Crone points out, the earliest reference to a book called the "Qur'an", outside the Islamic literary tradition, is from a dialogue between an Arab and the monk at Bet Hale in the late Umayyad period.[47]

On the other hand, if the Qur'an was not fully canonized until at least the end of the 8th century, almost 165 years after Muhammad's death, what do we do about these earlier inscriptions and textual fragments of the "Qur'an"? Do they not prove that the Qur'an was present in the 7th century? Rippin believes that the fragments are inconclusive and states that "the simple existence of written portions of the Qur'an in manuscript form, for example, does not tell us the full picture of the history of the text any more than the traditional collection stories or the language and structure of the text itself do."[48] In other words, the earlier fragments may have been gathered later into the final canonized Qur'an, but that does not mean that the Qur'an as we know it today first existed as a perfect, completed form in the days of Muhammad. Rippin also points out that the evidence does not support a "canonized closed text" in the first 50 years after Muhammad's death. First of all, he

---

[44] Toby Lester, "What Is the Koran?", chap. in *What the Koran Really Says: Language, Text, and Commentary* (New York: Prometheus Books, 2002), p. 122.

[45] Crone, *Hagarism*, p. 3.

[46] Crone, *Hagarism*, p. 18.

[47] Crone, *Hagarism*, p. 18. It is important to note that the Islamic literary tradition dates to the late 8th century, **after** the dialogue of the Arab and the monk at Bet Hale.

[48] Wansbrough, *Quranic Studies*, xvii

says that there were too many contradictory texts floating around in the late 7th and early 8th centuries. It is not until the end of the 8th century that a consistent text can be accounted for.[49] What are the other fragments and variants, then? Some of them may be from earlier Christian liturgy translated into an early Arabic script by Christian missionaries trying to reach their Arabic neighbors. Some may have been translations of the Jewish Psalms and commentaries into Arabic from a Syriac text. Some may have been early poetry to the monotheistic God who would shortly be known as the Allah of Islam. Claude Gilliot even believes that parts of the Qur'an may have come from a Syriac form of the Diatessaron, an early Greek compilation of a harmony of the gospels.[50]

Robert Hoyland is not comfortable with this assessment and says that it is not necessary to believe that because there are variants in the inscriptions that the Qur'an was not necessarily standardized before the end of the 7th century. He goes on to say that

> Much has been made of these adaptations or deviations from the standard text of the Qur'an, often regarded as confirmation that the latter had not yet stabilized. But though we cannot exclude the possibility that it reflects the fact that different versions of the Qur'an circulated in early times, there are many other possible, and arguably more plausible, explanations for such divergences. Sometimes they may be to serve the interests of clarity.[51]

According to Hoyland, the religious devotional vocabulary found on early inscriptions attests to the presence of a body of religious ideas circulating in the time before Abd al-Malik and the Dome of the Rock. For example, he mentions that "the three most common wishes of these texts, particularly the graffiti, are to ask for forgiveness (*ghfr*), seek compassion (*rhm*) and to make a declaration of faith (*'mn*), each of these a prominent theme and root in the Quran (*ghfr* 234 times; *rhm* 339 times; *ammana*: 537 times; *mu'min*:

---

[49] Wansbrough, *Quranic Studies*, p. xvi. See also, Toby Lester, "What is the Koran?" p. 110. See also Gilchrist's conclusion on the Samarqand and the Topkapi manuscripts in *Jam' al-Qur'an*, where he dates both manuscripts no earlier than the end of the 8th century.

[50] Claude Gilliot, "Reconsidering the Authorship of the Qur'an: Is the Qur'an Partly the Fruit of a Progressive and Collective Work?", chap. in *The Qur'an in Its Historical Context*, Routledge Studies in the Qur'an (London: Routledge, 2008), p. 99. For example, part of Q. 48:29 resembles the combined pericope in Mark 4:26-7 and Matthew 12:23 found in the Diatessaron.

[51] Hoyland, "New documentary texts and the early Islamic State", p. 407.

230 times)."[52] He also notes that Qur'anic material tended to dominate early Islamic political discussions and theological disputes. However, the religious vocabulary found etched on rocks throughout the region could also attest to Christian and Jewish presence or the development of an intermediate monotheistic faith that was developing which combined some features from both religions. For example, the phrase *bismillah*, "in the name of Allah", which is found at the beginning of all but one of the suras in the Qur'an, is very similar to the Christian Syriac phrase, *besmillah*, which was used for centuries before Muhammad.[53] Could it be that the Arabic expression came from the Syriac? It is very possible that the canonization of the Qur'an as well as the formation of Islamic theology were both still in the developmental phases in the middle of the 8th century.

Two Early Qur'anic Manuscripts

Another argument raised by Muslims in defense of an early Qur'an is that they believe two of the most famous manuscripts, the Samarqand and the Topkapi,[54] are original Uthmanic recensions

---

[52] Hoyland, "New documentary texts and the early Islamic State", p. 406.

[53] Isaac Adams states that the phrase "Bi'smi 'llahi 'r rahmani 'r-rahmin" is of Jewish origin and would have been known by the Quraish tribe and by Muhammad through a comtemporary poet named Umaiyah of Taif. See Isaac Adams, *Persia by a Persian: Being, Personal Experiences, Manners, Customs, Habits* (London: E. Stock, 1906), p. 299.

[54] The *Samarqand* manuscript is housed in the library of the Telyashayakh Mosque in Tashkent, Uzbekistan. It is written in the Kufic script, which became popular in the 8th century, and includes only Sura 2.7 through Sura 43.10. The *Topkapi* manuscript is kept in the Topkapi Museum in Istanbul, Turkey. It is also written in the Kufic script without vowel or consonant markings. It is evident that they did not originate as copies from the same place since the Topkapi codex has eighteen lines to a page and the Samarqand varies from eight to twelve lines per page. It is evident that they are two of the earliest Qur'anic manuscripts that we have, but they cannot be dated earlier than 150 years after Muhammad's death. See John Gilchrist, The Qur'an: The Scripture of Islam, Chapter 5: The Compilation of the Text of the Qur'an, Muslim Evangelicalism Resource Centre, South Africa, 1995. Arthur Jeffrey, after a thorough comparison of the script with other early Qur'ans, assigns the Samarqand codex to the early third Islamic century (early 800s). See Arthur Jeffery, "The Orthography of the Samarqand Qur'an Codex", Journal of the American Oriental Society, V. 62, pp. 175-195, 1942.

dating from the mid 7th century.⁵⁵ On the other hand, John Gilchrist argues that the Samarqand manuscript cannot be an Uthmanic original, or even a copy. He reasons that

> It is precisely the appearance of the script itself that would seem to negate such a claim. It is clearly written in Kufic script and, as we have seen, it is asking too much of an objective scholar to believe that a Qur'an manuscript written at Medina as early as the caliphate of Uthman could ever have been written in this script. Medinan Qur'ans were written in the al-Ma'il and Mashq scripts for many decades before the Kufic script became the common denominator of all the early texts throughout the Muslim world and, in any event, Kufic only came into regular use at Kufa and elsewhere in the Iraqi province in the generations following Uthman's demise.⁵⁶

Gilchrist concludes, then, that the Kufic script reached its perfection during the late 8th century when Classical Arabic was standardized, and since both the Samarqand and the Topkapi Qur'ans are written in the Kufic script, they cannot be dated any earlier than the end of the 8th century, more than 150 years after Muhammad's death.⁵⁷ In fact, he says that none of the surviving Qur'an manuscripts, "whether in whole codices or sizeable fragments, can be dated earlier than the late eighth century" since they all use scripts that were not developed until that time.⁵⁸

Sidney Griffith reminds us, however, that the late 7th century inscriptions of Quranic verses around the base of the dome in the Dome of the Rock shrine in Jerusalem are written in "beautiful Kufic" script.⁵⁹ Was this an earlier form of Kufic script than what we have in the Topkapi and Samarqand, or could these manuscripts also be dated to the end of the 7th century? It is, of course, possible that the Kufic script developed earlier. Andrew Rippin argues, however, that a 7th century Kufic script would still not make a

---

[55] Muhammad Hamidullah, *The Emergence of Islam: Lectures on the development of Islamic world-view, intellectual tradition and polity*, Publication no. 90, Islamic Research Institute, Islamabad, 1993.

[56] John Gilchrist, *Jam' Al-Qur'an -- The Codification of the Qur'an Text: A Comprehensive Study of the Original Collection of the Qur'an Text and the Early Surviving Qur'an Manuscripts* (Mondeor, South Africa: Muslim Evangelism Resource Center of Southern Africa, 1989), p. 147.

[57] Gilchrist, *Jam' Al-Qur'an -- The Codification of the Qur'an*, p. 147.

[58] Gilchrist, *Jam' Al-Qur'an -- The Codification of the Qur'an*, p. 147.

[59] Sidney Griffith, *The Church in the Shadow of the Mosque* (Princeton: Princeton University Press, 2008), p. 33.

difference. His reasoning is based on the idea that a "proto-Qur'an", even if written in a Kufic script, would still not reach a "point of authority, acceptance, and stability" which would be required for final canonization, until the end of the 8th century.[60]

Variations at San'a

One of the most fascinating recent archaeological finds that sheds light on the development of the Qur'an is the 1972 discovery of thousands of fragments of old Qur'ans in the attic of a mosque in San'a', Yemen. A few scholars, like Gerd Puin, believe that some of the fragments may even date back to the late 7th century.[61] This veritable scriptural "gold mine" should have been lauded in the Muslim press, except that many of these old texts contain variations from the standard text of the Qur'an. Toby Lester comments that "such aberrations, though not surprising to textual historians, are troublingly at odds with the orthodox Muslim belief that the Koran as it has reached us today is quite simply the perfect, timeless, and unchanging Word of God."[62] The man behind much of the controversy is Gerd Puin, a "specialist in Arabic calligraphy and Koranic paleography", who was sent by the German government to help unravel the mass of decaying documents. As he studied the crumbling manuscripts and the 35,000 pictures of the texts he noticed many minor variations as well as the presence of palimpsests, even earlier versions that had been washed off so that the parchment could be used again. From his study Puin concluded that "the Koran is a kind of cocktail of texts that were not all understood even at the time of Muhammad ... *Many of them may even be a hundred years older than Islam itself.* Even within the Islamic traditions there is a huge body of contradictory information, including a significant Christian substrate" (my emphasis).[63] In

---

[60] Wansbrough, *Quranic Studies*, p. xvii. In fact, the Dome of the Rock verses could be part of a proto-Qur'an.

[61] Lester, "What Is the Koran?" p.108.

[62] Lester, "What is the Koran?", p. 108.

[63] Lester, "What is the Koran?", p. 112. See also Ibn Warraq, *What the Koran Really Says: Language, Text, and Commentary* (New York: Prometheus Books, 2002), p. 67: "The Hijazi fragments seem to suggest that, even in the eighth century C.E., the text of the Koran was yet

other words, it would not necessarily be a problem to find an early fragment, say mid-7th century, with Qur'anic-like verses on it because it may indeed be from a pre-Islamic source, even from the gospel of Jesus or Psalms.

The best evidence we have today seems to reveal a slow development of the Qur'an from non-Muslim sources, primarily Syriac, that were adopted and incorporated into an intermediate monotheism that was neither Christian nor Jewish, but which was influenced by beliefs from both. At first it was the religion of the elite, but as the Arabs became more successful and began to settle in their conquered cities, the leaders recognized that they would need to fortify their hegemony by establishing their religious beliefs, authorizing their own scriptures and supporting their own prophet. For many Christians at that time, like John of Damascus, this new religion was understood as just a heresy of Christianity with anti-Christian beliefs and a false prophet. As time went on, however, written Arabic, as well as the scripture written in Arabic, became standardized and Muhammad became established in a religion that would soon rival Christendom.

In the end, the Revisionists and Neo-Revisionists may not agree whether the first 100 years of Islam can be reconstructed or not, but through the use of philological tools in conjunction with historical, archaeological, numismatic, epigraphical and non-Muslim documentary accounts, they are all helping to assemble pieces of the puzzle and, hopefully, will provide a more accurate picture in time.

Bibliography

Adams, Isaac. *Persia by a Persian: Being, Personal Experiences, Manners, Customs, Habits*. London: E. Stock, 1906.

Berkey, Jonathan P., *The Formation of Islam: Religion and Society in the Near East, 600-1800*. Cambridge: Cambridge University Press, 2003.

---

to be defined, and the "reading" options that the meagre *rasm* allowed had to be limited by officially recognizing only a part of them as admissible *qira'at*."

Bright, Martin. "The Great Koran Con Trick." *The New Statesman*, December 10, 2001, 1-4.

Crone, Patricia. *Meccan Trade and the Rise of Islam*. Princeton, N.J: Princeton University Press, 1987.

Crone, Patricia, and Michael Cook. *Hagarism: The Making of the Islamic World*. Cambridge: Cambridge University Press, 1977.

Gilchrist, John. *Jam' Al-Qur'an -- The Codification of the Qur'an Text: A Comprehensive Study of the Original Collection of the Qur'an Text and the Early Surviving Qur'an Manuscripts*. Mondeor, South Africa: Muslim Evangelism Resource Center of Southern Africa, 1989.

Gilchrist, John. *The Qur'an: The Scripture of Islam*. Mondeor, South Africa: Muslim Evangelism Resource Center of Southern Africa, 1995.

Gilliot, Claude. "Reconsidering the Authorship of the Qur'an: Is the Qur'an Partly the Fruit of a Progressive and Collective Work?" in *The Qur'an in Its Historical Context*. Routledge Studies in the Qur'an. 88-108. London: Routledge, 2008.

Griffith, Sidney. *The Church in the Shadow of the Mosque*. Princeton: Princeton University Press, 2008.

Hoyland, Robert. *Seeing Islam as Others Saw it: a Survey and Evaluation of Christianity Jewish, and Zoroastrian Writings on Early Islam*. Princeton, N.J: Darwin Press, 1997.

Hoyland, Robert. "New Documentary Texts and the Early Islamic State." *Bulletin of SOAS*. 3 vols. 69. 395-416. UK: School of Oriental and African Studies, 2006.

Hoyland, Robert. "The Content and Context of Early Arabic Inscriptions." *Jerusalem Studies in Arabic & Islam* 21, 3 (1997): 77-102.

Hamidullah, Muhammad. *The Emergence of Islam: Lectures on the Development of Islamic World-View, Intellectual Tradition and Polity*. Publication no. 90. Islamabad: Islamic Research Institute, 1993.

Jeffery, Arthur. "The Orthography of the Samarqand Qur'an Codex." *Journal of the American Oriental Society* 62 (1942): 175-195.

Johns, Jeremy. "Archaeology and the History of Early Islam: The First Seventy Years." *Journal Ofthe Economic and Social History of the Orient* (Brill Academic Publishers) 46, 4 (2003): 411-436.

Lester, Toby. "What Is the Koran?" Chap. in *What the Koran Really Says: Language, Text, and Commentary*. 107-128. New York: Prometheus Books, 2002.

Luxenberg, Chrisoph. *The Syro-Aramaic Reading of the Koran: A Contribution to the Decoding of the Language of the Koran*. Berlin: Verlag Hans Schiler, 2007.

Nevo, Yehuda, and Judith Koren. *Crossroads to Islam: The Origins of the Arab Religion and the Arab State*. Amherst, New York: Prometheus, 2003.

Robinson, Francis, and Ira Lapidus. *The Cambridge Illustrated History of the Islamic World*. London: Cambridge University Press, 1996.

Saadi, Abdul-Massih. "Nascent Islam in the Seventh Century Syriac Sources." Chap. in *The Qur'an in Its Historical Context*. Routledge Studies in the Qur'an. 217-222. London: Routledge, 2008.

Sahas, Daniel. *John of Damascus on Islam*. Leiden: E.J. Brill, 1972.

Wansbrough, John. *Quranic Studies: Sources and Methods of Scriptural Interpretation*. New York: Prometheus Books, 2004.

Warraq, Ibn. "Introduction." In *The Origins of the Koran: Classic Essays on Islam's Holy Book*, Ibn Warraq. 9-35. New York: Prometheus Books, 1998.

Warraq, Ibn. *What the Koran Really Says: Language, Text, and Commentary*. New York: Prometheus Books, 2002.

Jihad:
What does the Qur'an really say?

Dr Bernie Power

Melbourne School of Theology

When President George Bush, a few days after the 9/11 disaster, declared from a Washington mosque that "Islam is a religion of peace", it is unclear on what basis he made this claim. Certainly he had some philological statistics on his side: the word 'jihad' is found only four times in the Qur'an (Q.9:24; 22:78; 25:52; 60:1)[1], although the 3,000 dead still lying under the rubble in New York might have told another story. On the other hand, the Catholic archbishop of Sydney, George Pell, complained that he could not finish reading the Qur'an due to its frequent incitements to violence.[2] Who was right: the politician or the churchman?

The philological one-liner about "only 4 references to *jihad*" cannot be the last word. Lots of important things are missing from the Qur'an: the *shahada*, Islam's testimony of faith, for example, is not found there, nor is any reference to *tawhid*, the key doctrine of 'unity', nor does circumcision get a mention, nor the five daily prayers. Quite apart from the word *jihad*, there are several other Qur'anic terms that express the concept of fighting for Islam.

Qur'anic terms related to fighting

1. 'strive' is *jaahada* جَاهَدَ which is related to *jihad* جِهَاد – (found in 31 verses)

---

[1] Qur'anic verses will be marked as e.g. 14:21 – the 14th chapter, 21st verse.
[2] http://www.smh.com.au/news/national/pell-challenges-islam--o-ye-of-little-tolerant-faith/2006/05/04/1146335872951.html

2. 'fight' is *qaatala* قَاتَلَ which is related to *qatal* 'kill' or 'murder' قَتَلَ (in 42 verses)
3. 'in the cause (or way) of God' *fi sabeel illah* فِي سَبِيلِ الله. In 55 verses it means "to be involved in *jihad*". It may have a different meaning in some other verses of the Qur'an.
4. 'war' *harb* حَرْب occurs in 15 verses
5. The spoils of war – there are different terms for booty, including normal booty *anfal* الأنفال, *fai* الفيء or booty won without fighting by surrender of the besieged enemy. There is even a special verb *ghalla* غَلَّ (Q.3:161) describing theft from the war booty before its distribution.
6. Other spoils of war included prisoners أَسْرَى *asraa*, who might become slaves or concubines ('those whom your right hands possess' *ma malakat aymanukum* ما ملكت أيمانُكُم) or be sold back to their families for ransom *fida'* فِداء. One writer comments: "Although ideological motivation was best, Islam itself acknowledged that the motivation of spoils may have been of greater importance for the success of the great conquests."[3]

The Qur'an provides a rich vocabulary for war and its accoutrements. Of its approximately 6200 verses, over 160 verses relate to fighting and war. The Qur'an has 114 *Suras* or chapters. Those *suras* containing verses on fighting and jihad are nos. 2, 3, 4, 5, 8, 9, 16, 22, 25, 29, 33, 47, 48, 49, 57, 59, 60, 61, 63, 66, 73, 100, 110. The concept of Jihad is found in 1 in 5 *suras*, and 1 in 40 verses. It is not just an incidental doctrine.

What about the peaceful verses in the Qur'an?

Some Qur'anic verses do promote peace and tolerance, but generally they were written in Muhammad's early Meccan period (610-622 AD) when Islam, as a persecuted minority group, was struggling to gain public acceptance as a new religion. This was the first stage in Muhammad's prophetic career.

---

[3] Reuven Firestone *Jihad: the Origin of Holy War in Islam* (Oxford: Oxford University Press, 1999), 161 n.85

Stage 1: Peaceful Witness in Mecca (mostly from Meccan suras)

Multiple more peaceful themes are associated with Muhammad's early phase of Ministry, as follows:

(a) Freedom of religion for non-Muslims was allowed: 2:256; 109:6
(b) Non-Muslims were to be persuaded peacefully: 29:46; 5:8; 16:125
(c) Non-Muslims were to be left alone if they refused to listen: 6:70; 6:108; 15:3, 94-97; 73:10
(d) Hatred of others should not result in unjust treatment towards them: 5:8; 42:15; 60:8
(e) Forgiveness was important: 3:134; 2:109; 5:13; 7:199; 45:14; 15:85 (abrogated)
(f) Killing was forbidden: 5:32 and peace-making was encouraged: 8:61
(g) Judgement and punishment was left up to God: 51:60; 73:11-14.
(h) Muslims should be patient 50:39

The situation changes

When Muhammad accepted the invitation to go to Yathrib, a city about 300 kms to the north, to resolve its tribal conflicts by becoming their leader, his approach changed. Along with the 200 or so Muslim *muhajirs* (immigrants) from Mecca, he was surrounded by the believing *Ansar* (helpers) from Yathrib, which was renamed *medinat ennabi* (the city of the Apostle) or simply Medina. Now yielding social, political, religious and military leadership, Muhammad had other resources at his disposal. This moved him into the second phase of his career, where some fighting was permitted.

Stage 2: Fight only in self-defence and for justice

(a) Muslims were told initially to fight only in self-defence, but this was later abrogated: 2:190, 194; 9:12, 13; 22:39,40a
(b) They were told to fight to protect the oppressed: 4:75
(c) The Jews in Medina were allowed religious freedom initially: This was incorporated into the earliest treaties of Medina: e.g.

"The Jews of Bani Auf, who are a party to this agreement and are the supporters of the Muslims, shall adhere to their religion and the Muslims to theirs."[4]

The third stage

It was not long before the third stage was implemented. The 200 immigrants had escaped Mecca with few or no resources, and the passing nearby of wealthy Meccan caravans proved too much of a temptation. Within less than a year of his arrival in Medina, Muhammad began leading *ghazwat* (campaigns or raids) on nearby villages and passing caravans. In this stage he mostly kept to the Arab tribal raiding traditions, but sometimes he contravened them. His biographer, Ibn Ishaq, claims that Muhammad took part in 27 battles.[5]

Stage 3: Attacking within limits

(a) Muslims were told to attack others only outside the holy months, but this was later abrogated[6]: 9:36; 9:5; 2:217
(b) Fighting in Mecca was prohibited unless there was resistance: 2:191

The Grand Mufti of Saudi Arabia, Sheikh Abdel Aziz al-Sheikh, outlined these earlier stages in a statement on the official Saudi news service, defending Muslims' divine right to resort to violence: "The spread of Islam has gone through several phases, secret and then public, in Mecca and Medina. God then authorised the faithful to defend themselves and to fight against those fighting them, which amounts to a right legitimised by God. This ... is quite reasonable, and God will not hate it."[7]

---

[4] Ibn Ishaq *Sirat Rasul Allah* trans.as *The Life of Muhammad* (tr. A. Guillaume), (Karachi: Oxford University Press, 1998), p.231-33

[5] Ibid, p.659

[6] The abrogation or cancelling is noted in Muhammad Taqi-ud-Din al-Hilali and Muhammad Muhsin Khan *Translation of the meanings of the Noble Qur'an in the English Language* (Madinah, K.S.A.: King Fahd Complex for the Printing of the Holy Qur'an, 1424 A.H.), p.45 n.2

[7] Mark Durie "The Creed of the Sword", *The Australian*, September 23, 2006

The full doctrine of Jihad against non-Muslims was revealed in Medina (622-632 AD) when Muhammad's forces were winning battles. The Islamic Law of Abrogation (cancelling or supplanting) usually resolves the conflict with earlier 'peaceful' verses by stating that, where there is a conflict, later verses abrogate or cancel the earlier ones. Of the 23 *suras* mentioning fighting or war, 18 of these were revealed in Medina. Clearly it was a doctrine that developed later in Muhammad's life. In a footnote to Q.1.190 which begins: "And fight in the Way of Allah those who fight you, but transgress not the limits", a Saudi-authorised edition of the Qur'an defines 'jihad' as follows:

> *Al-jihad* (holy fighting) in Allah's cause (with full force of numbers and weaponry) is given the utmost importance in Islam and is one of its pillars (on which it stands). By jihad Islam is established, Allah's word is made superior, ... and His Religion (Islam) is propagated. By abandoning jihad (may Allah protect us from that) Islam is destroyed and the Muslims fall into an inferior position; their honour is lost, their lands are stolen, their rule and authority vanish. *Jihad* is an obligatory duty in Islam to every Muslim, and he who tries to escape from this duty, or does not in his innermost heart wish to fulfil this duty, dies with one of the qualities of a hypocrite.[8]

Once the full doctrine of *jihad* was articulated, it cancelled out all previous standing orders. "[Islamic] legal scholars ... argued that the famous 'Sword Verse' ... (Q.9:5) abrogated no fewer than 124 other verses commanding 'anything less than a total offensive against the non-believers'."[9]

It is this fourth stage which receives the most attention in the Qur'an. It outlines a broad justification, methodology and proposed outcome for *jihad*.

---

[8] Muhammad Taqi-ud-Din al-Hilali and Muhammad Muhsin Khan *Translation of the meanings of the Noble Qur'an in the English Language* (Madinah, K.S.A.: King Fahd Complex for the Printing of the Holy Qur'an, 1424 A.H.), p.39 n.1

[9] Alexander Knysh "Multiple Areas of Influence" in Jane Dammen McAuliffe (ed.) *The Cambridge Companion to the Qur'an* (Cambridge: Cambridge University Press, 2006), 219

Stage 4: unconditional warfare

Incentives to be involved in Jihad were given

(a) Reticence to fight

(i) The Muslims did not want to fight, but were ordered to do so: 2:216; 3:156; 4:77; 9:38
(ii) Those who refused to fight were criticised and threatened with hell-fire: 3:168; 4:72-75; 9:24, 81, 86, 87,90,120; 33:16-20; 47:20; 48:11,16.
(iii) Providing material support was an acceptable alternative to fighting 4:95
(iv) Muhammad was criticized for giving in to those who refused to fight 9:43

(b) Examples from history:

(i) The Jews in Moses' time were ordered to fight, but they turned away 2:246; 61:14
(ii) Jesus called on his disciples to be the helpers of God: 3:52; 9:111; 61:14
(iii) Previous prophets fought for God: 3:146

(c) Spiritual incentives

(i) Willingness to fight was a test from God: 9:16; 47:4; 47:31;
(ii) Losing was a test: 3:116,140,167
(iii) Muhammad was ordered to fight and to encourage others to do so: 4:84; 8:65,66; 8:72; 8:75

(d) Emotional incentives

(i) Some wept because they could not be involved in Jihad: 9:92
(ii) The handicapped, sick and poor were exempted from Jihad: 9:91
(iii) Acts of mercy or spirituality are not as worthy as fighting: 9:19; 73:20

(e) Psychological incentives

(i) Morale must be maintained, don't become weak, since victory was assured: 3:139

(ii) Those who made treaties against the Muslims would not support each other: 59:14

How was Jihad to be conducted?

(a) Methods of warfare

(i) Prepare for war with all resources, even if their resources were few: 8:60; 9:41; 57:10
(ii) Villages were attacked in unexpected raids: 7:4; 100:1-5,
(iii) crops were destroyed: 59:5
(iv) Close neighbours are threatened: 33:60-62.
(v) Patience in warfare was necessary: 2:177
(vi) The Muslims were encouraged to fight wholeheartedly: 8:12; 9:14; 22:78; 29:6; 61:10,11
(vii) Pursue the enemy 4:104.
(viii) Those who did not fight should provide 'asylum and aid' – 8:74.
(ix) Retreat by the Muslims was punishable: 48:16; 8:15,16

Muhammad boasted: "I ... have been made victorious through terror." (Sahih al-Bukhari 4:220)

(b) Post-war behaviour

(i) Do not sue for peace if you have the upper hand: 47:35
(ii) Muhammad was ordered to kill instead of taking prisoners: 8:67
(iii) Be harsh with your enemies: 9:73; 9:123; 25:52; 66:9
(iv) When you are victorious, punish the enemy severely: 8:57; 4:104
(v) Do not seek for reconciliation with enemies: 4:89; 60:1
(vi) Muslims should try to reconcile with other Muslims: 49:9

The Goals of Jihad

(i) The destruction of other religions and supremacy of Islam: 2:193 8:39; 48:28

(ii) Collection of ransom or tribute and total subjugation of others: 9:29; 47:4

The classical commentator Ibn Kathir outlined the value (*khayr*) of fighting. War was good "because following the fighting is victory and triumph over the enemy and the capture of their towns, wealth, progeny and children."[10]

The results of Jihad

(i) Fighting would bring God's mercy and rich reward in this world (booty) and in the next: 2:218, 244, 245; 4:94,95, 96; 5:35; 8:60, 69,74; 9:20-22; 9:88; 9:111; 16:110; 29:69; 48:19,20.
(ii) Booty was not necessarily allocated to those who fought in the battles 59:7,8; 8:41
(iii) Fighting was a sign of true faith in God; 4:76; 9:44, 45; 49:15
(iv) Muslims are promised victory: 8:66; 48:22; 48:1; 61:13.
(v) God loves those who fight: 61:4
(vi) God fights on behalf of the Muslims: 3:13; 123-125; 9:25,26; 33:25; 33:26; 8:17; 59:2; 63:4; 110:1-3
(vii) Killing was with God's permission, according to His promise: 3:152
(viii) Dying "in the way (or cause) of Allah" assures entrance to Paradise: 2:154; 3:157, 158; 3:169; 3:195; 4: 66, 67, 74; 4:100; 9:89,111; 22:58; 47:4-6

The goals were clear. "The direct purpose of jihad is the strengthening of Islam, the protection of believers and voiding the earth of unbelief. The ultimate aim is the complete supremacy of Islam, as one can learn from K.2:193"[11]

---

[10] Ibn Kathir *Tafsir* vol 1. p.446 cited in Firestone 1999, p.61.

[11] Rudolph Peters *Islam and Colonialism: The Doctrine of Jihad in Modern History* (The Hague: Mouton, 1979), p.10

Greater jihad, lesser jihad?

In a much-quoted hadith, Muhammad on returning from battle remarked: "We have returned from the lesser Jihad to the greater Jihad." When asked what he meant by that he is said to have replied: "The greater *jihad* is the struggle against the self."[12] This is often used by Muslim apologists to fend off questions about Muhammad's (and subsequently Islam's) violent history. Unfortunately, it is fictitious: Muhammad never said it.

Firestone comments on this saying: "Its source is not usually given, and it is in fact nowhere to be found in the canonical collections".[13] It is challenged even by some Muslims. The Australian lawyer, university lecturer and Islamic spokesperson Waleed Aly admits: "This famous 'greater jihad' report is of highly questionable historical authenticity. It does not occur in any of the most authoritative collections of narrations of the Prophet, and probably surfaced for the first time among ascetic movements just before al-Ghazzali's time."[14] Muhammad died in 632 AD and Al-Ghazzali in 1111 AD. Nearly 500 years separated these two men – rather a large time gap for new quotes to start surfacing.

It does, however, have an earlier origin according to one source. It is "related as *marfu'* by al-Baihaqi with a *da'if isnad,* according to al-'Iraqi."[15] A quick explanation of these terms: *marfu'* 'elevated' means that it purports to be a quotation of Muhammad himself; *da'if* 'weak' means that the *isnad* or chain of transmitters of this saying is disputed. Perhaps some of them were known to be liars, or they never met each other, so could not have passed this saying along. Someone eventually identifies the source, but the speaker was not Muhammad. "Ibn Hajar said that it is actually a saying of Ibrahim b. Abi 'Ablah, a Successor. Cited from *Kashf al-Khafa'*, no.

---

[12] W. Montgomery Watt "Islamic Conceptions of the Holy War" in Thomas P. Murphy, ed. *The Holy War* (Columbus: Ohio State University Press, 1976), p.150

[13] Firestone 1999: 140

[14] Waleed Aly *People Like Us: How arrogance is dividing Islam and the West* (Sydney: Picador, 2007), 153

[15] Source: http://www.usc.edu/dept/MSA/fundamentals/hadithsunnah/scienceofhadith/aape.html#G26

1362."[16] A 'successor' is someone who lived after the time of Muhammad, and was not acquainted with him. It seems that this saying was fabricated by someone who lived years later, and then put it into the posthumous mouth of Muhammad.

Muhammad, of course, spoke much about jihad, if we are to believe the earliest documents. Every mention of the word 'Jihad' in the *sahih* (i.e. authentic) Hadith collections of al-Bukhari (57 references) and Muslim (13 references) refer to physical fighting. It is the same in the collections called *Muwatta* (7 references) and *Mishkat al-Masabih* (9 references). Only in one of Abu Dawud's fifteen references do we find the single claim: "The Prophet (peace be upon him) said: 'The best fighting (*jihad*) in the path of Allah is (to speak) a word of justice to an oppressive ruler'." (narrated by Abu Sa'id al-Khudri). In over 100 mentions of *jihad* in these Hadith collections, only one suggests that it involves something other than warfare.

Another often-quoted hadith suggests a three-fold nature of 'striving' – it does not use the word '*jihad*':

> The Messenger of Allah (peace be upon him) observed: 'There was never a Prophet sent before me by Allah to his nation who had not among his people (his) disciples and companions who followed his ways and obeyed his command. Then there came after them their successors who said that which they did not practise, and practised that which they were not commanded to do. He who strove against them with his hand was a believer, he who strove against them with his tongue was a believer, and he who strove against them with his heart was a believer, and beyond that there was no faith, not even as much as a mustard seed.

Abu Rafi' said: I narrated this hadith to Abdullah ibn Umar; he contradicted me. ... I asked Ibn Mas'ud about this hadith. He narrated it in the same way as I narrated it to Ibn Umar." (Sahih Muslim *Kitab al-Iman 20.80* (1:69,70)

Firstly, note that its veracity was doubted by some of the early Muslims – not all accepted it as a true saying of the Prophet. Secondly, it is in the past tense, relating to previous prophets, not to Muhammad and his followers. Thirdly, this 'striving' of hand,

---

[16]Source: http://www.usc.edu/dept/MSA/fundamentals/hadithsunnah/scienceofhadith/aape.html#G26

tongue and heart was not against those who opposed or rejected the faith preached by the former prophets, but against co-religionists who had drifted from orthopraxy.

An opportunity to implement this occurred after Muhammad's death, when the Arab tribes which had become Muslim immediately reverted to paganism. Muhammad's successor, Abu Bakr, raised up armies to reconquer these tribes, in the *al-ridda* 'apostasy' wars, forcing them back into the fold of Islam. Although it undoubtedly involved some 'heart' and 'tongue', most of it was done by hand. This, it appears, is the norm. Firestone states:

> When the term is used without qualifiers such as 'of the heart' or 'of the tongue', [*jihad*] is universally understood as war on behalf of Islam (equivalent to *jihad* of the sword), and the merits of engaging in such *jihad* are described plentifully in the most-respected religious works.[17]

The Grand Mufti of Saudi Arabia, however, explained that war was never the prophet Muhammad's first choice against non-Muslims:

> He gave three options: either accept Islam, or surrender and pay tax, and they will be allowed to remain in their land, observing their religion under the protection of Muslims.

The option of violence was only a last resort, if they refused to convert or surrender peacefully to the armies of Islam.[18]

This was not simply untested military theory. A Muslim writer gives the historical example of how Islam came to Oman. According to Islamic tradition, Prophet Muhammad (PBUH) sent his messenger, Amr ibn Al-As to Oman with a letter to the two princes Abd and Jeifer some nine years after the Prophet had resorted to Al-Madinah (*hijra*). That was the year 630 A.D. He called upon them to accept Islam. The wording of the letter was as follows:

> In the name of God, the most gracious, the most Merciful. From Muhammad the Messenger of God to Jeifer and Abd, the sons of Al-Julandy. Peace be upon those who follow the true religion. After compliments, I call upon you to embrace Islam - accept and

---

[17] Firestone 1999, p.17.

[18] Mark Durie "The Creed of the Sword", *The Australian*, September 23, 2006

you will be saved, for I am the Messenger of God to all humanity. (I have come) to warn the living that affliction will befall unbelievers. If you accept Islam, as I hope you will, all will be well, but if you refuse to accept it, your kingdom will vanish and my horses will trample your grounds and my religion will triumph over your Kingdom.' The letter was stamped with the seal of the Prophet which read, "There is no God but Allah and Muhammad is the Messenger of Allah."[19]

Criticisms of the four-stage theory

The four-stage approach outlined above has not been without its academic critics. Reuven Firestone takes a 'documentary hypothesis' approach to the Qur'an, similar to that taken by some Old Testament scholars. He suggests that the Qur'an was a conglomeration of various views which were combined into a single document. "The fact is that the conflicting qur'anic verses cannot prove an evolution of the concept or sanction for religiously authorized warring from a nonaggressive to a militant stance ... It is just as likely that the conflicting verses of revelation articulate the views of different factions existing simultaneously within the early Muslim community of Muhammad's day and, perhaps, continuing for a period after his death. Each faction would refer to the different scriptural sources available from the oral and as yet unedited and uncanonised compendium of revelation for support of its views."[20]

An alternative is proposed, but it is textually unwieldy. He claims that it is better to group Qur'anic verses in a way "independent of the verses among which they are situated. This method sometimes creates a rather awkward situation in which the verses seem to be taken entirely out of context, but it is necessary in order to avoid prejudging the analysis because of proximity to possibly unrelated verses or because of preconceived ideas of historical context based on late interpretations." Instead he groups verses according to the following division:

> 1. Verses expressing nonmilitant means of propagating or defending the faith.

---

[19] Ahmed Hamoud Al-Maamiry *Oman and Ibadhism* (Lancers Press, New Delhi, 1980), p.21
[20] Firestone 1999: 64,65

2. Verses expressing restrictions on fighting
3. Verses expressing conflict between God's command and the reaction of Muhammad's followers.
4. Verses strongly advocating war for God's religion."[21]

Islamic orthodoxy

Although Firestone rejects the 'evolutionary theory' of progression from non-confrontation to militancy, he begrudgingly admits that it has invariably been the major path of interpretation by Muslims. He refers to "Islam's overwhelming acceptance of the traditional 'evolutionary theory'.[22] He concedes that "Militant groups promoting aggressive behaviour toward opponents of Islam eventually won the day. Their program is supported by militant scriptural passages, especially in what are dated as the 'later' revelations according to the 'evolutionary theory' ..., and this faithful ammunition exceeds the number of scriptural supports that would have been cited by their opponents."[23]

It is not only Muslim commentators who have held this view of the primacy of *jihad*. The record of recent history seems to bear it out, not the least being the daily news of suicide bombings somewhere in the world. Five years before George Bush stood in the Washington mosque proclaiming Islam's peaceful nature, Samuel Huntingdon had noted: "Muslims make up about one-fifth of the world's population but in the 1990's they have been far more involved in intergroup violence than the people of any other civilization...two-thirds to three quarters of intercivilizational wars were between Muslims and non-Muslims. Islam's borders are bloody, and so are its innards."[24] Post 9/11, his words sound almost prophetic. One contributor for this sad state of affairs may be Islam's rediscovery of the concept of *jihad* in their ancient scriptures.

---

[21] Ibid, 69

[22] Ibid, 69

[23] Ibid, 68

[22] Samuel Huntingdon, *The Clash of Civilizations and the Remaking of World Order* (New York: Simon and Schuster, 1996), 256-257

Bibliography

Aly, Waleed *People Like Us: How arrogance is dividing Islam and the West* (Sydney: Picador, 2007)

Firestone, Reuven *Jihad: the Origin of Holy War in Islam* (Oxford: Oxford University Press, 1999)

Al-Hilali, Muhammad Taqi-ud-Din and Khan, Muhammad Muhsin *Translation of the meanings of the Noble Qur'an in the English Language* (Madinah, K.S.A.: King Fahd Complex for the Printing of the Holy Qur'an, 1424 A.H.)

Huntingdon, Samuel *The Clash of Civilizations and the Remaking of World Order* (New York: Simon and Schuster, 1996)

Ibn Ishaq *Sirat Rasul Allah* trans.as *The Life of Muhammad* (tr. A. Guillaume), (Karachi: Oxford University Press, 1998)

Knysh, Alexander "Multiple Areas of Influence" in Jane Dammen McAuliffe (ed.) *The Cambridge Companion to the Qur'an* (Cambridge: Cambridge University Press, 2006)

Al-Maamiry, Ahmed Hamoud *Oman and Ibadhism* (Lancers Press, New Delhi, 1980)

Peters, Rudolph *Islam and Colonialism: The Doctrine of Jihad in Modern History* (The Hague: Mouton, 1979)

Watt, W. Montgomery "Islamic Conceptions of the Holy War" in Thomas P. Murphy, ed. *The Holy War* (Columbus: Ohio State University Press, 1976)

Fighting the Unbelievers: Various perspectives on Qur'an 9:29 by Muslim theologians

Denis Savelyev

Melbourne School of Theology

Introduction

"Fight against those who believe not in Allah, nor in the Last Day, nor forbid that which has been forbidden by Allah and His Messenger and those who acknowledge not the religion of truth among the people of the Scripture, until they pay the *Jizya* with willing submission, and feel themselves subdued" Qur'an, Sura 9:29[1]

There are many different explanations for this verse. Some Muslims today argue that the verse does not call Muslims to aggression against people of other religions. Some translations of the Qur'an, as in the case with the English translation made by Rashad Khalifa interpret the first words of the verse 9:29 as "You shall fight back."[2] Edip Yuksel, one of the translators of the Reformist Translation of the Qur'an in his annotation to verse 9:29 states that the context of this verse is the War of Hunain, which was provoked by the enemy and that this verse is mistranslated by almost every translator.[3] This implies that it does not speak about the Jews and the Christians at all. In the paper "Jihad and the Islamic Law of War" published by the Royal Aal Al-Bayt Institute for Islamic Thought in Jordan it is

---

[1] *The Noble Qur'an*, (Trans. Dr. Muhammad Taqi'-ud-Din Ae-Hilali and Dr. Muhammad Muhsin Khan, King Fahd Complex for the Printing of the Holy Qur'an Madinah, 1414 a.h.), 248.

[2] *Qur'an: the Final Testament, Authorized English Version*, (Trans. Rashad Khalifa, Islamic Productions, 2003), 151.

[3] *Qur'an, A Reformist Translation*, (Trans. Edip Yuksel, Layth Saleh al-Shaiban and Martha Shulte-Nafeh, Brainbow Press: USA, 2007), 160.

said that the Muslims waged wars only in defence or as a pre-emptive measure as in case of Tabuk.[4] Furthermore it is argued that only the Shafi'i school of law promotes the view that a person's belief can be a reason for fighting against them. However this view is mitigated by the opposite view also attributed to Shafi'i.[5] It is also stated that the state of being humbled mentioned with regard to the paying of *jizya* by the People of the Book in the verse 9:29 is "a result of the previous hostility and enmity exhibited by the group against the Muslim community".[6]

Those who state that this verse does call Muslims to show aggression towards Christians and Jews are often accused of having a wrong understanding of the Qur'an, or not knowing the Arabic language and so on. In order to identify the reason for fighting the People of the Book in Sura 9:29 we will look at different types of Qur'anic *tafsirs* (commentaries) written by Muslims who lived in different times and in different places. In addition we will also look at the writings of some Muslim scholars and jurists.

Sura 9:29 in different Qur'anic commentaries

Zamakhshari (1075-1144)

Mahmud ibn Umar al-Zamakhshari was a theologian and philologist of Persian origin.[7] Despite his Mu'tazilah views in theology his *tafsir* is widely circulated among non-Mu'tazilite Sunni[8] and regarded by all as an invaluable source of linguistic and literary insights.[9]

---

[4] *Jihad and the Islamic Law of War*, (The Royal Aal Al-Bayt Institute for Islamic Thought, 2007), 24.

[5] *Jihad and the Islamic Law of War*, 36.

[6] *Jihad and the Islamic Law of War*, 47.

[7] 'Zamakhshari, Mahmud Al (1075-1144)' in the *Historical Dictionary of Islam*, (ed. Ludwig W. Adamec, The Scarecrow Press: Lanham, 2009), 336.

[8] 'Az-Zamakhshari, Abu al-Qasim Mahmud b. 'Umar'' in *A Concise Encyclopedia of Islam*, (ed. Gordon Newby, Oneworld: Oxford, 2004), 216.

[9] Mustansir Mir, 'Tafsir' in *The Oxford Encyclopedia of the Islamic World*, (6 vols.; ed. John L. Esposito, Oxford University Press: Oxford, 2009, vol.5), 302.

Al-Zamakhshari starts his commentary of verse 29 from the phrase "of those who were given the book."[10] He explains that these words mean ditheistic Jews and tritheistic Christians and after a short mention of aberrations in their beliefs and practices he turns to the regulations of *jizya*, which the Jews and the Christians should pay in order to be exempted from being killed. Zamakhshari dedicates most of the commentary on this verse to the question of *jizya*. The reason why the Jews and the Christians should be fought is stated in the comments in the previous verse (Sura 9:28). Since Muslims were afraid of poverty due to the loss of trade with pagan Arabs they were ordered to fight the People of the Book:

> [God will make you rich by His grace] And Allah ordered them (the Muslims) to fight the people of the book and they (the Muslims) became rich by *jizya*. And it is said: invade their lands and (take) their booty... [If He wanted] if Allah saw in His wisdom that you will be rich, then this benefits your religion... [Allah knows] your condition...[11]

Thus the reason for fighting the Jews and the Christians according to Zamakhshari is to improve the financial situation of Muslims.

Baidawi (d. 1286)

'Abd Allah ibn 'Umar al-Baidawi is also of Persian origin. His work *Anwar al-tanzil wa-asrar at-ta'wil* is a more or less expurgated version of al-Zamakhshari's work.[12] He assimilated it to orthodox theology while drawing from other sources as well. Baidawi's commentary has been considered the best by many Sunni theologians.[13]

Baidawi starts his commentary on Sura 9:29 from the explanation of the words "who believe not in God and the Last Day".[14] He

---

[10] Abu al-Qasim Jar Allah Mahmud Ibn 'Umar al-Zamakhshari', in *Al-Kashshaf 'an haqa'iq ghawamid al-tanzil* (Dar al-Fikr, Beirut, no date, vol. 2), 184-185.

[11] Abu al-Qasim Jar Allah Mahmud Ibn 'Umar al-Zamakhshari' in *Al-Kashshaf 'an haqa'iq ghawamid al-tanzil*, vol. 2), 184.

[12] Mustansir Mir, 'Tafsir' in *The Oxford Encyclopedia of the Islamic World*, vol.5, 302.

[13] Helmut Gatje, *The Qur'an and Its Exegesis* (Oneworld: Oxford, 2008), 37.

[14] Commentary of Baidawi on Sura 9:29 is cited in Helmut Gatje, *The Qur'an and its Exegesis* (Oneworld: Oxford, 2008), 138-139.

states that the belief of such people is no belief at all. In the second paragraph he explains that they deviated from their own religion, which has been annulled through Islam. And in the next passage he says that Islam "annuls and destroys the other religions". These words suggest that the reason for fighting the People of the Book according to Baidawi is their erroneous practices and beliefs. The last three quarters of the commentary on this verse are dedicated to the explanation of the accepting of *jizya*.

Al-Qurtubi (d. 1273)

Abu 'Abd Allah Muhammad ibn Ahmad al-Ansari al-Qurtubi is a Maliki scholar from Andalusia.[15] His *Al-Jami li-Ahkam al-Qur'an* is a juristic *tafsir*, but it also discusses linguistic and literary issues.[16] Because of that it can be considered an exegetical encyclopedia in the manner of al-Tabari.[17]

According to Qurtubi the main reason for fighting the Jews and the Christians is their denial of Muhammad: "When they denied him they became like criminals and the word 'infidel' applied to them. So he (Allah) made for them a purpose for fighting..."[18] Qurtubi quotes Ibn Arabi according to whom words "fight them" means "as a punishment", the reason for punishment is their disbelief and disobedience, and the purpose of punishment is to make them pay *jizya*, which "is permitted to compensate for the loss of commerce from the polytheists because the infidels could no longer visit the holy sites". Qurtubi says that there are fifteen issues concerning this verse. The last fourteen issues are dedicated to the question of *jizya*.

---

[15] 'Al-Qurtubi, Abu 'Abd Allah Muhammad b. Ahmad b. Abi Bakr b. Faraj al-Ansari al-Khazraji al-Andalusi' in *A Concise Encyclopedia of Islam*, 180.

[16] Mustansir Mir, 'Tafsir' in *The Oxford Encyclopedia of the Islamic World*, vol.5, 303.

[17] Claude Gilliot, 'Exegesis of the Qur'an: Classical and Medieval' in the *Encyclopedia of the Qur'an* (6 vols.; ed. Jane Dammen McAuliffe, Leiden, Brill, 2002, vol. 2), 114.

[18] Al-Qurtubi, *Al-Jami li-Ahkam al-Qur'an*, Commentary on Sura 9:29, http://www.altafsir.com/Tafasir.asp?tMadhNo=1&tTafsirNo=5&tSoraNo=9&tAyahNo=29&tDisplay=yes&UserProfile=0&LanguageId=1, viewed 3 June 2010.

Ibn Kathir (d. 1373)

Imad al-Din Ismail ibn Umar ibn Kathir was a leading Syrian historian, Qur'an commentator, and scholar of Hadith. He was a student of the foremost *Hanbali* jurist of the Middle Ages, Taqi al-Din Ahmad Ibn Taymiyya, but he considered himself a follower of the *Shafi'i* school of law. He is famous among Muslims around the world for his *tafsir*, which draws heavily on the Hadith.[19]

From the very beginning of the commentary on this verse Ibn Kathir clearly states that the reason for fighting the People of the Book is their disbelief in Muhammad: "...they disbelieved in the master, the mightiest, the last and most perfect of all Prophets. Hence Allah's statement, Fight against those..."[20] Ibn Kathir then says that after this verse was revealed on the ninth year of *hijra* Muhammad prepared his army to fight the Romans and marched to Tabuk. The last two thirds of the commentary on this verse are dedicated to the topic of *jizya*. Later in the commentary on verse 30 Ibn Kathir repeats the reason for fighting, stating that, "Fighting the Jews and Christians is legislated because they are Idolaters and Disbelievers."[21] He mentions the enrichment of Muslims by the *jizya* in the commentary on verse 28, but it looks more like a consequence of the fighting the People of the Book than the reason for fighting.[22]

Tafsir al-Jalalayn (Jalalu'd-Din Al-Mahali d. 1495, Jalalu'd-Din As-Suyuti d. 1505)

This *tafsir* is called "al-Jalalayn" because it was written by two people with the name Jalalu'd-Din. It was started by Jalalu'd-Din Muhammad ibn Ahmad al-Mahali (1389-1495). After his death his

---

[19] 'Ibn Kathir, Imad al-Din Ismail ibn Umar' in the *Encyclopedia of Islam*, (ed. Juan E. Campo, Facts On File: New York, 2009), 333.

[20] Ibn Kathir, *Tafsir ibn Kathir*, (10 vols.; ed. Shaykh Safiur-Rahman al-Mubararpuri, Riyadh, Darussalam, 2003, vol. 4), 404-405.

[21] Ibn Kathir, *Tafsir ibn Kathir*, ed. Shaykh Safiur-Rahman al-Mubararpuri, vol. 4, 408.

[22] Ibn Kathir, *Tafsir ibn Kathir*, 404.

work was continued by his student Jalalu'd-Din as-Suyuti,[23] an Egyptian scholar who is known for his prolific writings on Hadith, fiqh, Qur'anic studies, Arabic language, and related subjects.[24] *Tafsir Al-Jalalayn* represents an ongoing paraphrase of the text of the Qur'an with linguistic explanations, materials from the Tradition, and variants.[25]

The interpretation of Sura 9:29 is quite short. The authors expand a little on the Qur'anic text, explaining the fact that the people who were given the Book do not believe in Allah and the Last Day and this is evident from their denial of Muhammad. The permitting of such things as wine shows that they do unlawful deeds and do not follow the religion of Truth, which abrogates other religions[26]. The rest of the interpretation for this verse explains the details of receiving *jizya* from Jews and Christians, a poll tax that they are required to pay every year.[27] Although the reason why Jews and Christians should be fought is not given, it can be found in the interpretation to the previous verse (9:28). It is said that after the 9th year after *hijra* the idolaters should not come near to the al-Masjid al-Haram. And since this meant that Muslims could face impoverishment due to the loss of the trade with pagan Arabs, Allah would enrich Muslims "through conquest and *jizya*."[28] Thus the main reason for fighting the Jews and the Christians, who according to the authors of this *tafsir* do not follow the true religion, is enrichment of Muslims.

Sayyid Qutb (d. 1966)

Sayyid Qutb was an Islamic activist and one of the ideologues of the Muslim Brotherhood. He was born in Upper Egypt in 1906.

---

[23] Abdalhaqq Bewely, 'Preface', in *Tafsir al-Jalalayn*, (Jalalu'd-Din al-Mahali and Jalalu'd-Din As-Suyuti, trans. Aisha Bewley, Abdalhaqq Bewley (ed.) and Muhammad Isa Walley, Dar Al Taqwqa: London, 2007), xi-xii.

[24] E. M. Sartain, 'Suyuti, Al (1445-1505)' in the *Encyclopedia of Islam and the Muslim World*, (2 vols.; ed. Richard C. Martin, Macmillan Reference USA: New York, 2004, vol. 2,) 669.

[25] Helmut Gatje, *The Qur'an and Its Exegesis*, 37.

[26] Jalalu'd-Din al-Mahali and Jalalu'd-Din As-Suyuti *Tafsir al-Jalalayn*, (Trans. Aisha Bewley, ed. Abdalhaqq Bewley and Muhammad Isa Walley, Dar Al Taqwqa: London, 2007), 404.

[27] Jalalu'd-Din al-Mahali and Jalalu'd-Din As-Suyuti *Tafsir al-Jalalayn*, 404-406.

[28] Jalalu'd-Din al-Mahali and Jalalu'd-Din As-Suyuti *Tafsir al-Jalalayn*, 404.

Qutb is best known for two works: *Milestones*, and the voluminous Qur'anic commentary *Fi zilal al-Qur'an* (In the shade of the Qur'an).[29]

According to Qutb verses 29-35 of Sura 9 define the final shape of relations between the Muslim community and the people of earlier revelations, who deviated from the divine faith, both in beliefs and behavior and hence are no longer following divine faith.[30] Unlike the first passage of this Sura, which speaks about a specific situation at a specific place, verse 29 is applicable to all people of earlier revelations everywhere. It is explained by more general phraseology and by the fact that by the time of revelation of Sura 9, all military conflicts with the Jews had already taken place, but no such conflict took place with any Christians.[31] Qutb argues that the new ruling to fight the People of the Book until their submission is justified by the inevitable confrontation between the divine system of Islam and all other human systems.[32] In order to support this point of view Qutb makes an excursion into the historical domain of hostility of the Jews towards Muslims, blaming them for violations of the treaties with Muslims, assassination of Caliph Uthman, conflict between Ali and Mu'awiyah, for the victory of the Tartars, fall of the Islamic Caliphate, and for every calamity that has befallen the Muslims in the modern history.[33] Then he turns to Christians and states that Byzantines and Persians became reconciled in order to confront Islam. He continues with the recalling of the Crusades, Reconquista, Western Colonialism and Christian missionary activity. Qutb concludes that the enmity of the Jews and Christians towards Islam is a permanent reality.[34] Then he goes on to the explanation of Sura 9:29 and states that descriptions of the People of the Book mentioned in the beginning of this verse provide justification for fighting them.[35] He also writes that the very fact of

---

[29] Sohalil H. Hashmi, 'Qutb, Sayyid (1906-1966)' in the *Encyclopedia of Islam and the Muslim World*, vol. 2, 568-569.

[30] Sayyid Qutb, *In the Shade of the Qur'an*, (18 vols.; Transl. Adil Salahi, The Islamic Foundation: Leicestershire, 2003, vol. 8), 3.

[31] Sayyid Qutb, *In the Shade of the Qur'an*, vol. 8, 101.

[32] Sayyid Qutb, *In the Shade of the Qur'an*, vol. 8, 101-102, 110.

[33] Sayyid Qutb, *In the Shade of the Qur'an*, vol. 8, 113-115.

[34] Sayyid Qutb, *In the Shade of the Qur'an*, vol. 8, 116-119.

[35] Sayyid Qutb, *In the Shade of the Qur'an*, vol. 8, 120.

possessing these characteristics place the People of the Book at war with the divine faith and Islamic society.[36] The second issue, which places them at war with Islam, is the inherent conflict between Islam and ignorance (or *jahiliyya*) to which the people of the earlier revelations belong.[37] In the end Qutb makes practical conclusions that in order to liberate mankind from submission to anyone other than God, Muslims must smash the power of the authorities based on false beliefs and make them to pay *jizya* in submission.[38] He also notes that there is no point in going into polemics about the practical questions of *jizya*, since modern day Muslims do not engage in *jihad*, because in his opinion there is practically no Muslim community in the real sense of the term.[39]

Mawdudi (d. 1979)

Abu al-Ala Mawdudi was a leading Muslim revivalist thinker and founder of the Jamaat-I Islami movement in India-Pakistan.[40] His multi-volume Qur'an commentary *Tafhim al-Quran* originally written in Urdu has been translated and circulated widely in Muslim world.[41]

Mawdudi starts his commentary on Sura 9:29 with the statement that the People of the Book just pretended to believe in God and in the Hereafter, but in fact they did not believe.[42] After an explanation of their errors in the two abovementioned beliefs Mawdudi turns to the purpose for which the Muslims are required to fight the People of the Book. And the purpose is "to put an end to the sovereignty and supremacy of the unbelievers so that the latter are unable to rule over men".[43] The reason for fighting is that the authority to rule should only be vested in the true believers, namely the Muslims,

---

[36] Sayyid Qutb, *In the Shade of the Qur'an*, vol. 8, 123.

[37] Sayyid Qutb, *In the Shade of the Qur'an*, vol. 8, 123.

[38] Sayyid Qutb, *In the Shade of the Qur'an*, vol. 8, 123.

[39] Sayyid Qutb, *In the Shade of the Qur'an*, vol. 8, 124.

[40] 'Mawdudi, Abu al-Ala (Maudoodi)' in the *Encyclopedia of Islam*, 462.

[41] 'Mawdudi, Abu al-Ala (Maudoodi)' in the *Encyclopedia of Islam*, 463.

[42] Sayyid Abul A'la Mawdudi, *Towards Understanding the Qur'an*, (8 vols.; Tranls. Zafar Ishaq Ansari Leicester, The Islamic Foundation, 2001, vol. 3), 202.

[43] Sayyid Abul A'la Mawdudi, *Towards Understanding the Qur'an*, vol. 3, 202.

while all others should live in a state of subordination paying *jizya* every year. The second half of the interpretation for this verse is dedicated to the explanation and defence of *jizya*. Mawdudi was concerned that some nineteenth and twentieth-century Muslim writers were apologizing for *jizya*, while "God's religion does not require that apologetic explanations be made on its behalf."[44] Non-Muslims by paying *jizya* receive freedom to "cling to their false, man-made ways", but they have "absolutely no right to seize the reins of power in any part of God's earth" because this would lead to corruption and mischief. In such situations Muslims are "under obligation to do their utmost to dislodge them from political power and to make them live in subservience to the Islamic way of life."[45]

Sura 9:29 in the works of Muslim scholars and jurists

We will consider two *ikhtilaf*-works written by Al-Tabari and Ibn Rushd. Although these works are focused on the disagreements between different jurists, we can see what the jurists agreed on. Al-Tabari did not mention any opinion of Ibn Hanbal, because from his point of view Ibn Hanbal was a scholar of Tradition and not a jurist.[46] Therefore we will look at the work of a famous Hanbali jurist Ibn Taymiyya. In the end we will look at the work of a famous Muslim scholar and historian Ibn Khaldun.

Al-Tabari (d. 923)

Abu Ja'far Muhammad ibn Jarir ibn Yazid al-Tabari was born in Persia in 838/839 in the region of Tabaristan near the Caspian Sea. Originally a Shafi'i jurist, he founded his own school of law, which was named after him.[47] During the tenth century the Jariri school of law vied with the Shafi'i, Hanafi and other schools, but later the

---

[44] Sayyid Abul A'la Mawdudi, *Towards Understanding the Qur'an*, vol. 3, 202.

[45] Sayyid Abul A'la Mawdudi, *Towards Understanding the Qur'an*, vol. 3, 202.

[46] Peter G. Riddell, 'Al-Tabari' in *The Qur'an – An Encyclopedia*, 622.

[47] Peter G. Riddell, 'Al-Tabari' in *The Qur'an – An Encyclopedia*, 622.

Jariri school of law died out and most of Tabari's works are now lost.[48] We will consider a translation of Tabari's *Kitab al-Jihad* (The Book of Jihad), which is a part of his book *Kitab Ikhtilaf al-Fuqaha* (The Book of the Disagreement Among Muslim Jurists).

Al-Tabari starts his Book of Jihad with a justification of Jihad based on Qur'anic verses. He argues that the message brought by Muhammad was superior to the previous prophets and messengers.[49] He was sent to all mankind and Allah promised that Islam will prevail over all other religions. Muhammad did not die until Allah cleared the roads to success for his followers and gave them "laws and rules of dealing with peoples of other religion, to the enemy until they put them to death..."[50] Thus the aim of Jihad is to make Islam prevail over other religions. Tabari also does not refer directly to Q.9:29, but he states that there is unanimous agreement among Muslim jurists that Muhammad was always calling polytheists to embrace Islam before attacking them. Yasir Ibrahim, the translator of the Book of *Jihad*, mentions that Tabari uses the word *mushrikun* (polytheists) in relation to both the pagans and to the People of the Book.[51] Some scholars argued that there is a need to call both polytheists and the People of the Book to embrace Islam or to pay *jizya* before fighting. The other view by other scholars was that at that time all people had already heard about Islam, so they could be fought without additional invitation to become Muslims.

Ibn Rushd (d. 1198)

Abu Al-Walid Muhammad Ibn Muhammad Ibn Rushd, also known in the West as Averroes, was born in Cordoba in 1126. He was not only a famous philosopher, but also a judge, physician, politician and legal thinker. We will consider a chapter on jihad

---

[48] Christopher Melchert, 'Tabari, Al- (839-923)' in the *Encyclopedia of Islam and the Muslim World*, vol. 2, 671.

[49] *Al-Tabari's Book of Jihad* (Trans. Yasir S. Ibrahim, The Edwin Mellen Press: Lewiston, 2007), 57-58.

[50] Yasir S. Ibrahim, trans. *Al-Tabari's Book of Jihad*, 58.

[51] Yasir S. Ibrahim, trans. *Al-Tabari's Book of Jihad*, 53.

from his best-known legal handbook *Bidayat al-Mujtahid wa-Nihayat al-Muqtasid*, which belongs to the genre of *ikhtilaf*-works.[52]

Ibn Rushd mentions Sura 9:29 in the paragraph dedicated to the aims of warfare. He says that Muslim jurists agreed that the aim of warfare against the People of the Book is conversion to Islam, or payment of *jizya*, which is based on the abovementioned verse.[53] According to Ibn Rushd Muslim jurists disagreed on which polytheists in addition to the Jews and the Christians are allowed to pay *jizya*. This discussion between Muslim jurists shows that the People of the Book are considered a category of polytheists. The reason for fighting them could be found in the paragraph "The Enemy". Averroes states that scholars agree that all polytheists should be fought and that this is based on Qur'anic verse 8:39: "Fight them until there is no persecution and the religion is God's entirely".[54] Although for the English-speaking readers it may seem that the reason for fighting is persecution, as mentioned in this verse, it is not so, as can be seen from the rest of this paragraph.[55] Ibn Rushd states that it has been related by Malik that the Ethiopians and the Turks are not allowed to be attacked on the strength of the tradition of Muhammad: "Leave Ethiopians in peace as long as they leave you in peace". However, Malik, when questioned, did not acknowledge the authenticity of this tradition

---

[52] Rudolph Peters, *Jihad in Classical and Modern Islam* (Princeton: Markus Wiener Publishers, 2008), 27.

[53] The Chapter on Jihad from *Averroes' Legal Handbook Al-Bidaya*, in Rudolph Peters, *Jihad in Classical and Modern Islam* (Princeton, Markus Wiener Publishers, 2008), 40.

[54] The Chapter on Jihad from *Averroes' Legal Handbook Al-Bidaya*, in Rudolph Peters, *Jihad in Classical and Modern Islam*, 30.

[55] It should be noted that the word *fitna*, translated here as "persecution", in some English Qur'anic translations was rendered differently. For example it was translated as "opposition in favour of idolatry" [*The Koran*, Trans. George Sale (London: Frederick Warne and Co., no date, 172], as "disbelief and polytheism" (*The Noble Qur'an*, Trans. Dr. Muhammad Taqi'-ud-Din Al-Hilali and Dr. Muhammad Muhsin Khan, 236), or as "idolatry" [*The Koran*, Trans. N.J. Dawood (England, Penguin Books, 1993), 129]. These translations could be supported by some classical Qur'anic commentaries. In the *Tafsir Al-Jalalayn* the word *fitna* is explained as *shirk* (polytheism) (Jalalu'd-Din al-Mahali and Jalalu'd-Din As-Suyuti *Tafsir al-Jalalayn*, 385). Ibn Kathir gives the same meaning for *fitna*, and states that similar was said by Abu-Aliyah, Mujahid, Al-Hasan, Qatadah, Ar-Rabi bin Anas, As-Suddi, Muqatil bin Hayyan and Zayd bin Asam (Ibn Kathir, *Tafsir ibn Kathir*, ed. Shaykh Safiur-Rahman al-Mubararpuri, vol. 4, 314).

but said that "people still avoiding attacking them".[56] This implies that for Malik the war against other polytheists besides the Ethiopians and Turks was an offensive character, and for the other jurists war against all polytheists was of an offensive character. Thus the reason for fighting polytheists is not a defence, as it would be in the case of persecution, but an establishing of the dominion of Islam over all other religions.

Ibn Taymiyya (d. 1328)

Taqi al-Din Ahmad Ibn Taymiyya was a Syrian jurist and theologian from the Hanbali school of law. He has had a lasting effect on Islamic life through his influence on Ibn al-Wahhab.[57]

In his work *Al-Siyasa al-Shariyya* he emphasizes the obligatory character of jihad and shows the gradual changing in Allah's commands concerning fighting in the Qur'an from not permitting to fight and kill anyone, to permission to fight and finally to the imposing of fighting the unbelievers.[58] The aim of jihad "is that the religion is God's entirely and God's word is uppermost... therefore, those who stand in the way of this aim must be fought".[59] Ibn Taymiyya mentions two types of *jihad*: the first and the most serious is against unbelievers and people who refuse to abide by certain prescriptions of Shari'a; and second is a defensive *jihad*. Although he does not refer directly to verse 9:29, he alludes to it in stating that the People of the Book "are to be fought until they become Muslims or pay *jizya* having been humbled."[60] He also mentions that the expedition to Tabuk represented the offensive form of *jihad* waged in order to propagate the religion, to make it triumph and to intimidate the enemy.[61]

---

[56] The Chapter on Jihad from *Averroes' Legal Handbook Al-Bidaya*, in Rudolph Peters, *Jihad in Classical and Modern Islam*, 30.

[57] Oliver Leaman, "Ibn Taymiyya, Taqi Al-Din" in *The Qur'an – An Encyclopedia*, 280.

[58] *Al-Siyasa Al-Sharyyia*, in Rudolph Peters, *Jihad in Classical and Modern Islam* (Princeton: Markus Wiener Publishers, 2008), 44-45.

[59] *Al-Siyasa Al-Sharyyia*, in Rudolph Peters, *Jihad in Classical and Modern Islam*, 49.

[60] *Al-Siyasa Al-Sharyyia*, in Rudolph Peters, *Jihad in Classical and Modern Islam*, 50.

[61] *Al-Siyasa Al-Sharyyia*, in Rudolph Peters, *Jihad in Classical and Modern Islam*, 54.

Ibn Khaldun (d. 1406)

Abd al-Rahman ibn Muhammad Ibn Khaldun was a medieval scholar famed for his philosophy of history and insights into the rise and fall of civilizations. He was born in Tunis and later immigrated to Andalusia, where he acquired a thorough education in Qur'anic studies, hadith and fiqh – especially that of the Maliki school of law.[62] His *Muqaddima* (Introduction) has become one of the most important works on medieval historiography for modern scholars.[63]

In the chapter *On Dynasties, Royal Authority, Government Ranks and All That Goes With These Things*, Ibn Khaldun has a paragraph where he compares relations between political and religious authorities in Islam, Judaism and Christianity. He states that for the Muslim community the holy war waged in order to convert everybody to Islam either by persuasion or by force is a religious duty. Because of this political and religious power are united in Islam. Other religious groups unlike the Muslims did not have a universal mission, so the holy war for the Jews and the Christians was a duty only in case of defense.[64] Their religious leaders were concerned with establishing their religion and not with politics, because they are not "under obligation to gain power over other nations, as is the case with Islam".[65] In order to illustrate this Ibn Khaldun then briefly recalls the history of the Jews starting with the time of Moses, and the history of the origination and propagation of Christianity. He also mentions in passing religious disagreements between Christians, which led to the emergence of different Christian groups, noting that there is no need to "blacken the pages of this book with discussion of their dogmas of unbelief".[66] He does not cite Sura 9:29, but he alludes to it when he mentions that their religious dogmas are all unbelief and that Muslims have no need in

---

[62] "Ibn Khaldun, Abd al-Rahman ibn Muhammad" in the *Encyclopedia of Islam*, 334-335.

[63] R. Kevin Jaques, "Ibn Khaldun (1332-1404)" in the *Encyclopedia of Islam and the Muslim World*, ed. Richard C. Martin, 2 vols. (New York, Macmillan Reference USA, 2004, vol. 1), 335-336.

[64] Ibn Khaldun, *The Muqaddimah: An Introduction to History*, (Trans. Franz Rosenthal Princeton, Princeton University Press, 1989), 183.

[65] Ibn Khaldun, *The Muqaddimah: An Introduction to History*, 183.

[66] Ibn Khaldun, *The Muqaddimah: An Introduction to History*, 188.

discussing or arguing with them about those things, but must let them choose between "conversion to Islam, payment of the poll tax, or death."[67]

Comparison and Analysis

According to the two Qur'anic commentaries – *Tafsir Al-Jalalayn* and the *tafsir* by Zamakhshari - the reason for fighting the People of the Book referred to in Qur'an 9:29 is the enrichment of Muslims because of the loss of trade with pagan Arabs. At the same time the authors of these commentaries note that Jews and Christians are disbelievers. Ibn Kathir mentions enrichment of Muslims, but in his opinion it is a consequence of fighting Jews and Christians while the reason for fighting them is their disbelief and denial of Muhammad. Baidawi, Qurtubi, Qutb and Mawdudi as well as Ibn Kathir mention the disbelief of Jews and Christians as the primary reason for fighting them. Sayyid Qutb states that the expedition to Tabuk was of a pre-emptive character, but at the same time he asserts that the possessing of the characteristics given in the first part of the verse (not believing in Allah and the Last Day, not forbidding what was forbidden by Allah, and not acknowledging Islam) would put Jews and Christians at war with Islam anyway. Mawdudi expands the explanation and says that they should be fought because disbelievers must not rule over humanity. None of the commentators mentioned above stated that the reason for fighting in this verse is as a defence. All commentators except Qutb and Mawdudi, spend much more time explaining regulations concerning *jizya*, suggesting that the main question for the commentators was not whether to fight the People of the Book or not to fight, but what to do with them when they are conquered. In contrast to other commentators, who lived in the times when offensive *jihad* was widely practiced, Qutb and Mawdudi do not go into details when writing about *jizya*, because for them this question was more historical than practical. They were more concerned with justification for fighting the People of the Book, and convincing their readers that Muslims must put an end to the sovereignty and supremacy of unbelievers.

---

[67] Ibn Khaldun, *The Muqaddimah: An Introduction to History*, 188.

According to Al-Tabari, Ibn Rushd, Ibn Taymiyya, and Ibn Khaldun, the People of the Book are a subcategory of polytheists. All these authors agree that the war against polytheists is waged in order to make Islam prevail over other religions. Sura 9:29 is mentioned because of the choice – conversion to Islam, paying of *jizya*, or death – contained in it. Al-Tabari and Ibn Khaldun allude to Sura 9:29 in relation to the prerequisites for warfare, while Ibn Rusd and Ibn Taymiyya mention this verse in relation to the aim of warfare.

Conclusion

The main reason for fighting the People of the Book according to the writings of different Muslim commentators and jurists examined in this paper is the beliefs and practices of the Jews and Christians or, in the words of these authors, their disbelief.

None of these authors mention defence as a reason for fighting the Jews and the Christians, and only one, namely Sayyid Qutb, mentions the pre-emptive character of the expedition to Tabuk, at the same time stating that the state of disbelief of the Jews and the Christians makes them at war with Islam per se.

Qur'anic commentators devote much more time to the explanation of *jizya* than to the reason for fighting, and jurists use verse 9:29 more often in relation to the threefold choice, which implies that the main question for them was not whether to fight the People of the Book or not, and why to fight them, but what to do before the fighting and after they are defeated.

Bibliography

Al-Mahali, Jalalu'd-Din and As-Suyuti, Jalalu'd-Din *Tafsir al-Jalalayn* (Trans. Aisha Bewley, ed. Abdalhaqq Bewley and Muhammad Isa Walley, London: Dar Al Taqwqa, 2007).

Al-Qurtubi, *Al-Jami li-Ahkam al-Qur'an*,
http://www.altafsir.com/Tafasir.asp?tMadhNo=1&tTafsirN

o=5&tSoraNo=9&tAyahNo=29&tDisplay=yes&UserProfile=0&LanguageId=1

"Al-Qurtubi, Abu 'Abd Allah Muhammad b. Ahmad b. Abi Bakr b. Faraj al-Ansari al-Khazraji al-Andalusi" in *A Concise Encyclopedia of Islam* (ed. Gordon Newby, Oxford: Oneworld, 2004)

Al-Zamakhshari, Abu al-Qasim Jar Allah Mahmud Ibn 'Umar *Al-Kashshaf 'an haqa'iq ghawamid al-tanzil*, (4 vols., Beirut: Dar al-Fikr, no date, vol. 2).

"Az-Zamakhshari, Abu al-Qasim Mahmud b. 'Umar" in *A Concise Encyclopedia of Islam* (ed. Gordon Newby, Oxford: Oneworld, 2004).

Bostom, Andrew G. *The Legacy of Jihad* (New York: Prometheus Books, 2008).

Gatje, Helmut *The Qur'an and Its Exegesis* (Oxford: Oneworld, 2008).

Gilliot, Claude "Exegesis of the Qur'an: Classical and Medieval", in the *Encyclopedia of the Qur'an* (6 vols., ed. Jane Dammen McAuliffe, Leiden: Brill, 2002, vol. 2).

Hashmi, Sohalil H. "Qutb, Sayyid (1906-1966)" in the *Encyclopedia of Islam and the Muslim World* (2 vols., ed. Richard C. Martin, New York, Macmillan Reference USA, 2004, vol. 2).

"Ibn Kathir, Imad al-Din Ismail ibn Umar" in the *Encyclopedia of Islam* (ed. Juan E. Campo, New York: Facts On File, 2009).

Ibn Kathir, *Tafsir ibn Kathir* (10 vols., ed. Shaykh Safiur-Rahman al-Mubararpuri, Riyadh: Darussalam, 2003, vol. 4).

"Ibn Khaldun, Abd al-Rahman ibn Muhammad" in the *Encyclopedia of Islam*, (ed. Juan E. Campo, New York: Facts On File, 2009).

Ibn Khaldun, *The Muqaddimah: An Introduction to History*, tr. Franz Rosenthal, Princeton, Princeton University Press, 1989

Ibrahim, Yasir S. tr. *Al-Tabari's Book of Jihad*, Lewiston, The Edwin Mellen Press, 2007

Jaques, R. Kevin "Ibn Khaldun (1332-1404)" in the *Encyclopedia of Islam and the Muslim World* (2 vols., ed. Richard C. Martin, New York, Macmillan Reference USA, 2004, vol. 1).

Jihad and the Islamic Law of War (Jordan: The Royal Aal Al-Bayt Institute For Islamic Thought, 2007).

Leaman, Oliver "Ibn Taymiyya, Taqi Al-Din" in *The Qur'an – An Encyclopedia* (ed. Oliver Leaman, London: Routledge, 2006).

"Mawdudi, Abu al-Ala (Maudoodi)" in the *Encyclopedia of Islam* (ed. Juan E. Campo, New York: Facts On File, 2009).

Mawdudi, Sayyid Abul A'la *Towards Understanding the Qur'an* (8 vols., Trans. Zafar Ishaq Ansari, Leicester: The Islamic Foundation, 2001, vol. 3).

Melchert, Christopher "Tabari, Al- (839-923)", in the *Encyclopedia of Islam and the Muslim World* (2 vols., ed. Richard C. Martin, New York: Macmillan Reference USA, 2004, vol. 2).

Mir, Mustansir "Tafsir", in *The Oxford Encyclopedia of the Islamic World* (6 vol., ed. John L. Esposito, Oxford: Oxford University Press, 2009, vol.5).

Peters, Rudolph *Jihad in Classical and Modern Islam* (Princeton: Markus Wiener Publishers, 2008).

Qur'an, A Reformist Translation (Trans. Edip Yuksel, Layth Saleh al-Shaiban and Martha Shulte-Nafeh, USA: Brainbow Press, 2007).

Qur'an: the Final Testament, Authorized English Version (Trans. Rashad Khalifa, Islamic Productions, 2003).

Qutb, Sayyid *In the Shade of the Qur'an* (tr. Adil Salahi, Leicestershire: The Islamic Foundation, 2003).

Riddell, Peter G. "Al-Tabari", in *The Qur'an – An Encyclopedia* (ed. Oliver Leaman, London: Routledge, 2006).

Sartain, E. M. "Suyuti, Al (1445-1505)" in the *Encyclopedia of Islam and the Muslim World* (2 vols., ed. Richard C. Martin, New York: Macmillan Reference USA, 2004, vol. 2).

The Koran (Trans. George Sale, London: Frederick Warne and Co., no date).

The Koran (Trans. N.J. Dawood, England: Penguin Books, 1993).

The Noble Qur'an (Trans. Dr. Muhammad Taqi'-ud-Din AL-Hilali and Dr. Muhammad Muhsin Khan, Madinah, King Fahd Complex for the Printing of the Holy Qur'an, 1414 a.h.).

"Zamakhshari, Mahmud Al (1075-1144)" in the *Historical Dictionary of Islam* (ed. Ludwig W. Adamec, Lanham, The Scarecrow Press, 2009).

The Kharijites: Ideologues for Contemporary Islamic Extremism

Dr John Kingsbury

Even among students of Islam, the early sect of the Kharijites is scarcely known, yet its ideological influence can arguably be traced throughout the entire history of Islam to present-day militant jihadist groups. But more than simply being an inspirer of *jihad* in the sense of war against non-Muslim infidels, it is this sect that in both practice and theory has provided the impulse for the bewildering contemporary phenomenon of Muslims in violent opposition to other Muslims. While we can understand for example, how the Pakistani *Taliban* could instigate the May 2010 New York Time Square car bomb plot, it is almost incomprehensible to an outside observer how this same group could conduct suicide attacks amongst their coreligionists at home. Is such behaviour to be regarded as so deviant from mainstream Islamic teaching that its protagonists have forfeited the right to bear the name 'Muslim', or alternatively is it to be recognized as a genuine face of Islam among the myriad of personas that this diverse faith manifests?

In this paper I will demonstrate how the persistence of an idea or ideology can continue to be potent even in the absence of the tangible entity that birthed it. Similar to how, for example, neo-Nazism in Germany has survived post the demise of the Third Reich, so the ideology of the violent Kharijite movement, 'long relegated to the dustbin of history' in the opinion of a modern soldier[1], continues to hold sway among the theorists of *jihad*. In an essentially chronological format I will trace the development of

---

[1] J. W. Jandora, 'Osama bin Laden's Global Jihad: Myth and Movement', *Military Review* (November – December 2006), 44.

radical thinking that has advocated and incited violence within the House of Islam itself. Both individuals and movements will be discussed, and sometimes concurrently when a person and an organization together constitute an entity. Restraint will be exercised in confining the survey to readily discernible Kharijite traits, rather than attempting a purview of any individual's contribution to *jihadi* thought in general. And rather than devoting a discrete section to Kharijite doctrine, I will introduce features of it at points where it is of particular prominence on the chronological pathway.

While the dates and precise details of many events in the earliest decades of Islam are disputed, the origins of the Kharijites are not.[2] They came into being as a third sect at the time of the much more commonly known division of Islam into its two main branches of Sunni and Shi'a Muslims. In 656, 'Uthman, the third of the four Rightly Guided Caliphs was murdered.[3] His successor to the caliphate, 'Ali (whom Shi'as follow as the legal successor to the Prophet Muhammad), was immediately challenged by Mu'awiyya, a cousin of 'Uthman's, and the long-established governor of Syria. The two met in battle in July or August 657, at Siffin in northern Iraq close to the border with Syria. Fighting had been commonplace in the fledgling religion from the days of Muhammad, but this particular confrontation had a novel feature. With the tide of battle turning against them, the Syrian troops resorted to the expediency of raising copies of the Qur'an on their lances, demanding that the dispute be settled by means of arbitration. 'Ali reluctantly agreed and for his pains not only suffered the ignominy of a ruling against his claim to the caliphate, but also faced the wrath of a group of his own supporters who objected to arbitration in principle.

The dissenters argued that conflicting leadership claims were not to be resolved by human decision making processes, but rather should adhere to the Qur'anic injunction that 'there is no judgement except that of God' (*lā hukma illā li-llāhi*).[4] They deemed 'Ali's compromise to be sin, and in doing so ushered in a major characteristic of historical Kharijite ideology and one that has permeated much of

---

[2] The Arabic singular is *khariji* and the plural *khawarij*.

[3] On the succession of grievances that contributed to 'Uthman's demise, see W. Montgomery Watt, *The Formative Period of Islamic Thought* (Edinburgh: University Press, 1973), 9-12.

[4] This translation is from A. Rippin, *Muslims: Their Religious Beliefs and Practices*, 3rd edition (London and New York: Routledge, 2005), 75.

Islamic extremism to the present day. Not only was 'Ali a sinner but he and his supporters were declared to be no longer Muslims.[5] Separation from such apostates was the logical necessity, and so these self-appointed judges of what constitutes a true Muslim, withdrew from the wider group and became known as Kharijites (or 'seceders').[6] In contrasting them with the major sects, Sookhdeo states: 'The puritanical Kharijites took the most extreme stance, deeming that every Muslim who committed a major sin was an apostate and therefore an enemy.'[7] Unlike the Sunnis who would recognize a caliph from Muhammad's tribe, or the Shi'a, who insisted on a descendant of 'Ali, the Kharijites maintained that any suitably pious Muslim ought to be able to exercise the role.

Declaring a fellow Muslim to have abandoned the faith and deserving of death, is the essence of the Kharijite doctrine of *takfir*.[8] Following a strict and literal interpretation of the Qur'an, the Kharijites were able to view life through sharply dichotomous lenses: 'Their world was neatly divided between belief and unbelief, Muslims (followers of God) and non-Muslims (enemies of God), peace and warfare'.[9] While not necessarily in the specifics, this black and white Kharijite understanding of reality is clearly recognizable as the dominant trait in any religious manifestation that we might label 'fundamentalist'. Further, the underlying quest for truth and purity is an inherent impulse in any committed adherent of any faith. Where the Kharijites differ though, historically, and in their contemporary reincarnations, is in their willing recourse to extreme violence as a means of tangibly marking the division. In discussing *takfir*, Ruthven has no hesitation in

---

[5] The term for a person who had committed a grave sin, and was to be excluded from membership of the community, was *sāhib kabīra*, W. Montgomery Watt, 'Conditions of Membership of the Islamic Community', *Studia Islamica* 21(1964), 7.

[6] From *kharaja*, to 'go out'. Watt details four specific ways in which the term can be understood in relation to the Kharijites, *The Formative Period of Islamic Thought*, 15. The two most pertinent for this paper are 'those who have gone out from among the believers', and 'those who go out and take an active part in the *jihad*'.

[7] P. Sookhdeo, *Global Jihad: The Future in the Face of Militant Islam* (McLean, VA: Isaac, 2007), 217.

[8] J. O. Hunwick describes *takfir* as a verbal noun from the verb *kaffara* 'to declare someone a *kāfir* or unbeliever', *Encyclopedia of Islam* (Leiden: Brill, 1990), 122.

[9] J. L. Esposito, *Unholy War: Terror in the Name of Islam* (Oxford: Oxford University Press, 2002), 42.

linking this doctrine from the early centuries with present day instances of what he calls 'anarchic terrorism', and he goes on to associate it with the broader activity of Islam's 'sixth pillar': 'Ideologically Islamist terror depends on the murderous conjunction of *takfir* and *jihad*.'[10]

Before moving on to trace the Kharijite impulse as it has surfaced and been developed through various scholars, groups and movements, completeness requires a brief sketch of their rise and demise as an historical entity. A year after the battle of Siffin 'Ali was able to subdue the break-away group, but not sufficiently enough to prevent them from spreading geographically over a period of more than 200 years. Expressing their militant DNA the Kharijites continued in a state of constant rebellion, with 'no scruples about shedding the blood of fellow coreligionists.'[11] They themselves divided into various sects, establishing a presence in parts of Arabia and Iran in the late seventh century and then subsequently in Basra, Iraq.[12] They also spread into North Africa, where the local Berber population rallied under the Kharijite call to holy war.[13] Then in the late ninth century the sect made its final thrust for power in an extraordinarily diverse cultural context. The lowly black African Zanj slaves in the Iraqi empire fomented a revolt under the leadership of an Iranian Kharijite that lasted for twelve years and in its expansion almost reached Baghdad. The end came though in 883 with military defeat, and a symbolic finality as recorded by Karsh: 'Their leader was killed and his head sent on a pole to Baghdad.'[14] Time, however, would prove that the Kharijites were in fact both a hydra and a phoenix.

---

[10] M. Ruthven, *Islam in the World* (London: Granta, 2006), 403-404. Ruthven, in describing *takfir*, does not limit it to intra-Muslim strife today, but certainly recognizes this feature of it: '... declaring one's opponent to be a *kafir* or infidel, regardless of whether he or she formally subscribes to Islam and the religious duties it enjoins'.

[11] E. Karsh, *Islamic Imperialism: A History* (New Haven and London: Yale University Press, 2007), 37. For further details see also page 49.

[12] P. Crone describes the Basran sect of the Kharijites as 'anarchists ... notorious for its militant intolerance', 'Ninth-Century Muslim Anarchists', *Past and Present* 167 (2000), 4.

[13] Though they are not within the scope of this paper it should be noted that the Kharijites still exist in Oman, East Africa, Tripolitania and southern Algeria as an identifiable sect called the 'Ibadis. They are described as a 'moderate' sect, and it is likely that their origins can be traced back to the mid $1^{st}/7^{th}$ century in association with a group of the *ka'ada* (quietist), T. Lewicki, 'al-Ibādiyya' in *Encyclopedia of Islam*, 648.

[14] E. Karsh, *Islamic Imperialism*, 49.

To all intents and purposes Kharijite-style thinking remained latent for more than 350 years through until the emergence of a medieval scholar and occasional warrior-against-heretics, Ibn Taymiyya (1268-1328). In the assessment of Espostio, Ibn Taymiyya is the scholar from this period of history who has had more influence on radical Islamic ideology than any other.[15] This notwithstanding, care needs to be taken in distinguishing between his extensive writing on *jihad* in general[16], and those aspects of it that pertain to this paper's focus on *jihad* against rebellious Muslims *á la* the Kharijites. Like these forerunners, Ibn Taymiyya wanted to see a reformed and pure version of Islam, free from legal innovations, as defined by a literalist understanding of the Qur'an and *sunna*. And like many Christians today who speak idealistically about the 'early Church', he longed for a return to the supposed simplicity of the times of the Prophet and the first caliphs, and the associated greatness of the religion. Ibn Taymiyya also employed the sharply differentiated thinking of the Kharijites that divided the world into two essential groupings, the House of Islam or *dar al-Islam*, and the non-Muslims, the House of War or *dar al-harb*.

Ibn Taymiyya's understanding of the world and its peoples in these diametrically opposed camps is simply standard Islamic thought that naturally feeds the theology of *jihad*. But what is notable in his writing, and a direct linkage with the Kharijites, is his willingness to include some Muslims as part of *dar al-harb*, and not in a hypothetical sense either but with reference to a particular grouping of people. The focus of his vehemence was the Muslim Mongols who in their military excursions ended up crossing swords with the Muslim Mamluks in Syria and Egypt. Because the former did not adhere to Islamic Sharī'a, and because according to Cook they fought with the backing of a multi-religion coalition ('... Christian Armenians, Georgians, still-pagan Mongols, and Shi'ites, in addition to Sunni Muslims'[17]), they were declared by Ibn Taymiyya

---

[15] J. L. Esposito, *Unholy War*, 45.

[16] For example his 'Governance according to God's Law in Reforming both the Ruler and His Flock', emphasizes the religious justification for *jihad*. Cited by P. Sookhdeo, *Global Jihad*, 76.

[17] D. Cook, *Understanding Jihad* (London, Berkeley and Los Angeles: University of California Press, 2005), 65.

to be unbelievers according to the doctrine of *takfir*. Further, the scholar-activist who was so intolerant of innovation and accretion in law, went on to promulgate a new instruction that the Mongols were not only infidel and apostate, but had to be opposed with even more vigour than the traditional enemies such as Christians.[18]

Cook describes Ibn Taymiyya's fatwa judging the relative quality of other Muslims' Islam as a 'novel conclusion'.[19] One-time novelties though, by definition, become commonplace, and so it has come about that this medieval decree has become part of the theological arsenal of contemporary militant Muslims. Even occasional followers of Islamic matters will know of the visceral hatred that Osama bin Laden had for the ruling elite of Saudi Arabia, both because of their corruptly opulent life style, and also their refusal to accept his offer of military support in the war against Saddam Hussein's Iraq. This condemnation of rulers as 'un-Islamic' was also a mark of Egypt's high profile Islamic Jihad in the latter part of last century. Like Ibn Taymiyya, its members wanted to create a true Islamic state and society, the starting point of which was a declaration that the Egyptian state and rulers were 'atheists'.[20] While these contemporary movements are legitimate examples of the Kharijite-inspired *takfir*, it is important to note that they, like many other Islamist groups, practice a dual *jihad* that also emphatically targets the West. For instance, no Westerner will recognize Bin Laden's antipathy to the Saudi regime before first identifying his preeminent role as the September 11, 2001 arch-terrorist.

If making the jump from Ibn Taymiyya to the likes of Bin Laden and Islamic *Jihad* seems to be stretching excessively the chain of Kharijite influence, then that can be compressed and strengthened by the inclusion at this point of a puritanical eighteenth-century group. Muhammad ibn 'Abd al-Wahhab (1703-1792) was the founder of the movement that still bears his name today, and in the assessment of Esposito, Ibn Taymiyya was his 'exemplar'.[21] Ibn 'Abd al-Wahhab was similarly a scholar, studying Islamic law and theology in Mecca and Medina, but he was much more able to

---

[18] D. Cook, *Understanding Jihad*, 65.

[19] D. Cook, *Understanding Jihad*, 65.

[20] J. L. Esposito, *Unholy War*, 90.

[21] J. L. Esposito, *Unholy War*, 47.

meld the theoretical and military-political aspects of radicalism than Ibn Taymiyya was. Rather than simply participating in a few jihadist forays like his predecessor, Ibn 'Abd al-Wahhab forged an alliance with one Muhammad ibn Saud, that over time, and with a checkered passage, has become the rigorously Islamic Wahhabist kingdom of Saudi Arabia. In the early years, violence against other Muslims was regarded as a legitimate means of achieving a religious end: 'Like the Kharijites, the Wahhabi viewed all Muslims who resisted as unbelievers (who could be fought and killed).'[22] Presumably something of this mentality undergirded the Saudi Arabian efforts against Islamic Iraq in both Gulf Wars. In suggesting this, it is important not to overlook the irony that the puritanical kingdom is itself the object of derision by the Kharijite-animated al-Qaeda.

Having discussed the ideologically separatist and practically confrontational doctrines of *takfir*, and *dar al-Islam* versus *dar al-harb*, a third theoretical component can be added to the doctrinal mix, one consistent with the Kharijite view of the world, and brought into greater prominence by the Wahhabis. Ibn 'Abd al-Wahhab likened Arabian society in the eighteenth century to the period of ignorance, or *jahiliyya*, that supposedly characterized life on the Arabian peninsula in pre-Islamic pagan times. The remedy for *jahilyya* was two-fold. Firstly, Muslims had to return to a strict and literalist understanding of the Qur'an and *sunna*, which at times of militancy included a ban on any ritual practices not specifically permitted by the Prophet.[23] Ibn 'Abd al-Wahhab explicated his solutions for *jahilyya* society in writings like the tract entitled *Nawaqid al-Islam* (The Things Which Nullify Islam) which sets fences around what a Muslim may believe or do in order to still remain within the community of faith. Rippin says of this tract, that it 'harkens back to the moral stance of the Khawārij'.[24]

Coupled with the prescriptive constraints was a proactive campaign by the Wahhabis to rid the Islamic world of its *jahilyya* accretions.

---

[22] J. L. Esposito, *Unholy War*, 48.

[23] Ruthven notes that in theory at least Wahhabism permitted anything not explicitly forbidden in the Qur'an and *sunna*, *Islam in the World*, 267.

[24] A. Rippin, *Muslims*, 167.

Any other expression of Muslim devotion was a fair target for their iconoclastic fervour. Consistent with Cook's description of it as 'probably the most radical of all the anti-Muslim [sic] jihad movements'[25], the Wahhabi-Saud alliance began its rampage with a declaration of *jihad* against other Muslims in 1746. Prior to its defeat in 1813 the militant state variously attacked and occupied the Shi'a city of Karbala, Islam's sacred cities of Mecca and Medina, and destroyed Shi'a as well as Sufi shrines. Albeit in opposition to an entirely different religion, the *Taliban's* desecration of Afghanistan's 1500 year-old Buddhist statues on March 11 2001 in Bamyan, has eerie similarities with the purifying zeal of the Wahhabis. While the phoenix-like quality of the original Kharijites emerged primarily in an ideological resurrection following their defeat in 883, the Wahhabis have not only managed to transmit their theology to other radical groups, but have survived in a very concrete form after their 1813 'defeat'. A telling comment by Cook serves as a caution against ever writing off any manifestation of militancy. On the Wahhabi attempt to 'purify' Islam, he states that it 'would be merely a footnote in history were it not for the fact that the Saudi Arabian state, revived in the early twentieth century ... today again controls the holy cities of Islam.'[26]

Just as aspects of Ibn Taymiyya's radical doctrines found expression, and sometimes fuller development, in the writings of Ibn 'Abd al-Wahhab, so has the latter's thought been embraced and honed by the twentieth century's 'godfather and martyr' of Islamic extremism, the Egyptian Sayyid Qutb (1906-1966).[27] Before outlining the Kharijite manifestations in Qutb's thought, it is helpful to understand how he has been differentiated from traditional Wahhabism. Sookhdeo describes a 'citation analysis' study of medieval and modern *jihadi* scholars conducted by a US group, the Combating Terrorism Center. He notes that Sayyid Qutb ranks first among modern authors, and refers to him as a 'Salafi-*Jihadi*' author.[28] Salafiyya, or neo-Wahhabism, is characterized by an even more literal interpretation of the sacred text than its parent body,

---

[25] D. Cook, *Understanding Jihad*, 74.

[26] D. Cook, *Understanding Jihad*, 75.

[27] J. L. Esposito, *Unholy War*, 59.

[28] P. Sookhdeo, *Global Jihad*, 309.

and strives for 'a return to a primitive and pure form of Islam'.[29] The US study identifies three types of Salafi thinkers, placing Qutb in the most extreme category of *jihadi* theorists who include 'the overthrow of apostate regimes' among their goals.[30] So in Qutb, there is no sense at all of moderation in intra-Islam *jihad* after fourteen centuries, but arguably a hardening of attitude.

The development of Qutb's radical ideas cannot be divorced from his dramatic life experiences, but space precludes even a sketch of the biographical pathway from educated intellectual to militant ideologue of Egypt's Muslim Brotherhood.[31] It will suffice to mention simply those aspects of his life that served to sustain the Kharijite impetus within his version of Islam. Qutb was implicated in a plot to assassinate the country's leader Gamal Abdel Nassar. Through the experiences of imprisonment on several occasions, being tortured, and witnessing the brutality of the authorities against fellow members of the Brotherhood, including a prison massacre, the once irenic and open-minded scholar became progressively radicalized in his thinking and vehement about the necessity of violent action to overthrow the government of his country. This process of doing theology in a real life context, and concluding the need for militant engagement, has striking parallels with some of the early expressions of Christian liberation theology in the contexts of oppressive Latin American regimes. Cook, in pertinent imagery, describes the import of Qutb's real life experiences as 'the anvil upon which radical Islam in Egypt was forged'.[32]

Consistent with his extremist forebears, Sayyid Qutb vigorously promoted the doctrines of *takfir* exclusion, and the *dar al-Islam dar al-harb* dichotomous perception of the world, as discussed above. But his most significant contribution in my view, with respect to Kharijite doctrine, is the depth of his thinking on the related notion of *jahiliyya* or *jahili* society. Stemming from his early revulsion with

---

[29] M. Nazir-Ali, *Conviction and Conflict: Islam, Christianity and World Order* (London and New York: Continuum, 2006), 94.

[30] P. Sookhdeo, *Global Jihad*, 310.

[31] For detailed accounts of Qutb's life see J. L. Esposito, *Unholy War*, 56-61, and D. Cook, *Understanding Jihad*, 102-106.

[32] D. Cook, *Understanding Jihad*, 102.

sinful American society, it is a given that the West would be encompassed within the orbit of a *jahili* grouping, one that 'does not dedicate itself to submission to Allah alone in its beliefs and ideas, in its observances of worship and in its legal norms'.[33] What is particularly notable, though, is the way he pushes out the boundaries of inclusivity in the *jahili* society with respect to Islam itself. Potentially, none are spared this invidious appellation, as he details it in his famous *Milestones along the Way* (*Ma'alim fi al-tariq*). He argues that the state of *jahiliyya*, or Satanic-induced barbaric ignorance, prevailing prior to the time of Muhammad has returned in an even more insidious form, because whereas it was once the nomenclature for pagans, it now afflicted Muslim societies as well. This is attributed to the syncretistic blending of Qur'anic ideals with an amalgam of foreign accretions 'from Greek philosophy and ancient Iranian legends to Jewish scriptures and traditions'.[34]

Qutb's vitriol is directed not only against his own 'un-Islamic' Egyptian state but against all so-called 'Muslim' societies. Belief in Allah is almost incidental, because the issue at stake is complete *submission* to him and a congruent refusal to subject oneself to any other legislative authority. Inevitably Qutb's expansion of *jahiliyya* beyond its original Kharijite practice of condemning un-Islamic rulers and regimes to the whole of society, engendered debate as to what precisely constituted 'society'. This issue is of critical practical importance and it relates directly to the question posed at the outset about how Islamists in present-day Pakistan can kill coreligionists in the name of a shared faith. If society itself is deemed to be *jahili*, then the legitimate objects of internal *jihad* extend beyond ruling regimes, and military and bureaucratic institutions, to its civilian members. Sookhdeo states the reality bleakly and bluntly: 'If the entire society, not just the government is *jahili*, then this legitimizes attacks on civilians who are effectively apostates. There is no neutral ground.'[35] Qutb was executed in 1966, but like his militant predecessors stretching all the way back to the battle of Siffin, even in death he has managed to pass on the perpetually reinvigorated mantle of Kharijite thought. For example, Ruthven states that

---

[33] S. Qutb *Milestones*, 66-68.

[34] E. Karsh, *Islamic Imperialism*, 215.

[35] P. Sookhdeo, *Global Jihad*, 282.

Sayyid Qutb's intellectual influence is such that 'there is a direct line of transmission that links him with Osama bin Laden.'[36]

It remains now to examine how the bin Laden-assisted *Taliban* can be viewed as the latest link in the ideological chain that started in the seventh century. Jandora refers to bin Laden's 'sensitivity to being branded a neo-Kharijite.'[37] Are the *Taliban* similarly reticent about claiming this designation, or are there elements of doctrine and praxis that they would readily identify with? With regard to this question, it is necessary to be cognizant of the relative paucity of material on the ideology of the *Taliban*. This I would suggest has to do with the fact that like their Wahhabi antecedent, the *Taliban* for a time essentially disappeared off the radar screen of contemporary militancy. Even exceptionally well-informed writers, offering their commentaries within this decade, effectively speak of this Pakistan-birthed group in the past tense. Esposito, writing in 2002, refers to the Afghan Northern Alliance backed by the United States, as having 'defeated the *Taliban*.'[38] Ruthven's new 2006 edition recalls its 'overthrow by US armed forces in 2002.'[39] And in a similar vein, Sookhdeo in 2007 speaks of the 'disintegration of their rule.'[40] On the contrary, and as the world is readily aware of, the phoenix has risen from the ashes and is baring its vicious talons in both Afghanistan and Pakistan. So, whether wanted or not, the opportunity is again before scholars to ponder more deeply the tenacity of this particular brand of Islamic militancy.

Notwithstanding this premature truncation of research, the origins of the *Taliban* (students or pupils) and their *modus operandi* place them firmly in the neo-Kharijite camp. Consistent with their nomenclature the *Taliban* are the product of madrassas (or traditional Islamic schools) and mosques, situated throughout the turbulent North-West Frontier of Pakistan.[41] Historically these

---

[36] M. Ruthven, *Islam in the World*, 405.

[37] J. W. Jandora, 'Osama bin Laden's Global Jihad', 46.

[38] J. L. Esposito, *Unholy War*, 12-13.

[39] M. Ruthven, *Islam in the World*, 395.

[40] P. Sookhdeo, *Global Jihad*, 279.

[41] This region was home to me during the years 1989-1994, and unbeknown to me (or most Westerners), the *Taliban* were being nurtured and radicalized virtually on our doorstep. Their ability to survive and regroup is evidenced in a photograph in the *Nelson Mail*, 20 October,

madrassas were not seedbeds of radicalism, but were rather characterized by what Nazir-Ali calls the 'traditional quietism of Deoband'[42], a Sunni reformist movement originating in India. However, with the largesse from Saudi oil revenues, these institutions and their largely Pathan (or Pashtun) clientele increasingly came under the sway of that country's puritanical Wahhabi Islam. Ruthven even refers to the group as the 'Salafist Taliban'[43], which, by implication from the Salafi-Sayyid Qutb link established above, brings the *Taliban* within the orbit of the latter's influence. Esposito describes the content and outcome of this Wahhabi (or perhaps more accurately Salafiyya, or neo-Wahhabism?) education as a 'myopic, self-contained, militant worldview in which Islam is used to legitimate their tribal customs and preferences.'[44] Large numbers of men and boys from the more than 3 million refugees in Pakistan from the Afghan-Soviet war were ripe for, and vulnerable to, the intolerant and anti-modernity tenets of this contextualized Wahhabi Islam. The *madrassas* became veritable factories churning out warriors for *jihad* in Afghanistan.[45]

Even more explicit links with their Kharijite forebears can be established with reference to the violent practices of the *Taliban*. While I do not agree with Esposito's historically naïve perception of *jihad* in classical Islam as purely a 'defense', he is surely correct in noting how the *Taliban* have transformed a conventional understanding of holy war into one 'that targets unbelievers, *including Muslims* and non-Muslims *alike*' [my emphases].[46] One newspaper article, from a plethora of similar recent material I have collected, provides graphic evidence of the Kharijite-like proclivity to engage in violence against one's coreligionists. '*Suicide bombers target military neighbourhood*' is a Reuters report from Lahore, published on 13 March 2010. It describes the actions of two *Taliban* suicide bombers who killed at least 45 people at a military facility in

---

2009, that shows residents from South Waziristan fleeing the *Taliban* and arriving in an overloaded ute in our home town of Dera Ismail Khan, 5.

[42] M. Nazir-Ali, *Conviction and Conflict*, 162.

[43] M. Ruthven, *Islam in the World*, 395.

[44] J. L. Esposito, *Unholy War*, 16.

[45] Sookhdeo mentions the Haqqania School near Peshawar that closed down in 1997 and sent all of its more than 2800 pupils to Afghanistan to fight against the Northern Alliance, *Global Jihad*, 347.

[46] P. Sookhdeo, *Global Jihad*, 16.

the city, including nine soldiers.[47] Presumably the civilian casualties were not simply 'collateral damage' in military-speak, but rather legitimate targets in the all-encompassing *jahili* society as promulgated by Qutb. The Afghan cousins of the Pakistani *Taliban* have been equally ruthless in their own setting. For example, their attacks on the Shi'a Hazara at Mazar-e Sharif in northwestern Afghanistan in 1998, have been labeled by Ruthven as 'genocidal'.[48]

It may be that Osama Bin Laden has qualms about this fratricidal behaviour within Islam, but if so his sensitivity needs to be understood in relative and not absolute terms. Jandora, in describing Bin Laden's second set of targets as 'so-called apostate rulers' goes on to state that for Bin Laden 'it is more difficult to justify Muslims killing other Muslims than it is to justify Muslims killing infidels', but notes significantly that this leader of global *jihad* finds justification for the former action in the writings of Ibn Taymiyya.[49]

Because Islam as a world faith is characterized by such great diversity, no objective student is going to conclude that militant strands within it make it *ipso facto* a religion of violence. There are, however, some in both the political and scholarly communities, who go to the other extreme and are keen to downplay violent *jihad* by arguing that it is contrary to the very essence of Islam as a religion of peace. Invariably, as a subset of *jihadi* Islam, the Kharijites are caught up in the same debate. With respect to the political front, few will have forgotten the stringent efforts made by British Prime Minister Tony Blair, and US President George Bush following the 9/11 atrocities, to drive a sharp divider between the 'terrorists' and Islam as a 'peaceful religion'. In a similar vein, but specific to this study, British Foreign Office Minister Mike O'Brien contrasted an essentially peaceful Islam with radical heretical terrorists who he labelled as 'the modern Kharijites'.[50]

---

[47] *Nelson Mail*, 13 March, 2010, 9.

[48] M. Ruthven, *Islam in the World*, 395. Between 2,000 to 5,000 members of the Hazara community were massacred.

[49] J. W. Jandora, 'Osama bin Laden's Global Jihad', 44.

[50] Michael O'Brien, *The Threat of the Modern Kharijites* (London: Paper presented at the Meeting of the Royal United Services Institute for Defense Studies 2002), cited by P. Sookhdeo, *Global Jihad*, 424.

A number of scholars of Islam, while not making such a sharp differentiation between Islam and the modern-day successors of the Kharijites, nonetheless advocate (as distinct from cogently arguing, in my view) a considerable distancing between the two, implicitly or explicitly. For example, Foss writing on the Kharijites as Islam's first terrorists, records their demise in the ninth century, noting that only the Ibadis lasted, and that 'terrorism and extremism failed'.[51] Esposito maintains, with reference to the Kharijites, Assassins and al-Qaeda, that 'mainstream Islam, in law and theology as well as in practice, in the end has always rejected or marginalized extremists and terrorists'.[52] And Lewis, writing on holy war, states that 'at no point do the basic texts of Islam enjoin terrorism and murder'.[53] Rather than regarding the Kharijite impulse as being extra-Islam, or aberrant to it, I have argued that in both thought and practice, it must be considered as a legitimate expression of a multi-faceted faith. In contradistinction to the likes of Esposito, I agree with the judicious evaluation of Rippin, who says of the Kharijites, that 'the tendency displayed in their thought has always provided a tension *in* Islam' [my emphasis].[54]

Bibliography

Cook, D. *Understanding Jihad* (London, Berkeley and Los Angeles: University of California Press, 2005).

Crone, P., 'Ninth-Century Muslim Anarchists', *Past and Present*, 2000.

Encyclopedia of Islam (Leiden: Brill), 1990.

---

[51] C. Foss, 'Islam's First Terrorists' (2007), no pages, http://web.ebscohost.com.ezproxy.canterbury.ac.nz/ehost/detail?vid=1&hid=6&sid=3a. Cited 8 April 2010.
[52] J. L. Esposito, *Unholy War*, 128. Cook, writing on Esposito's understanding of *jihad* says, 'Esposito deliberately spiritualizes what is an unambiguously concrete and militant doctrine, without a shred of evidence from the Qur'an or any of the classical sources, in which jihad and fighting is against real human enemies, and not the devil ... But then Esposito loses his way again, maintaining that Islam expanded during the early stage by "preaching, diplomacy and warfare", and once again inverts the natural order. He seems to have an aversion to dealing with Islamic history as it really was', *Understanding Jihad*, 42.
[53] B. Lewis, *The Crisis of Islam: Holy War and Unholy Terror* (New York: Random House, 2003), 38.
[54] A. Rippin, *Muslims*, 76.

Esposito, J. L., *Unholy War: Terror in the Name of Islam* (Oxford: Oxford University Press, 2002).

Foss, C., 'Islam's First Terrorists', no pages, http://web.ebscohost.com.ezproxy.canterbury.ac.nz/ehost/detail?vid=1&hid=6&sid=3a (2007).

Jandora, J. W., 'Osama bin Laden's Global Jihad: Myth and Movement', *Military Review* (2006).

Karsh, E., *Islamic Imperialism: A History* (New Haven and London: Yale University Press, 2007).

Lewis, B., *The Crisis of Islam: Holy War and Unholy Terror* (New York: Random House, 2003).

Nazir-Ali, M., *Conviction and Conflict: Islam, Christianity and World Order* (London and New York: Continuum, 2006).

Qutb, S., *Milestones* (Indianapolis: American Trust Publications, 1988).

Reuters, 13 March, 2010, 'Suicide bombers target military neighbourhood', *Nelson Mail*.

Rippin, A., *Muslims: Their Religious Beliefs and Practices*, (3rd ed., London and New York: Routledge, 2005).

Ruthven, M., *Islam in the World*, London: Granta, 2006).

Sookhdeo, P., *Global Jihad: The Future in the Face of Militant Islam*, (McLean, VA: Isaac. 2007).

Washington Post/Reuters, 20 October, 2009, 'Civilians flee anti-militant advance', *Nelson Mail*.

Watt, W. Montgomery, 'Conditions of Membership of the Islamic Community', *Studia Islamica* 21. (1964).

Watt, W. Montgomery, *The Formative Period of Islamic Thought* (Edinburgh: University Press, 1973).

CSIOF Occasional Papers No. 1 & 2 (2009 & 2010)

Greater and Lesser Jihad: Competing or Complementary Perspectives?

Dr Peter Francis

Malyon College

There is little doubt that the events of 9/11 have again challenged modern-day Islam to determine whether it is to be properly regarded as a religion of violence or of peace. Is the concept of the lesser *jihad,* particularly that which takes the form of an offensive *jihad,* a competing doctrine with that of the greater *jihad* of the soul, or is it complementary?

On 2nd March 2010 Dr Muhammad Tahir ul-Qadri issued a 600-page fatwa on Suicide Bombings and Terrorism which absolutely condemned all forms of terrorism. While his words seemed to echo a range of similar edicts made by other Muslim clerics since the 9/11 attacks, Dr Qadri maintained that his fatwa, which declares terrorists and suicide bombers to be unbelievers, goes further than any previous denunciation.[1] Dr Qadri said he "felt compelled to issue the edict because of concerns about the indoctrination of British Muslims at university -- Umar Farouk Abdulmutallab, the accused Nigerian Christmas Day bomber, has said he was radicalized while studying in London in 2008 -- and the failure of Muslim clerics and scholars to condemn such extremism".[2] As a scholar of Sufism, with its long tradition of emphasis upon peace, tolerance and moderation, it was not surprising to hear Dr Qadri railing against aggressive jihad. In the introduction to his fatwa, Qadri insisted, "They can't claim that their suicide bombings are

---

[1] M. Holden, http://www.nationalpost.com/news/story.html?id=2634649 viewed 3 May 2010.

[2] Muhammad Tahir ul-Qadri, "Launch Speech: Fatwa on Suicide Bombing and Terrorism" http://www.fatwaonterrorism.com/ viewed 3 May 2010.

martyrdom operations and that they become the heroes of the Muslim Umma. No", he said, "they become heroes of hellfire, and they are leading towards hellfire. There is no place for any martyrdom and their act is never, ever to be considered *jihad*."[3]

This fatwa issued by Dr Qadri has raised yet again the perennial question for Islam and that is whether the Qur'anic concepts of *jihad* are competing or complementary.

To answer that question we will begin by examining the Qur'anic origins of the concept of *jihad*, noting the historic development of the doctrine. From there we will look more closely at the concepts of the greater *jihad* and the lesser *jihad*, investigating the range of ways in which scholars have suggested that the lesser *jihad* might legitimately be engaged throughout history. A necessary part of this consideration will be an exploration of the perceived purposes of *jihad*. In conclusion we will also consider some of the modern perspectives on *jihad*, including some of the influential figures who have helped to shape the more radical views of offensive *jihad*, before finally highlighting the significant challenge that the notion of *jihad* still presents to Muslim leaders in this modern age.

Qur'anic Origins of Jihad

Riaz Hassan asserts that "the concept of *jihad* pre-dates Islam and has its origin in pre-Islamic Arabia".[4] He notes that "etymologically, the word *jihad* is derived from the Arabic word *jahada* or *juhd*, meaning ability, exertion or power".[5] However, in modern Arabic, the word *jihad* embraces a wide semantic spectrum, the breadth of which can be seen in the variety of ways in which the term was used within the Qur'an.

In the first instance Qur'an 22:41 declares that the principal purpose of *jihad* is to "establish prayer, give zakat (alms), command good and forbid evil".[6] The early ideology of *jihad* was essentially

---

[3] Muhammad Tahir ul-Qadri, "Launch Speech: Fatwa on Suicide Bombing and Terrorism" http://www.fatwaonterrorism.com/ viewed 3 May 2010.

[4] R. Hassan, *Inside Muslim Minds* (Melbourne: Melbourne University Press, 2008), 103.

[5] Hassan, *Inside Muslim Minds*, 104.

[6] Qur'an 22:41.

instructive, instructing believers to strive for the establishment of an Islamic social and moral order. Patrick Sookhdeo suggests that "while not normally included in the five pillars of Islam (though some Muslims do add it as a sixth pillar), the struggle for Islam (*jihad*) is one of the most basic religious duties glorified in the Qur'an and *hadith* and prescribed in Islamic law (*shari'a*)".[7] John Esposito reinforces this perspective as he maintains that "in its most general meaning, it (*jihad*) refers to the obligation incumbent on all Muslims, as individuals and as a community, to exert themselves to realize God's will, to lead virtuous lives, and to extend the Islamic community through preaching, education, and example, and writing".[8]

However, as we trace the early beginnings of Islam we discover that idea of *jihad* soon took on a secondary meaning which included the right, indeed the obligation, "to defend Islam and the Muslim community from aggression".[9]

The earliest Qur'anic verses sanctioning the defensive struggle against unbelievers were revealed soon after the *hijrah* (emigration) when Muhammad and his followers were forced to flee from Mecca to Medina in 622. Yet, even at that point, Shaltut maintains that "whenever they (the followers of Muhammad) felt the urge to resist the oppression and to revenge themselves on the oppressors, the Prophet held them back, bidding them to be patient in expectation of a command from Allah".[10] However, when they were almost overcome by desperation, Muhammad received the first fighting verses, Qur'an 22:39-40.[11] Hassan observes that "after the establishment of the Islamic state in Medina, the situation changed, and hardly anything, with the possible exception of prayers and *zakat*, received greater emphasis than *jihad*".[12]

---

[7] P. Sookhdeo, *Islam. The Challenge to the Church* (Pewsey: Isaac Publishing, 2006), 19.

[8] J.L. Esposito, *Islam. The Straight Path* (Oxford: Oxford University Press, 2005), 93.

[9] Esposito, *Islam. The Straight Path*, 254.

[10] Shaltut and R.Peters (ed.), "The Koran and Fighting" in *Jihad in Medieval and Modern Islam* (Leiden: E.J.Brill, 1977), 42.

[11] Qur'an 22:39-40, "Leave is given to those who fight because they were wronged – surely God is able to help them – who were expelled from their homes wrongly for saying, 'Our Lord is God'".

[12] Hassan, *Inside Muslim Minds*, 107.

Once the nascent Islamic state was established in Medina, the Qur'anic revelations began to expand the concept of *jihad* to include the promise of reward for those killed in *jihad* as well as the inclusion of threats of severe punishment in the hereafter for those refusing to participate.[13] Qur'an 3:169 provides the reassuring promise, "Think not that those who are slain in Allah's way as dead. Nay, they live, finding their sustenance in the Presence of their Lord; They rejoice in the bounty provided by Allah".[14] Riddell and Cotterell note further that "allied to the promise of paradise came a further promise, the forgiveness of sins".[15] The eminent theologian Muslim records the following tradition:

> A man stood up and said, "Messenger of Allah, do you think that if I am killed in the way of Allah, my sins will be blotted out from me?" The Messenger of Allah (peace be upon him) said: "Yes, in case you are killed in the way of Allah, you were patient and sincere and you always fought facing the enemy, never turning you back on him."[16]

Unlike the earlier verses, with their 'instructive' orientation, "these verses are orientated towards 'motivating' and 'mobilizing' believers to participate in *jihad*".[17] A significant shift was beginning to take place in regard to the meaning of *jihad*. While Esposito notes that "the Qur'an provided detailed guidelines and regulations regarding the conduct of war: who is to fight and who is to be exempted (48:17,9:91), when hostilities must cease (2:192) and how prisoners should be treated (47:4)"[18], an important set of verses known as the "sword verses"[19] cannot be ignored. The question of whether these verses can be harmonized with other Qur'anic verses such as 17:19, 29:5-6, 47:31 and 76:22, which portray *jihad* as "the constant struggle against the wayward self"[20], is one which must be addressed.

---

[13] Qur'an 9:81, 48:16.

[14] Qur'an 3:169.

[15] P. Riddell & P. Cotterell, *Islam in Context* (Grand Rapids: Baker, 2003), 28.

[16] Abdul Hamid Siddiqi (ed), Muslim, *Sahih Muslim* (Lahore: Ashraf, 1980, Vol 3), Al-Imara, chap.1285, no.4646, 1046-47.

[17] Hassan, *Inside Muslim Minds*, 105.

[18] Esposito, *Islam. The Straight Path*, 255.

[19] Qur'an 2:190, 9:5, 9:13, 9:29.

[20] C.T.R. Hewer, *Understanding Islam. The First Ten Steps* (London: SCM Press, 2006), 153.

Competing or complementary perspectives on jihad

A key sword verse is 9:5 which says, "When the sacred months have passed, slay the idolaters (the Meccans) wherever you find them, and take them, and confine them, and lie in wait for them at every place of ambush"[21]. Such verses represent a clear shift in the focus of *jihad* from defence to offence. Qutb notes the shift, pointing out that Muslims were "first restrained from fighting; then they were permitted to fight; they were commanded to fight against aggressors; and finally they were commanded to fight against all polytheists".[22]

Hassan observes that "according to traditional Muslim understanding of this revelation, the verse was thought to have abrogated all earlier limitations on the use of violence against unbelievers".[23]

Mahmud Shaltut on the other hand argues that the method of Qur'anic exegesis which sees about 70 verses being abrogated "since they are incompatible with the legitimacy of fighting" does "scant justice to the fact that the Koran is the primary source of Islam".[24] Accordingly, he argues for what he describes as "the exemplary method of Koran-interpretation".[25] In applying this exegetical method, Shaltut seeks to demonstrate that when the verses in the Qur'an are properly understood in their context it becomes self-evident that, "the Koran instructs us clearly that Allah did not wish people to become believers by way of force and compulsion, but only by way of study, reflection and contemplation".[26]

He sees in the Qur'an only two grounds upon which the legitimate use of force might be applied. The first was the resolution of issues between Muslim brothers, where some have erred and because of their rebellion must forcibly be brought back into submission to the

---

[21] Qur'an 9:5.
[22] S. Qutb, *Milestones* (Indianapolis: American Trust Publications, 1988), 115.
[23] Hassan, *Inside Muslim Minds,* 107.
[24] Shaltut, "The Koran and Fighting", 26.
[25] Shaltut, "The Koran and Fighting", 27.
[26] Shaltut, "The Koran and Fighting", 31.

will of Allah. The whole purpose of such use of force is to "preserve the unity of the Islamic state (*ummah*) and to protect the community against the evils of rebellion and mutual hostility".[27] According to Shaltut's exegetical method, the only other justification for the use of force is when the Muslim state is itself under assault. Shaltut further notes that Qur'an 2:190-194 "prohibit the provocation of hostility and this prohibition is reinforced by Allah's repugnance to aggression and by his dislike for those who provoke hostility".[28]

Ruthven appears to have great sympathy for this view, asserting that "traditional scholarship argued that these verses and similar verses should be taken in conjunction with the Qur'anic message as a whole (which includes the unambiguous injunction of 2:256: 'There shall be no compulsion in religion')".[29] He contends further that the sword verses "should be strictly understood in the historical context of the Prophet Muhammad's campaigns against the Makkans, and if applied subsequently the doctrine of *jihad* should be restricted to collective self-defence".[30]

In a somewhat similar vein Kateregga presents a picture of Islam as essentially a religion of peace, suggesting that, while the idea of *jihad* includes the struggle against a visible enemy, its primary purpose has to do with the inner struggle against the temptations of the devil and one's own passions.[31] In much the same way as Donohue and Esposito[32] focus primarily on the defensive nature of physical conflicts, so Kateregga prefers to see the "*lesser* jihad" the physical conflict, as being only an enforced extension of the "greater *jihad*", the internal struggle for piety and a life which honours God. As Hewer puts it, "The journey as an obedient servant of God must always begin in the individual Muslim's heart. Unless evil is conquered in the heart, then the Muslim is in no position to right the wrongs of the world".[33] Thus for these commentators, the primary purpose of *jihad* is the purifying of one's own soul and the

---

[27] Shaltut, "The Koran and Fighting", 39.

[28] Shaltut, "The Koran and Fighting", 44.

[29] Ruthven, *Islam in the World* (Oxford: Oxford University Press, 2006), 403.

[30] Ruthven, *Islam in the World*, 403.

[31] B.D Kateregga and D. W. Shenk, *Islam and Christianity: A Muslim and Christian Dialogue* (Grand Rapids: Eerdmans, 1980), 77.

[32] J.J. Donohue and J.L. Esposito, *Islam in Transition. Muslim Perspectives* (Oxford: Oxford University Press, 2007), 399-401.

[33] Hewer, *Understanding Islam*, 154.

appropriate focusing of their lives on the things that advance the name and cause of God.

Those who prefer to place the primary emphasis upon the "greater *jihad*", the spiritual *jihad,* often quote a *hadith* in which Muhammad describes physical battle as "'the lesser *jihad (jihad-e-asghar)*' i.e. inferior to the struggle for personal purity which he called 'the greater *jihad (jihad-e-akbar)*'. One version runs:

> A group of Muslim soldiers came to the Holy Prophet (from a battle). He said: Welcome, you have come from the lesser jihad to the greater jihad. It was said: What is the greater jihad? He said: The striving of a servant against his low desires. *Al-Tasharraf,* Part 1, p.70. [34]

Nevertheless there can be no escaping the explicitly violent nature of the sword verses referred to. In an effort to find some complementary harmony between the concept of the "lesser *jihad*" and the "greater *jihad*", commentators such as Ruthven argue the case for the classical formulations of *jihad* which saw it being applied to "the moral effort against evil, including one's own evil impulses, and the military struggle against the enemies of Islam".[35] Indeed, in tracing the influence of Arabian Wahhabism on the modern-day understanding of *jihad,* Ruthven goes on to state that "the personal or 'inner' (greater) *jihad* against evil furnishes the preparation of the external (lesser) *jihad* which aims to destroy evil in the world".[36] For Ruthven there is an inseparable link between the two. The greater *jihad* must always precede, inform and moderate the lesser *jihad.*

The history of offensive jihad

Whilst noting the attempt by numerous scholars to argue for the complementary nature of the "greater *jihad*" of the soul and the necessary defensive form of the "lesser *jihad*", it is impossible to ignore the evidence of the aggressive or offensive form of *jihad*

---

[34] P. Sookhdeo, *Understanding Islamic Terrorism* (Pewesy: Isaac Publishing, 2004), 95.

[35] Ruthven, *Islam in the World*, 403.

[36] Ruthven, *Islam in the World,* 280.

embraced particularly during the period of the expansion of the Islamic empire.

Donohue and Esposito freely acknowledge that during the post-Prophetic era, classical jurists unanimously divided *jihad* into two main modalities. "The first we may refer to as 'aggressive *jihad*', which is proactive and, according to the majority, constituted a communal requirement to be carried out at least once every year. The second modality was the 'defensive *jihad*', which was waged whenever Muslim lands were attacked".[37]

During the post-Prophetic period as the Islamic empire was growing and coming in constant contact with competing ideological systems, it became necessary for scholars to develop a more coherent doctrine of *jihad*. Thus, Muslim jurists al-Shaybani (d.804) and Shafi'i (d.820) joined forces, bringing together the Qur'anic texts and *hadiths* to formulate a definitive doctrine of *jihad* which essentially divided the world into the Abode of Islam (*Darul-Islam*) and the Abode of War (*Darul-Harb*). In the first, "Islamic law and sovereignty prevailed", while the second "included lands that were not yet under the moral and political authority of Islam".[38] According to this doctrine, "The Abode of Islam would be in a permanent state of warfare with the Abode of War until the latter submitted".[39]

In an effort to justify this notion of the permanent state of war, Fred Donner maintains that:

> In this society (the Arabian world of the 7th century), war (*harb*, used in the senses of both *activity* and *condition*) was in one sense the normal way of life; that is, a "state of war" was assumed to exist between one's tribe and all others, unless a particular treaty or agreement had been reached with another tribe establishing amicable relations.[40]

With this in mind, Donohue and Esposito argue that the Qur'anic texts enjoining *jihad* on the followers of Allah were simply

---

[37] Donohue and Esposito, *Islam in Transition*, 399.

[38] Hassan, *Inside Muslim Minds*, 110.

[39] Hassan, *Inside Muslim Minds*, 110.

[40] F. Donner, J. Kelsay (ed.) and J.T. Johnson (ed.), "The Sources of Islamic Conceptions of War" in *Just War and Jihad: Historical and Theoretical Perspectives on War and Peace in Western and Islamic Tradition* (New York: Greenwood Press, 1991), 34.

"responding to the existing state of affairs by effectively redirecting energies that were already being expended. Moreover, peace, i.e., the repelling of aggression, rather than conversion to Islam was the ultimate aim in this fighting".[41] The overarching purpose of *jihad* seen in this way was to provide for the security and freedom of the Muslims in a world that kept them under threat.

However, Muhammad Sa'id al-Buti of Damascus University takes the repelling of aggression one step further, arguing a case for pre-emptive aggression, as a defensive measure in the battle with the enemies of Islam. He says:

> "It becomes axiomatic that the responsibility for guarding and defending these two possessions [Islam's territorial abode, and the Islamic society] cannot be fulfilled by peaceful *jihad*, by tongue or *da'wa* [proclamation]. It is a task that can only be achieved by driving back aggressors, repelling them and foiling any dangers likely to be caused by them".[42]

In David Cook's reflection on this statement he asserts that, for al-Buti, belligerent *jihad* is legitimized "when Muslims are aware of the obviously aggressive intentions of a foreign power or state and reserve the right for themselves to strike pre-emptively against their enemy".[43]

Nonetheless, Esposito insists that contrary to popular belief, the early conquests did not seek to spread the faith through forced conversion, but to spread Muslim rule. In saying this he does, however, concede that "as Islam penetrated new areas, people were offered three options: (1) conversion, that is full membership in the Muslim community, with its rights and duties; (2) acceptance of Muslim rule as 'protected' people and payment of a poll tax; (3) battle or the sword if neither the first nor the second option was accepted".[44]

---

[41] Donohue and Esposito, *Islam in Transition*, 398.

[42] S. Al-Buti, quoted in *Understanding Jihad* by D. Cook (London: University of California Press, 2005), 122.

[43] D. Cook, *Understanding Jihad*, 122.

[44] Esposito, *Islam*, 35.

The problem with this aggressive form of *jihad* is that it left their enemies with little option. If they were to avoid conflict then they could either convert or become the tax-paying subjects of an occupying force. Bat Ye'or contends that in reality:

> *Jihad* divides the people of the world into two irreconcilable groups: the Muslims – inhabitants of the dar-Islam regions subject to Islamic law; and infidels – inhabitants of the dar-al-harb (*Harbis*), the territory of war; destined to come under Islamic jurisdiction, either by conversion of its inhabitants [through da'wa] or armed conflict [through *jihad* in its non-Sufi, militaristic sense].[45]

Lee Harris concludes that "Islamic *jihad*, from its commencement, refused to recognize the legitimacy of any status quo other than that achieved in Dar el-Islam, or 'the domain of peace'".[46]

Modern perspectives on offensive jihad

From the seventeenth to the nineteenth centuries, the Muslim world was increasingly faced with economic and social dispossession as European countries embarked upon their campaigns of expansion and colonization. Hassan observes that:

> resistance among the local populations against the foreign rulers, at least in the initial stages, was organized by politico-religious movements under the banner of *jihad*.[47]

Indeed much of the *jihad* called for came under the revivalist motif as the faithful were called, not only to exercise defensive *jihad*, but also offensive *jihad* in an effort to reclaim what rightly belonged to Allah.

By way of illustration Abdullah Saaed cites the response to British colonization of the Indian subcontinent where a number of ulama declared that India was no longer an 'abode of Islam' (*dar al-islam*) but an 'abode of war' (*dar al-harb*). "In the early 1800s, Hajji Shariat Allah argued that India was an abode of war and declared *jihad*

---

[45] B. Ye'or, *Islam and Dhimmitude: Where Civilizations Collide* (Cranbury NJ: Fairleigh University Press, 2002), 43.

[46] L. Harris, "Jihad Then and Now" in *Policy Review*, no.139 (2006), 72.

[47] Hassan, *Inside Muslim Minds*, 112.

against the British in Bengal".[48] Similar *jihad* movements were called for in places like Africa where the "Sanusis in the North waged a *jihad* against the French and Italians. In Sudan, Muhammad Ahmad, otherwise known as the Mahdi of Sudan, declared a *jihad* against the British and killed General Gordon in 1855".[49]

Even by the middle of the twentieth century when Muslim countries had reclaimed their independence from direct colonial rule, the struggle for Islam was far from over. Most now independent Muslim countries "were ruled by authoritarian, oppressive and corrupt regimes".[50] Thus, with the 'national project' failing, a new ideology of the Islamic state began to emerge. The Pakistani social thinker Abul A'la Mawdudi (1903-1979) is largely regarded as the founder of the modern concept of the Islamic state. Mawdudi believed that Islam is about much more than a set of religious rituals. His goal was "the complete transformation of individual, society and politics in line with Islamic ideology".[51] It was his view that it was not enough for society to be composed of Muslims – "it must also be Islamic in its basic structure".[52]

Sayyid Qutb, the chief ideologue of the Muslim Brotherhood in Egypt, was greatly influenced by Mawdudi. His seminal work *Ma'alim fi al-Tariq*, translated as *Signposts on the Road* or *Milestones*, has became the primary ideological source of contemporary radical Islamic movements. While Qutb did not see himself as a radical, but rather a traditionalist, his writings, along with those of Mawdudi, have proven to be enormously influential in inspiring the modern revivalist movement which has included terrorism.

Bennett observes that, "like Mawdudi, Qutb dismissed the view that *jihad* could only be defensive".[53] In Qutb's view, to reduce *jihad* to

---

[48] A. Saaed, *Islamic Thought: An Introduction* (London: Routledge, 2006), 133.

[49] Saaed, *Islamic Thought*, 134.

[50] Hassan, *Inside Muslim Minds*, 113.

[51] P. Sookhdeo, *Global Jihad. The Future in the Face of Militant Islam* (Mclean, VA: Isaac Publishing, 2007), 281.

[52] Sookhdeo, *Global Jihad*, 281.

[53] C. Bennett, *Muslims and Modernity. An Introduction to the Issues and Debates* (London: Continuum, 2005), 204.

self-defence is to "diminish the greatness of the Islamic way of life".[54] In fact Qutb argues that *jihad* does not have to be justified by any particular condition. Rather, "*jihad* is the justifiable instrument of choice for establishing God's authority on earth, for arranging human affairs according to the true guidance provided by God and for abolishing 'all Satanic forces'".[55] According to Bennett, Qutb's insistence that Muslims can take the initiative in using violence, without waiting until they are attacked, cements his place as "the intellectual father of modern Islamic terrorism and the inspiration behind 9/11".[56]

Conclusion

Since 9/11 there have been many disparate voices from within the Islamic world on this matter. Clerics such as Mohammed al-Asi, the elected Imam of the Islamic Centre in Washington DC, appear to support the complementary nature for offensive *jihad* on the grounds that Muslims cannot at present "enjoy freedom of conscience and will, and a truly independent state". Therefore he says:

> "Our understanding of the Qur'an and the Sunnah obliges us to carry the burden of *jihad* to deter all forms of persecution, discrimination, and hurt and injury premeditated by inimical forces. Muslims like all other people, are entitled to security: security for their lives, their possessions and their faith".[57]

Articulating the justification for offensive *jihad* even more clearly is Azzam Tamimi, who "described *jihad* in terms of a struggle against all political or economic oppression or tyranny".[58] He asserts that:

> "Not only does the Islamic faith permit a Muslim to resist despotism and rebel against it, but it makes it incumbent upon him to do so with whatever means available to him. It is understandable that a Muslim may lose his life struggling against oppression, and for this he or she

---

[54] S. Qutb, *Milestones* (Indianapolis: American Trust Publications, 1988), 130.
[55] Qutb, *Milestones*, 127.
[56] Bennett, *Muslims and Modernity*, 208.
[57] M. Al-Asi, "Qur'anic Teaching on the Justification for *Jihad* and Qital" in *Crescent International* (1-15 June 2003), 7.
[58] Sookhdeo, *Global Jihad*, 366.

is promised a great reward in the life after death. In other words, the effort made is not wasted and the sacrifice is not in vain".[59]

Against this, as we have already noted, there have been numerous voices of notable clerics such as Muhammad Tahir ul-Qadri who, recognizing the competing nature of offensive *jihad*, have roundly condemned all forms of offensive *jihad*, especially those which involve terrorism and suicide bombing. He, along with others such as Louay Fatoohi, would argue that armed *jihad* is at best just a temporary measure for self-defence, but peaceful *jihad*, in the sense of self-improvement and preaching Islam and working for good, is permanent.[60]

The dilemma facing the Muslim community of the world today is that under the classical formulation of *jihad*, when it became clear that *jihad* was necessary, it could only be called by the legitimate Muslim ruler. Normally it was the Caliph who would call for the *jihad*.[61] But since there has been no Caliphate since 1924, there is now today no one leader who is able to provide authoritative direction on behalf of the worldwide *umma*.

Commentators such as Donohue and Esposito warn Muslims against the "fallacy of assuming that realities of yesterday pass automatically into today or that the factual or historical assessments of the Muslims past constitute authoritative doctrines that are binding on the Muslims of the present".[62] However, in the absence of any unifying and authoritative leadership within the wider Muslim community, it is hard to see how there will ever be a satisfactory resolution to the question of the complementary or competing nature of the great *jihad* of the soul and the lesser *jihad* of external struggle for the Islamic community as a whole.

What is certain is that scholars such as Shaltut who argue against the idea that the latter verses of the Qur'an concerning offensive *jihad* abrogate the earlier, more moderate verses on *jihad*, might well

---

[59] A. Tamimi, "Concepts of Life Beyond Death: Martydom, Resurrection, Heaven & Hell", in *Institute of Islamic Political Thought* (26 March, 2004).

[60] L. Fatoohi, *Jihad in the Qur'an: The Truth from the Source* (Kuala Lumpur: A.S. Noordeen, 2002), 34-35.

[61] Hewer, *Understanding Islam*, 154.

[62] Donohue and Esposito, *Islam in Transition*, 407.

be accused of engaging in their own form of abrogation, by denying the highly elevated position afforded by the Qur'an to the exercise of offensive *jihad*. There can be no doubt that in the minds of many revivalists the concepts of the greater *jihad* and the offensive lesser *jihad* are not only complementary, but essential, having been mandated by the Qur'an itself.

Bibliography

Ahmed, A.S. *Discovering Islam: Making sense of Muslim history and society* (London: Routledge, 1990).

Al-Asi, M. "Qur'anic Teaching on the Justification for *Jihad* and Qital" in *Crescent International* (1-15 June 2003).

Bennett, C. *Muslims and Modernity. An Introduction to the Issues and Debates* (London: Continuum, 2005).

Cook, D. *Understanding Jihad* (London: University of California Press, 2005).

Donner, F. "The Sources of Islamic Conceptions of War" in *Just War and Jihad: Historical and Theoretical Perspectives on War and Peace in Western and Islamic Traditions.* (ed. J. Kelsay and J.T. Johnson, New York: Greenwood Press, 1991).

Donohue, J.J. *Islam in Transition: Muslim Perspectives* (Oxford: Oxford University, and Esposito: J.L. Press, 2007).

Elias, J.J. *Islam: Religions of the World* (London: Routledge, 1999).

Esposito, J.L. *Islam: The Straight Path* (New York: Oxford University Press, 1988).

Fatoohi, L. *Jihad in the Qur'an: The Truth from the Source* (Kuala Lumpur: A.S. Noordeen, 2002).

Guillaume, A. *Life of Muhammad (a translation of Ibn Ishaq's Sirat Rasul Allah)* (Karachi: Oxford University Press, 1955).

Haeri, S.F. *The Elements of Islam* (Melbourne: Element Books, 1993).

Harris, L. "Jihad Then and Now" in *Policy Review,* no.139 (2006), 72.

Hallaq, W.B. *The Origins and Evolution of Islamic Law* (Cambridge: Cambridge University Press, 2005).

Hassan, R. *Inside Muslim Minds* (Melbourne: Melbourne University Press, 2008).

Hewer, C.T.R. *Understanding Islam: The First Ten Steps* (London:

Humphreys, R.S. *Islamic History* (London: I B Tauris, 1991).

Karsh, E. *Islamic Imperialism: A History* (London: Yale University Press, 2006).

Kateregga B.D and Grand Shenk, D. W., *Islam and Christianity: A Muslim and Christian Dialogue* (Rapids: Eerdmans, 1980).

Lapidus, I.M., *A History of Islamic Societies* (Cambridge: Cambridge University Press, 2002).

Qutb, S. *Milestones* (Indianapolis: American Trust Publications, 1988).

Qutb, S. *Islam: The Religion of the Future* (Safat, Kuwait: Sahaba Islamic Press, 1974).

Rahman, F. *Islam* (London: Weidenfeld & Nicholson, 1966).

Ramadan, T. *Western Muslims and the Future of Islam* (Oxford: Oxford University Press, 2004).

Riddell, P.G. and Cotterell, P., *Islam in Context: Past, Present and Future* (Grand Rapids: Baker Academic, 2003).

Rippin, A. *Muslims: Their Religious Beliefs and Practices* (London: Routledge, 2005, 3rd ed.).

Ruthven, M. *Islam in the World,* (2nd ed, London: Penguin, 1991).

Saaed, A. *Islamic Thought: An Introduction* (London: Routledge, 2006).

Schacht, J. and Bosworth, C.E. (eds) "Islamic Religious Law" in *The Legacy of Islam* (2nd ed., Oxford: Oxford University Press, 1979), 392-403.

Shaltut, M. "The Koran and Fighting" in *Jihad in Medieval and Modern Islam* (ed. R. Peters, 26-53, Leiden: E.J. Brill, 1977).

Sookhdeo, P. *Global Jihad: The Future in the Face of Militant Islam* (McLean VA: Isaac Publishing, 2007).

Sookhdeo, P. *Islam: The Challenge to the Church* (Pewsey, UK: Isaac Publishing, 2006).

Sookhdeo, P. *Understanding Islamic Terrorism* (Pewsey, UK: Isaac Publishing, 2004).

Tahir ul-Qadri, M. "Launch Speech: Fatwa on Suicide Bombing and Terrorism" http://www.fatwaonterrorism.com/ viewed 3 May 2010.

Tamimi, A. Concepts of Life Beyond Death: Martydom, Resurrection, Heaven & Hell", in *Institute of Islamic Political Thought* (26 March, 2004).

Ye'or, B. *Islam and Dhimmitude: Where Civilizations Collide* (Cranbury NJ: Fairleigh University Press, 2002).

PART TWO

CONTEXT

CSIOF Occasional Papers No. 1 & 2 (2009 & 2010)

The Vision for Pakistan: Muslim state or Islamic state?

John L. Bales

Minister, Greenacre Anglican Church, Sydney

Pakistan was created on 14th August 1947 as a homeland for the Muslims of India. From the start there were tensions about its identity as a secular, Muslim or Islamic state, tensions which have led to ongoing confusion and conflict. In this paper we examine some different visions of Pakistan's identity and the consequences of the failure to find an agreed understanding.

The division of India in 1947 was based on the 'two nations' theory that the Muslims and Hindus of India were distinct 'nations' with their own histories, cultures, languages and traditions. Muslims feared that under democratically elected majority rule, the Hindus would dominate and oppress them. The nineteenth century reformer Sayyid Ahmad Khan sought to combine Islam with Western rationalism as part of the movement towards Muslim modernism. In 1875 he established the Muhammadan Anglo-Oriental College in Aligarh to provide modern education for the Muslims of India. He was opposed to the independence movement of the National Congress, advising Muslims to support the British government. He was concerned that Muslims, as a distinct nationality, would be outnumbered and so dominated in an independent India.[1]

This was taken a stage further by Muhammad Iqbal. In his speech as president of the Muslim League in 1930[2] Iqbal called for the

---

[1] See texts in Wm. Theodore de Bary (ed.), *Sources of the Indian Tradition,* compiled by Stephen Hay and I. H. Qureshi (Columbia University Press: New York, 1958, Vol. II), 190, 194f.

[2] de Bary (ed.), *Sources of the Indian Tradition*, 211-216.

creation of a separate state for Muslims in the North-West of India. For Iqbal, religion was not just a private experience but should form the basis for an Islamic social order that requires the construction of a national polity. He argued that "the Indian Muslim is entitled to full and free development on the lines of his own culture and tradition in his own Indian home-lands."[3]

The political realisation of this idea was pursued to its fruition by the leader of the Muslim League, Muhammad Ali Jinnah, known as the Qaid-i-Azam.

Jinnah was a lawyer of Khowaja background with liberal religious views. As a member of the Indian National Congress he advocated Hindu-Muslim unity as the best way to independence from the British. In 1913 he also joined the Muslim League. When Gandhi organised the first campaign of civil disobedience against the British in 1920 Jinnah withdrew from the Congress.[4] By 1930 Jinnah had become disillusioned, leaving Indian politics and basing himself in London to practice law. Under pressure from friends, including Iqbal, he returned to India in 1934 and from then on fought for a separate state of Pakistan.[5] In March 1940 at Lahore Jinnah gave the presidential address when the Muslim League adopted the Lahore Resolution calling for a separate Muslim homeland.[6]

From 1934 till his death in 1948 Jinnah's primary goal was to see a Muslim nation emerge in north India. Gradually the Islamic elements in his speeches grew but he never wanted a theocratic Islamic State in the traditional sense.[7]

---

[3] de Bary (ed.), *Sources of the Indian Tradition*, 214.

[4] A good account of the various influences leading to Jinnah's conversion is found in Ahmed, *Jinnah, Pakistan and Islamic Identity*, 61-85.

[5] Pakistan means the 'land of the pure.' The name, taking letters from Punjab, Afghanistan, Kashmir, Sind and Baluchistan had been suggested by Rahmat Ali, a student at Cambridge in 1933. See de Bary (ed.), *Sources of the Indian Tradition*, 275ff.

[6] Selections from Jinnah's speech in de Bary (ed.), *Sources of the Indian Tradition*, 283-286.

[7] Some have viewed Jinnah as using Islam for his own political ends, for example Christophe Jaffrelot (ed.), *A History of Pakistan and its Origins* (Trans. Gillian Beaumont, Anthem Press: London, 2002), 14: "Jinnah and most of his lieutenants were not religious, but they used Islam as a focus for an evocation of nationalism, playing on its emotional power..."; Ira Lapidus says "The Pakistan program was the program of secularized elites who were forced by disunity of the Muslim population and by competition with the Hindu majorities to call their political society 'Islamic'." *A History of Islamic Societies* (Cambridge University Press: Cambridge, 2002, 2nd ed.), 637. But this fails to take into account the changes in Jinnah's thinking during the 1920s and 30s; see Ahmed, *Jinnah, Pakistan and Islamic Identity*, 19-32 for a critical assessment of scholarship on Jinnah.

If we examine some of his speeches in the last two years of his life we see his developing views.[8] Muslim nationhood was based on culture rather than religion: "Not only are most of us Muslims but we have our own history, customs and traditions and those ways of thought, outlook and instinct which go to make up a sense of nationality."[9]

Several times he spoke against the idea of a theocracy.[10] In a talk broadcast to the people of America Jinnah said "I do not know what the ultimate shape of this constitution is going to be, but I am sure it will be of the democratic type, embodying the essential principles of Islam... Islam and its idealism have taught us democracy. It has taught equality of men, justice and fair play to everyone... In any case Pakistan is not going to be a theocratic State -- to be ruled by priests with a divine mission."[11]

In his opening address as President to The Constituent Assembly[12] he did not evoke Islam but spoke in general terms of law and order, bribery, corruption, and nepotism. He appealed to the members to "Concentrate on the well-being of the people, and especially of the masses of the poor... If you change the past and work together in a spirit that everyone of you, no matter what community he belongs, no matter what relations he had with you in the past, no matter what is his colour, caste or creed, is first, second and last a citizen of the State with equal rights, privileges and obligations, there will be no end to the progress you will make."[13] Minorities were to be free and protected: "You are free; you are free to go to your temples, you are free to go to your mosques or any other place of worship in this state of Pakistan. You may belong to any religion or caste or creed -- that has nothing to do with the business of the State... We

---

[8] Ahmed, *Jinnah, Pakistan and Islamic Identity*, 177, rightly notes that Jinnah's views remained vague.

[9] In a broadcast to the people of Australia, 19 February 1948 in M. A. Jinnah, *Speeches and Statements 1947-1948*, (Oxford University Press: Karachi, 2000), 118ff.

[10] In Jinnah, *Speeches and Statements 1947-1948*, 15, 118, 125, "Pakistan is not a theocracy or anything like it".

[11] Jinnah, *Speeches and Statements 1947-1948*, 125, 111, and Jaffrelot (ed.), *A History of Pakistan and its Origins*, 62, quoting a speech of 9 June 1947.

[12] Jinnah, *Speeches and Statements 1947-1948*, 25-29 on 11 August 1947. The Assembly was established in 1947 to frame the constitution for Pakistan.

[13] Jinnah, *Speeches and Statements 1947-1948*, 27f.

are starting with this fundamental principle that we are all citizens and equal citizens of one State."[14]

Some have viewed this speech as a total reversal of Jinnah's 'two-nations' theory[15] but it must be interpreted in the light of other statements of the time and the context that Pakistan was nearly a reality. In these two years he frequently mentions Islam and even speaks of Pakistan as an Islamic State.[16] In another address he says that, "The idea [of Pakistan] was that we should have a State in which we could live as free men and women and which we could develop according to our own lights and culture and where principles of Islamic social justice could find free play."[17] Again, at the opening of State Bank on 1 July 1948 he said he would "watch with keenness the work of your Research Organization in evolving banking practices compatible with Islamic ideals of social and economic life... The adoption of Western economic theory and practice will not help us in achieving our goal of creating a happy and contented people."[18]

Jinnah's vision then was of Pakistan as a democracy, with equality for all, including minorities and a modernist interpretation of Islam with British-type constitutional arrangements. Sadly he died just over a year after the founding of Pakistan. While it took till 1956 for the Constituent Assembly to produce a constitution, a significant step came in 1949 when they adopted the 'Objectives Resolution'[19] under the guidance of Prime Minister Liaquat Ali Khan. It is a compromise between the liberal, democratic ideas of Jinnah and a more 'Islamic' line pushed by the *ulama* (clergy/scholars) and other traditional elements.

The Resolution begins by asserting that 'sovereignty over the entire universe belongs to God Almighty alone and the authority which He has delegated to the State of Pakistan through its people for

---

[14] Jinnah, *Speeches and Statements 1947-1948*, 28, see also the interview on pages 14-15.

[15] For example, Ishtiaq Ahmed writes that "a more candid statement in favour of secularism and against a religious state is difficult to find ... the speech contradicted the whole rationale of Pakistan." *The Concept of an Islamic State in Pakistan*, (Vanguard: Lahore, 1991), 79.

[16] See *Speeches and Statements 1947-1948*, 40, 123, 201.

[17] *Speeches and Statements 1947-1948*, 51.

[18] *Speeches and Statements 1947-1948*, 231.

[19] de Bary (ed.), *Sources of the Indian Tradition*, 290-291. This has remained the basis for the constitutions of 1962 and 1973. The current version, now incorporated as the preamble is available online at <www.pakistani.org/pakistan/constitution/preamble.html>

being exercised within the limits prescribed by Him is a sacred trust.' Further "the principles of democracy, freedom, equality, tolerance, and social justice, as enunciated by Islam, shall be fully observed"; "fundamental rights including equality of status, of opportunity, and before law ..." shall be guaranteed and the judiciary will be independent.[20] Although acceptable to many, the resolution failed to address the variety within Islam, nor is it clear on the relation of the State and judiciary to the *ulama*. Thus a door opened for those who wanted to introduce traditional Islamic law (Shariah) into Pakistan.

Introducing the Objectives Resolution, Liaquat Ali Khan reiterated that Pakistan is not a 'theocracy.' For Khan theocracy is "a government by ordained priests, who wield authority as being specially appointed by those who claim to derive their rights from their sacerdotal position."[21] In his analysis of the Islamic State in Pakistan Ishtiaq Ahmed defines a 'theocracy' as 'a state in which the ultimate sovereign is God.[22] This broader definition is more applicable to the Pakistan context.

Maulana Abul A'la Maududi was the most influential advocate of a theocracy, the imposition of Islamic social order.[23] He was a prolific writer and around 1940 established the Jamaat-i Islami (The Islamic Party) as a vanguard of true community. Although opposed to the establishment of Pakistan[24] he moved to Lahore in 1947. Maududi accepted the Objectives Resolution and saw it as a springboard for his Islamic polity. For him Islam seeks to establish the "kingdom of God" and so is a "theocracy", not as rule by a priestly class but as

---

[20] On the process of making the 1956 Constitution and its interpretation, see Manzooruddin Ahmed, *Pakistan: The Emerging Islamic State* (Allies Book Corporation, Karachi, 1966).

[21] Ahmed, *Pakistan: The Emerging Islamic State,* 293; see also Oxford Dictionary. In this sense the polity of Ayatollah Khomeini would be closer to a theocracy than any other system. Esposito, *Islam and Politics* (Syracuse University Press: New York, 1998, 4th ed.), 324ff.

[22] Ahmed, *The Concept of an Islamic State in Pakistan,* 28.

[23] There is vast literature on Maududi. A useful work is Seyyed Vali Reza Nasr *Maududi and the Making of Islamic Revivalism* (New York & Oxford: OUP, 1996); also Charles J. Adams 'Mawdudi and the Islamic State' in J. L. Esposito, *Voices,* 99-133.

[24] mainly because of his pan-Islamic views and because the movement was led by modernist, liberal Muslims.

the Muslim community living under the Shariah.[25] He prefers the term theo-democracy, emphasising the role of the community in electing the government. Others have called Maududi's system 'nomocracy' (rule of law) but as the law involved is the Shariah, the divine Law, it is reasonable to call this theocracy. Such a use will include both Maududi and the views of other traditional *ulama*.

Khurshid Ahmad has published a number of Maududi's political writings in *Islamic Law and Constitution*.[26] We will mainly focus upon a paper entitled "Political Theory in Islam" written in 1939.[27]

Maududi's foundation for the social and moral system of Islam is the Unity and Sovereignty of Allah.[28] Allah is the only real sovereign and law-giver. An Islamic state must be based on the law of God in the Qur'an and traditions of Muhammad. In contrast to the traditionalists Maududi does permit the use of *ijtihad* or 'effort to ascertain the real intent' of an Islamic injunction.[29] Thus a Muslim government may enact legislation which, based on the revealed Law is specific to the conditions of modern life. There is freedom in matters not dealt with under Sharia. However, Islam has 'divine limits'; certain principles, checks and balances are "prescribed in order that man may be trained to lead a balanced and moderate life".[30] Much legislation laid down in the Sharia, such as religious duties, Zakat, marriage, divorce and retaliation (qisas) is unalterable because it has been enacted by God.[31]

Such a State is the antithesis of Western democracy which is based on the sovereignty of the people, a blasphemous idea for Maududi. But Islam does include democracy as the ruler chosen by the (believing) people.

---

[25] Maududi, *Islamic Law and Constitution,* (Trans. Khurshid Ahmad, Islamic Publications: Lahore, 1992, 11th edition), 139.

[26] Note 24. The book has been frequently updated and revised.

[27] Maududi, *Islamic Law and Constitution,* 124-152. Like most of Maududi's writings this has also been published separately and is reproduced in *Islam: Its Meaning and Message,* ed. Khurshid Ahmad and Salem Azzam (London: Islamic Foundation, 195), 147-171.

[28] Maududi, *Islamic Law and Constitution,* 136ff.

[29] Maududi, *Islamic Law and Constitution,* 76, see the whole chapter "Legislation and 'Ijtahad' in Islam", 71-92.

[30] Maududi, *Islamic Law and Constitution,* 142.

[31] Maududi, *Islamic Law and Constitution,* 144.

The stated purpose of the Islamic State according to the Shariah is to establish the kingdom of God by preventing exploitation, safeguarding liberty and especially establishing a well-balanced society of social justice.[32] Such an ideological State is "universal and all-embracing", its sphere of activity applying to all areas of life. It can only be ruled by upright believers. Non-Muslims have the status of *dhimmi*s, citizens who may participate but without being in key decision-making positions.[33]

Maududi revises the classical Islamic theory of the Caliphate by interpreting *khalifah* ('vicegerency') as the whole community of believers instead of a single appointed Caliph: "every believer is a Caliph of God in his individual capacity."[34] This is the foundation for Islamic democracy. There are no class divisions but equality for all and no room for dictatorship of any individual or group, the ruler being answerable to both God and the community.[35] The Islamic order gives anequilibrium between individualism and collectivism.[36]

Maududi's ideas of the sovereignty of Allah, *ijtihad* and *khalifah* constitute a radical reinterpretation of traditional Islam. His influence on modern Islamism has been enormous.[37] In Pakistan his ideas and the agitation of the Jamaat-i Islami led to an increasing Islamisation of the law and society especially during the presidency of General Zia-ul Haq (1977-88).

We have examined only two models for Pakistan, Jinnah's liberal, modernist understanding of Islam with a secular political order and Maududi's theocracy based on the sovereignty of God expressed in Islamic law. Between these there are a host of other interpretations of the Islamic state. Ishtiaq Ahmed outlines four different approaches among Pakistani writers: the sacred state excluding or

---

[32] Maududi, *Islamic Law and Constitution*, 145.

[33] Maududi, *Islamic Law and Constitution*, 147. Maududi dealt with the status of non-Muslims in greater detail in a paper, "Rights of Non-Muslims in an Islamic State" reproduced in *Islamic Law and Constitution*, 273-300.

[34] Maududi, *Islamic Law and Constitution*, based on Surah 2.24, 25.

[35] This is the basis of the Jamaat-i Islami's objection to prolonged martial rule.

[36] Maududi, *Islamic Law and Constitution*, 152.

[37] including Sayyld Qutb and the Muslim Brotherhood. See J. L. Esposito, *The Islamic Threat* (New York and Oxford: OUP, 1999, 3rd ed.), 128-138.

including the human will and the secular state admitting or excluding the divine will.[38] Similarly, Marc Gaborieau[39] distinguishes three groups: the secularizing elite, the modernists and the "men of religion." While they differ slightly in their categories it is clear that there is no consistent understanding of the relation of Islam to the ideology of Pakistan. This failure to settle on a definite ideology has been a constant source of disturbance and strife. In the remainder of this paper we look at some of these issues.

Firstly, Pakistan has struggled to deal with its ethnic diversity.[40] Already in 1948 Jinnah insisted on the use of Urdu as the national language.[41] Seen as a denial of Bengali culture it led to riots in Dacca. The 'language problem' symbolised a deeper issue: neither 'Muslim culture' nor Islam as a religion has been able to weld the different ethnic groups together. Punjab was the most populous province in West Pakistan and Punjabis or Muhajirs (refugees from India following 1947) controlled much of the army, civil service, wealth and industry of Pakistan. This 'Punjabi hegemony' offended and marginalised the other provinces. Finally the Bengalis revolted in 1971 and, with India's help, fought for independence as Bangladesh. Similar problems continued in Sind and Baluchistan, with, strikes, violence and independence movements. In Karachi the Muharjirs set up their own political party in 1984,[42] at times fighting pitched battles with Sindhis and Pathans.

---

[38] 1. the sacred state excluding human will- traditional ulama and Maududi; 2. sacred state including the human will - Muhammad Asad, Ghulam Perwez, Abdul Hakim and Javid Iqbal; 3.the secular state admitting divine will - S. M. Zafar and Muhammad Usman; 4. the secular state excluding the divine will- Muhammad Munir. After discussing each writer in detail Ahmed presents a very useful comparative chart of the differences between them, Ahmed, *The Concept of an Islamic State in Pakistan*, 190-193.

[39] in Jafferlot (ed.), *A History of Pakistan and its Origins*, 238-240. Secularists (Jinnah and Munir), modernists (Muhammad Iqbal, Fazlur Rahman and Abdul Hakim) and the "men of religion", (the ulama and the fundamentalists like Asad and Maududi). Another useful analysis is E. I. J. Rosenthal, *Islam in the Modern National State* (Cambridge: Cambridge University Press, 1965), 125-153, looking at Asad and Maududi.

[40] Rosenthal, *Islam in the Modern National State*, 16-38, outlines this history of ethnic tensions. Frances Battacharya, in the same volume, devotes a chapter to 'East Bengal', 39-60.

[41] See his remarks in a speech to the students of Dacca University on 24 March 1948 in Jinnah, *Speeches and Statements 1947-1948*, 157. Urdu is the language of the Muslims of north India, especially in Uttar Pradesh. As this was the province most concerned with the Pakistan movement Urdu became a symbol of Muslim culture.

[42] The Muhajir Qaumi Movement (the refugee national movement) now renamed as the 'Mutahida Qaumi Movement (United National Movement) but still basically a Muhajir movement.

A second problem has been debate over the definition of Islam. An example is the agitation against the Ahmadiyya,[43] followers of Mizra Ghulam Ahmad (1838-1908) who believed he was endowed with the spiritual qualities of a prophet. This claim contradicts the finality of the prophet Muhammad[44] and Ahmadiyya have been persecuted as heretics. In the 1950s there were anti-Ahmadiyya demonstrations involving both traditional *ulama* and the Jamaat-i Islami, all calling for them to be declared non-Muslims. The inquiry and report led by Justice Munir examined the different Islamic groups and found that there was no agreement over who is a Muslim.[45] The issue lapsed under martial rule but re-emerged when Zulfikar Ali Bhutto became Prime Minister. In 1974 Bhutto, seeking to appease the Islamic elements, declared the Ahmadiyya to be non-Muslims.[46]

This procedure of identity-making by exclusion has opened the door to increasing sectarian violence. The Shi'ite community has been subjected to periodic attacks from radical Sunni groups, but even within the Sunnis there are regular outbreaks of violence between the Deobandis and Barelwis.[47]

In his discussion of the diversity of Islam in Pakistan Gaborieau concludes "the composite nature of Islam in Pakistan is in jeopardy more than ever. There are many deep-seated causes of sectarian conflict... But above all, such conflict is a symptom of an ideological conflict which means that both the state and the Islamic parties feel the need constantly to reiterate the fact that Pakistan is a Muslim country, and to define a 'true' Muslim in ever narrower terms".[48]

Jinnah repeatedly assured the minorities that they were welcome and equal citizens with Muslims. However pressure from the *ulama* and fundamentalists has reduced them to the status of '*dhimmis.*'

---

[43] See Marc Gaborieau in Jafferlot, *A History of Pakistan and its Origins,* 228ff.

[44] Qur'an Surah 33.40.

[45] Munir later wrote up the story in his book *From Jinnah to Zia* (Lahore: Vanguard Books, 1991).

[46] their worship places not to be called mosques and the call to prayer not to be used by them.

[47] Gaborieau, in Jafferlot, *A History of Pakistan and its Origins,* 233ff.

[48] Gaborieau, in Jafferlot, *A History of Pakistan and its Origins,* 234.

Under Zia laws of evidence and blasphemy were introduced which have marginalised the minority communities.[49]

The controversy over the underlying ideology of Pakistan is also linked to the failure to establish democracy in Pakistan. Democracy requires strong civil institutions and a sense of national unity. The divisions of ideology and ethnic tensions have created great instability. The army is one of the few institutions which has a real sense of the nation but it has been too easy for the Generals to step in when there are civil disturbances.[50] The instability of democracy is increased by the pressure to give in to the Islamic parties.[51]

Pakistan today is still searching for its identity. In some ways the two-nations theory had merit but in fact India is made up of hundreds of nations. The religion of Islam has not been able to hold Pakistan together and the failure to come to an agreed understanding, either broad or narrow, has led to much conflict and violence. Martial law keeps the lid on the violence for a time but the basic desire for democracy and popular representation is very strong in the country. It is hard to see how the strife can be stopped without the emergence of some strong political leaders who can guide the nation into a new self-understanding.

Bibliography

Adams, Charles J. 'Mawdudi and the Islamic State' in J. L. Esposito (ed.), *Voices of Islamic Resurgence* (Oxford University Press: New York, 1983).

Ahmad, Khurshid (ed.), *Islam – its Meaning and Message* (The Islamic Foundation: London, 1976).

---

[49] On Zia's Islamisation see Kamal Faruki 'Pakistan: Islamic Government and Society' in John Esposito, *Islam in Asia* (New York & Oxford: OUP, 1987), 58-76. For an account of the situation of Christians in Pakistan see Patrick Sookhdeo, *A People Betrayed: The Impact of Islamization on the Christian Community in Pakistan* (Christian Focus Publications: Fearne, Ross-shire: 2002).

[50] Military rule has been imposed in Pakistan from 1958-1971 (Ayub Khan and Yaha Khan), 1977-1988 (Zia-ul Haqq) and Pervez Musharraf 1999-2008, although with some restricted form of parliament operating at times.

[51] For example, despite many people acknowledging the injustice of the current Blasphemy law, no-one has been able to emend it.

Ahmad, Khurshid and Zafar I. Ansari, *Mawdudi: An Introduction to his Life and Thought* (The Islamic Foundation: Leicester, 1986).

Ahmed, Akbar S. *Discovering Islam: Making Sense of Muslim History and Society* (Vanguard Books: Lahore, 1988).

Ahmed, Akbar S. *Jinnah, Pakistan and Islamic Identity: The Search for Saladin* (Routledge: London, 1997).

Ahmed, Ishtiaq, *The Concept of an Islamic State in Pakistan* (Vanguard: Lahore, 1991).

Ahmed, Manzooruddin, *Pakistan: The Emerging Islamic State* (Allies Book Corporation: Karachi, 1966).

de Bary, Wm. Theodore (ed.), *Sources of the Indian Tradition*, compiled by Stephen Hay and I. H. Qureshi (New York: Columbia University Press, 1958, vol. 2).

Esposito, J. L., *Islam and Politics*, (4th ed., New York: Syracuse University Press, 1998).

Esposito, J. L., *Islam: The Straight Path* (3rd ed., Oxford and New York: Oxford University Press: 1998).

Esposito, J. L., *The Islamic Threat*, (3rd ed., Oxford and New York: OUP, 1999).

Esposito, J. L. (ed.), *Islam in Asia: Religion, Politics and Society* (Oxford and New York: OUP, 1987).

Esposito, J. L. (ed.), *Voices of Islamic Resurgence* (New York: Oxford University Press, 1983).

Faruki, Kemal A., 'Pakistan: Islamic Government and Society' in John Esposito, *Islam in Asia* (Oxford an New York: OUP, 1987).

Gandhi, Rajmohan, *Understanding the Muslim Mind* (Penguin Books: New Delhi, 1987).

Hardy, P., *The Muslims of British India* (Cambridge University Press: Cambridge, 1972).

Ikram, S. M., *Modern Muslim India and the Birth of Pakistan*, (5th ed., Lahore: Institute of Islamic Culture, 1990).

Iqbal, Muhammad and Seyd Abdul Vahid (ed.), *Thoughts and Reflections of Iqbal* (Lahore: Muhammad Ashraf, 1964).

Jafferlot, C. (ed.), *A History of Pakistan and its Origins,* (Transl. Gillian Beaumont, London: Anthem Press, 2002).

Jalal, Ayesha, *The Sole Spokesman: Jinnah, the Muslim League and the Demand for Pakistan* (Cambridge: Cambridge University Press, 1985).

Jinnah, M. A. *Speeches and Statements 1947-1948,* with Introduction by S. M. Burke (Karachi: Oxford University Press, 2000).

Keddie, N. R. 'Ideology, Society and the State in Post-Colonial Muslim Societies", in F. Halliday and AH. Alavi (eds.), *State and Ideology in the Middle-East and Pakistan* (Houndmills, England: Macmillan, 1988).

Lapidus, Ira, *A History of Islamic Societies,* (2nd ed., Cambridge: Cambridge University Press, 2002).

Maududi, S. Abul A.la, *First Principles of the Islamic State,* (Trans. Khurshid Ahmad, Lahore: Islamic Publications, 1960).

Maududi, S. Abul A.la, *Islamic Law and Constitution* (Trans. Khurshid Ahmad, Lahore: Islamic Publications, 1960).

Munir, M., *Pakistan from Jinnah to Zia: a Study in Ideological Convulsions* (unknown binding, 1980).

Naim, C. M. (ed.), *Iqbal, Jinnah, and Pakistan: The Vision and the Reality* (New York, Syracuse University: Maxwell School of Citizenship and Public Affairs, 1979).

Nasr, Seyyed Vali Reza, *Maududi and the Making of Islamic Revivalism* (Oxford and New York: OUP, 1996).

Rosenthal, E. I. J., *Islam in the Modern National State* (Cambridge: Cambridge University Press, 1965).

Smith, W. C., *Modern Islam in India: a Social Analysis* (Lahore: Muhammad Ashraf, 1946).

Sookhdeo, Patrick, *A People Betrayed: The Impact of Islamization on the Christian Community in Pakistan* (Christian Focus Publications: Fearne, Ross-shire, 2002).

Wolpert, S., *Jinnah of Pakistan* (Oxford, 1994).

A New Day for Islamist Politics in Modern Turkey: The AK Party and Gülen Movement[1]

Richard Duncalfe

Postgraduate researcher, Laidlaw-Carey Graduate School, Auckland

In a textual landscape where many books on Islam seem incapable of going beyond terrorism, jihad or Islamist rhetoric, a pressing need exists to demonstrate the multiple faces and diversity of voices within Islam, and the variety of ways with which secularism and modernity are dealt with. Despite an increasing yearning for civil society and democracy, the future of many Middle Eastern states remains uncertain.

The persistence of authoritarian rulers in maintaining their crowns however, has led to Turkey becoming an increasingly popular locus of socio-political attention.[2]

While internal conflict has hamstrung many Middle Eastern efforts at democratization, in Turkey certain Islamic actors have been able to negotiate the terms of a dominant secular state tradition and a procedurally functional democracy. In the absence of any monolithic Turkish Islamist movement, what is to be learned from the phenomenal rise of Islamic politics in this overwhelmingly Muslim majority nation?[3] What can occur if Islamist movements

---

[1] Ed.: This article predates the dramatic changes that occurred in Turkey after 2014.

[2] Turkey has long occupied a strategic location on the world stage. Situated between the West and the Islamic world, it is an important player in NATO, Middle Eastern alliances, and stands at the crossroads of almost every issue of importance to the United States and the EU on the Eurasian continent.

[3] According to the CIA World Factbook, at a ratio of approximately 99.8% Muslim, Turkey is one of the most Muslim countries in the world. See https://www.cia.gov/library/publications/the-world-factbook/geos/tu.html. Moreover, a survey dated May-June 2006 indicates that a majority in Turkey define themselves as *Islamist*

lessen their combative stance and begin to cooperate with secular states? This paper will explore how contemporary Turkey is negotiating the struggle between religion and politics. In this respect, beginning with the general rise of Islamic politics in modern Turkey, particular attention will be given to the Islamism of the AK Party and the Gülen movement.[4]

It is important at the outset to distinguish the term *secular* from *laic*, as many have mistakenly used secular or employed them interchangeably. Secularism is not merely the separation of religion and state, but includes the removal of the domination of religious authority from diverse spheres of society. The Turkish state's position on religion however, is more accurately represented by *laicism*, the subordination of religion to the state, whereby the state aims to control all public expressions of Islamic practice. This is a crucial difference in the Turkish context.[5]

Like White (2002), this paper will use the term *laic* instead of the more common yet less accurate *secular* to describe the Turkish state's policy toward religion and the related popular ideology. The author will use *secular* to refer to those self-identified as non-religious or who believe in the privatization of religious belief and practice.

(48.4%), as opposed to *Laicist* (20.3%). See www.tesev.org.tr/etkinlik/Presentasyon-2006.pdf. See footnotes below for definitions of these terms and their derivatives.

[4] The terms *Islamic* and *secular* are used in this paper as distinctly different from Islamist and secularist. As noted well by Turam (2007, 165-166) the former two are non-confrontational in that they passively or actively promote freedom for their own views and lives, and thereby engage in a negotiation of the boundaries between religion and politics. In contrast to the former, Islamists and secularists actively challenge competing ideologies, in order to fashion social order and polity after their own religious or secular blueprints of the world. Islamism is a political ideology then, whereas Islamic is an adjective utilised to indicate a view, thought, style or practice that makes reference to Islam as a religion, but not part of an Islamist ideology per se.

[5] The essence of *laicism* is spelled out in the AK Party principles: *laicism* is "the state's impartiality toward every form of religious belief and philosophical conviction", meaning that, "the state, rather than the individual, is restricted and limited by this." As cited in Jenny White, *Islamist Mobilisation in Turkey: A Study in Vernacular Politics* (Seattle: University of Washington Press, 2002), 274. White's compelling ethnography of "vernacular politics" in Turkey rightly points out (2002, 35), "The state controls the education of religious professionals and their assignments to mosques and approves the content of their sermons. It also controls religious schools and the content of religious education and enforces laws about the wearing of religious symbols and clothing in public spaces and institutions."

Tracing the development of new Islamist parties in modern Turkey

Beginning in the 1950s and peaking in the 1980s, a number of developments greatly enhanced Turkey's modernisation. These same events transformed Turkish politics and cultivated the fertile soil from which Islamist parties would finally begin to yield a harvest. During this period many Islamist policy supporters moved from provincial towns and villages to urban centers, where they were more likely to gain access to formal education and opportunities for upward social mobility. Supporters consisted largely of conservative Sunni Muslims from central Anatolia and the hinterlands, who had to some degree either resisted modernisation or despite latent desire had rarely benefited from it. Thus Islamism in Turkey has to some extent grown as a response to social, economic and political discontent.[6]

Meanwhile Islamist groups responded to the needs and aspirations of the newly urban university students, professionals, businessmen and merchants. They offered financial and practical assistance to the graduates and whoever was in need. By the late 1980s a new urban middle class and business elite had emerged whose members often came from provincial towns.[7] Instead of rejecting market competition and capital accumulation, newly rich Islamists began formulating a cultural disposition for competitive engagement with

---

[6] With the transition to a multiparty system in 1946, Islamic groups began to form covert and overt alliances with the ruling parties. With the provision of civil liberties in the 1961 constitution, Islamist groups began to operate legally, though their activities were technically banned. Until Necmettin Erbakan established the National Order Party in 1970, Islamists had either formed conservative factions within other parties or had remained underground. This signalled the first time in which Islamists had an autonomous party through which they could campaign their agenda. See Nilufer Narli, "The Rise of the Islamist Movement in Turkey" in *Revolutionaries and Reformers: Contemporary Islamist Movements in the Middle East*, ed. Barry Rubin (New York: State University of New York Press, 2002), 125-127, 133.

[7] Having their origins in Anatolian towns, the new business elite desired to assert its provincial identity and preserve its values and traditions. Consequently, its members, dubbed "Anatolian Lions" follow the pro-Islamic leadership of MUSAID (the Association of Independent Industrialists and Businessmen) rather than its more urban, Westernised counterpart TUSIAD (The Turkish Businessmen's and Industrialist's Association). See Narli, 128.

the global economy, with the view that Turkey would potentially become an industrial and economic powerhouse in the region.[8]

One of the main pillars of the Turkish "Republican Project", the making of a Westernised, secularised and modern nation state, has been laicism. This overarching project not only privatized religion but effectively marginalised and even repressed Islamic actors since the 1920s.[9]

The Turkish Republic has continued to display pendulum swings between repression and toleration of Islam. Each time Islamic social forces gained power and were thought to impose an Islamist agenda upon the populace or pose a threat to the secular state, the Turkish military would intervene in the political process through a *coup d'etat*.[10] Particularly through the 1990s, religious associations, sects and centers were regularly under surveillance and sporadically attacked by police.[11]

The institutionalisation of laicism and modernity involved not a direct exclusion of Islam but rather the engineered inclusion of Islam within the modern political system. This particular understanding had to be carefully forged and implemented. For it to take hold, it had to be an innovative, hybrid adaptation tailored to the particularities of Turkey's sociopolitical practices and

---

[8] Yıldız Atasoy, Turkey, *Islamists and Democracy: Transition and Globalization in a Muslim State* (New York: I.B. Tauris, 2005), 177-182.

[9] For a comprehensive argumentation on the terms *laic* and *secular* and their derivatives, see Andrew Davison, "Turkey, a 'Secular' State? The Challenge of Description", *South Atlantic Quarterly* 102, 2/3 (2003), 333-350. See also İştar Gözaydın, "Religion, Politics, and the Politics of Religion in Turkey", in *Religion, Politics and Turkey's EU Accession,* ed's. Dietrich Jung and Catharina Raudvere (New York: Palgrave Macmillan, 2008), 159-160. Despite laicism being a founding principle and an immensely significant element of the Turkish secular constitutional system, its institutionalization was by no means one of consensus or democratic process. The Turkish nation-state was built upon three decades of harsh authoritarian measures, oppression and elimination of rivals through dictatorial means.

[10] The Constitutional Courts have closed down four pro-Islamic parties, in 1971, 1980, 1998 and 2001. See Berna Turam, *Between Islam and the State: The Politics of Engagement* (California: Stanford University Press, 2007), 6. See also Alev Çınar, *Modernity, Islam and Secularism in Turkey: Bodies, Places and Time* (Minneapolis: University of Minnesota Press, 2005), 14-15. Çınar contends that the founding elite conjured up quite an original modernity project, made possible by establishing a critical distance from two extremes. On the one hand a blind submission to Westernism would run the risk of losing its national distinctiveness. On the other hand, if the Ottoman style Islamic legal frame of reference were maintained, Turkey would not be able to modernize and become part of the Western "civilized" world as it deeply aspired to. Hence, a healthy distance from both excessive Westernism and stagnant Islamism created an unique in-between hybrid modernity *á la Türka*.

[11] Berna Turam, 2007, 7.

Ottoman Islamic frames of reference. The Atatürkist innovation would bring Islamic authority under the full and absolute control of the secular state.[12]

Some contended that the Turkish State was so inherently authoritarian and illiberal that it was doomed to repress and eventually obliterate all national Islamic movements. Şerif Mardin (1973) argues that westernizing modernity failed to win the hearts of Muslims because of state repression and the abuse of power by westernizing bureaucrats. Civil and military bureaucratic cadres wielded state power in an effort to retain their control of the "centre" over the "periphery." This socio-cultural state domination undermined community and culture, eventually generating feelings of resentment, estrangement, hostility and insecurity among the masses.[13]

Mardin (1986) later contends that *Kemalism*[14] ultimately provided no viable means to make life meaningful for the majority of the population.[15] Where it failed to create a social ethos that appealed to the heart as well as the mind, modern Turkish Islamists succeeded.

The mid-1980s witnessed the rise of the Refah (Welfare) Party. Refah won its first significant electoral victory in the local elections of 1994, when it came to power in the city administrations of several major cities in Turkey, including Ankara and Istanbul.[16] The

---

[12] Alev Çınar, 2005, 16.

[13] Şerif Mardin, "Center-Periphery Relations: A Key to Turkish Politics", *Daedalus* Vol. 102, 1 (1973):169-190.

[14] *Kemalists* are supporters of the official secularist ideology. *Kemalism* is a highly charged worldview, whose adherents are committed to preserving not only the state's control over Islam but also state domination over society in general. Kemalist Republicans hold the religious expression of Islam to be a private affair. Thus religion was taken out of the classroom and all state public functions, and religious symbols and clothing were banned from public institutions.

[15] Şerif Mardin, "Religion and Politics in Modern Turkey", in *Islam in Political Process,* ed. James Piscatori (Cambridge: Cambridge University Press, 1986), 138-159.

[16] The party attracted a much greater variety of supporters than any previous Islam-inspired party. Followers included conservative townspeople and poor urban migrants, but now also professionals, intellectuals and wealthy industrialists. Many working class and conservative women became political activists for the first time, going door-to-door to garner support for Refah (Welfare). Despite a wide divergence among its constituents of political interest and opinion, Welfare and its successors competently mobilised its hybrid membership into a multifaceted, integrated and organized activism. In this way, rather than being restricted to

party rose to national power in 1996, showing that laicism could no longer enjoy the position of unrivalled authority in the public sphere. Political Islam in Turkey was now an undeniably prominent contender, fully equipped to challenge the status quo on its own terms (via modern parliamentary democracy) and on its own grounds (in the larger metropolitan cities where secular modernity had been so deeply entrenched).

The Refah Party's Islamism was not fundamentalist in nature. Instead of seeking to retrieve doctrines, beliefs and practices from a sacred and bygone golden era, their discourse was a liberal one based on vernacular religion. Islamic identity was not forged for the larger transnational Islamic community (the umma), but was tailored exclusively for a Turkish speaking audience living in Turkey.

Furthermore, rather than taking Islam as a religion, with excessive citations from the Qur'an, it portrayed it as a culture deeply rooted in the Ottoman past. Refah promoted the idea of an Ottoman-Islamic civilization as Turkey's "true national culture",[17] and as a valid alternative to the country's official secular, Western-oriented and ethnic –based identity.[18] It was then a return and restoration of what was believed to be Turkey's true culture and its potential as a "glorious civilization."

Others took an opposite stance, claiming that the rise of political Islam and the victory of Refah demonstrated that Islam was a real threat in Turkey. After a decree issued by the National Security

---

the politics of the marginalised or economically weak, the Islamic political movements of modern Turkey used Islam as a strategic resource for building frames of reference and cross-class alliances. See Yıldız Atasoy, 2005, 5.

[17] Alev Çınar, 2005, 12. As merely one contemporary cultural example among many, modern Islamist women began wearing a distinctive style of Islamic dress called *tesettür*. *Tesettür* affords a long, loosely-tailored, feminine coat which is paired with a larger than normal silk headscarf. It is a reinterpretation of colourful, stylish, late Ottoman elite clothing and serves as another everyday manifestation of the nostalgia for Ottoman respectability that permeates Turkish Islamism. Likewise Jenny White (2002, 49-54) also identifies how the Ottoman era has been mined by Islamists for everyday models of Islamic practice, communal organisation and administration. Examples include Islamists increasing employment of a form of Turkish replete with Arabic or Persian words, the Ottoman *millet* administration system has gained currency, and many Kemalist icons have been undermined and where possible transformed by Ottoman imperial symbols or portraits of sultans. Islamists have also been at the forefront of a renaissance of sorts into Ottoman music and historical archives.

[18] Whilst firmly against Westernism of the state on the grounds that it is incompatible with Turkey's true national culture Refah never expressed any animosity to the West itself.

Council against this "rising threat of political Islam" in 1997, Refah was forced out of office before being forcibly closed down entirely in 1998. As is so often the case, it reemerged from the ashes under a new name, Fazilet (Virtue) Party, which became the main opposition party in the 1999 general elections.[19]

Those most concerned in the late 1990s were primarily threatened secularists, fearfully anticipating the decay of Atatürkism and the ultimate demise of official laicism.[20] In 2001 the Fazilet Party also ceased to exist, this time reorganizing under the name Saadet (Felicity) Party. It is at this juncture, the moderate wing, largely representing the younger generation, broke away and founded the Adalet ve Kalkınma Party (AK Party, AKP or Justice and Development Party).

The rise and road of the AK Party

Under the leadership of former Istanbul mayor Recep Tayyip Erdoğan AKP swept to power with a two-thirds majority government in the November 2002 elections.[21] It was an historic occasion which would significantly transform the political landscape. For the first time in the history of Turkey, a political party with Islamist origins had come to power with a sufficient

---

[19] The organizational structure, basic ideological tenets, and the cadre of the party remained essentially intact through to 2001. They did begin however, to openly endorse secularism, promoting the concept that under true secularism the state and religion should remain separate. In not recognizing freedom of conscience and in meddling in religious affairs, it was the state that was portrayed as being anti-secular and undemocratic. Despite this important strategic shift, the state and military remained unconvinced and in 2001 the Fazilet Party was also dismembered.

[20] Turam (2007, 8) comments however that, as the AKP has persisted with a European-oriented secular regime under a pro-Islamic government despite opposition, the numbers of disgruntled secularists has actually shrunk over the last decade. The attitudes of a growing number of secular actors towards Islam have been moderating from intolerant forms of secularism and laicism to more tolerant forms, particularly since the late 1990s. This change has been especially hard for Kemalists who have predominantly perceived this transition of perception as a defeat to pervasive Islamisation.

[21] Alev Çınar, 2005, 180. Among the 20 parties that competed for seats, only two reached the required 10 percent threshold for representation. After numerous fragile coalitions, corruption scandals and widespread socio-economic discontent the 2002 election result represented a popular repudiation of the authoritarian elitist establishment who had shared power between them for several decades.

majority to change the constitution. With an almost brand new crop of parliamentarians the elections effectively swept away an entire generation of established politicians. A new social contract had been entered into, based upon a greater respect for democracy, human rights, integrity and social justice.

The AK Party did not represent a direct continuation of either of its predecessors, Refah or Fazilet. Instead, under the leadership of Erdoğan they pursued a more liberal, less confrontational political line, by further endorsing secularist ideals, full acceptance into the EU, downplaying Islamist agendas, and giving priority to economic liberalization and development.

Even though the party continues to disassociate itself from assertive political Islam, it nevertheless maintains a liberal-Islamist perspective imbued with conservative religious values and morality, and a national identity and culture that positions moderate Islam as its essential defining value.[22]

Erdoğan frequently stated their party's duty was to serve not just their supporters but the larger public, regardless of their political opinions. Instead of turning to the Qur'an and resorting to claims of being the only true representatives of Muslims, as Refah had done, AKP employed a liberal discourse, demanding from the state recognition of basic individual rights and liberties, including freedom of conscience and practice of religion.

These new Islamists designated Istanbul, not Ankara, as the centre of Ottoman-Islamic civilization and the true heart and soul of the nation. In so doing they unsettled the established norms of nationhood centred in Ankara in an attempt to advance their alternative nationalist project.[23] The gateway cities of Turkey became portrayed as in dire need of their guardianship and

---

[22] Notwithstanding such diverse patterns of reform and cooperation, a primary agenda remains the revitalization of faith and the acquisition and legitimacy of faith-based lives in the secular institutional milieu of Turkey. Drawing on an impressive array of primary and secondary sources, and quantitative data, Arda Can Kumbaracıbaşı's (2009) detailed assessment of AKP's development as an organisation is highly recommended. With cogent analysis he traces the AK Party's electoral roots, internal power structure, strategy, leadership and critical future challenges.

[23] Çınar, 2005, 170. The unofficial commemoration of the conquest of Istanbul on 29 May, 1453 by Islamists relocated the national founding moment from an early twentieth century secular-Turkish time to an Ottoman-Islamic time frame. It was an alternative, yet equally authoritative nationalist discourse, retaining the formula "one nation= one state=one history."

transformative intervention, and they projected themselves as the only agents morally and politically capable of securing the needed changes.[24]

The rising popularity of the AKP has been maturing beyond the mere traditional political and institutional channels. To understand something of the inertia one must delve into the heart of everyday life. Indeed, as noted by Çınar, "The secular constitutional system and the Islamist challenges brought to it accentuate the importance of daily activity and public life in the making of and negotiation of the national subject."[25] For example, the ongoing dispute over wearing the Islamic headscarf illustrates the way in which an everyday activity, getting dressed for work, university or school, is integrally related to the negotiation of the norms of constitutional order, namely laicism, democracy and nationalism.[26]

---

[24] In August 2001, Recep Tayyip Erdoğan founded the Justice and Development Party, whose acronym in Turkish is "AK", meaning "pure white", "clean" or "unblemished." The very name invokes principles of social justice and incorruptability, connoting a much needed response to economic inequality and state oppression. Intentionally, they identify themselves as moderate yet sincere Muslims who have the moral fortitude and integrity to bring much needed change to decades of political corruption and manipulative power struggles. To the surprise of many commentators at the time, the party symbol is a lightbulb. It is deliberately open to multiple readings and is a radical departure from the animal, plant or openly Islamic or nationalist symbolism of most previous parties. Together with the shining bulb were used slogans such as, "Open to brightness, closed to darkness", and "Forward to a bright tomorrow." See Béatrice Hendrich, "Post-nationalist Semiotics? The Emblem of the Justice and Development Party AKP" in *Turkey Beyond Nationalism: Towards Post-Nationalist Identities*, ed. Hans-Lukas Kieser (New York: I.B.Taurus, 2006), 152. Interestingly, of the 71 party founders, which included 12 women, none were politicians but rather represented a range of ages, well educated professionals active across many spheres of society. The horizontal and more egalitarian characteristics of the grassroots organisation penetrated the very structure of the party itself, developing a new style of party altogether. See White, 2002, 273-274.

[25] Çınar, 2005, 27.

[26] The headscarf has become a potent symbol of political Islam worldwide, a simple item of clothing loaded with ideological meaning and potentially disruptive power. For some veiled women it became an issue that evoked liberal democratic values, namely freedom of conscience and individual rights. For Islamists, the controversy stems from a clash between an Islamic worldview which deems areas such as a woman's hair and neck as being private, and a secular code which sees them as public. The Islamic code of dress operates on the assumption that the public is by default male. Publicness is defined by that which is visible to the male gaze. However, a woman's private parts are only to be revealed before other women or to her husband in the privacy of her home. Under the patriarchal values of Islam then, these private parts are to be safeguarded by her father or husband, and their protection is the ultimate measure of his authority and honour. By demanding its removal in the public sphere not only is she unprotected from the probing and offensive male gaze, but her privacy is violated, her man's honour is threatened and the authority of Islam over her body is

It is this concern with forging and defining a national subject that impels the state to monitor and intervene in daily social activity. Other realms of everyday interaction range from rites of passage to entertainment, celebration to education. Negotiation is the key principle of operation, as it draws attention to the constitution as a never-finalised set of guiding principles that are under constant debate and contestation.[27]

More recently, Islamic political and societal leaders have become increasingly vocal in their desire for greater recognition of faith-based and morally conservative ways of life. Whereas the Westernised elite have looked down upon such suggestions, moderate Islamic actors have successfully undergone personal reform and in the process accumulated social, economic and intellectual capital and power, emerging as an alternative pro-Western and secularisation-friendly social force.[28] Even as the AK Party has largely come to be seen as an icon for reform and democracy, consideration must also be given to Fethullah Gülen, the founder of what has undoubtedly become Turkey's largest and most influential non-governmental Islamist movement.

The Gülen Movement

Like the AK Party, Fethullah Gülen's ability to reconcile traditional Islamic values with modern life and science has won the movement a large and receptive audience.[29]

---

compromised. Conversely to wear the veil allows Islamist women to enter the public sphere, to take up positions and professions of office, and to feel more secure and less threatened. In the Islamist feminist struggle against traditionalism, to have the capacity to lead an active public life is a powerful asset against a mindset that would seek to confine them to their homes. See Ayşe Zengin, "Namus Kavramı ve Örtü" (The Notion of Honour and the Veil), *Milli Gazete*, 17 June 1996.

[27] Alev Çınar, 2005, 28.

[28] Another popular form of Islamic associations are religious orders called *tarikat*. Sustained via social and personal networks, these religious orders may have intricate relations with specific political parties, but to what extent any influence is felt or anti-secular ideology is present is questionable.

[29] Bülent Aras and Ömer Caha, "Fethullah Gülen and his Liberal 'Turkish Islam' Movement" in *Revolutionaries and Reformers: Contemporary Islamist Movements in the Middle East*, ed. Barry Rubin (New York: State University of New York Press, 2002), 141. For a scholarly treatment of the Gülen movement's intellectual and religious formation, including detailed analysis of how Gülen utilizes educational networks to achieve spiritual enlightenment and

Emerging out of the 1980s fragmentation of the Nur Islamic movement, Gülen expanded internationally throughout the 1990s, and has attained the mantle of the most dynamic, transnational, autonomous, faith-inspired, societal movement to have spawned from Turkey.[30]

The dynamism of Nurcu and neo-Nurcu groups is rooted in their text-based network of media, business, publishing and educational establishments, around which their founder's writings remain very much centred. There are now several hundred Gülen inspired educational institutions alone across the world, with particular strength in the Middle East, Central Asia, the Caucuses, and many areas of Central and Eastern Europe. The schools stress a modern curriculum and the notion that all knowledge, whether religious or otherwise, brings one closer to God. The teachers are normally pious followers of Gülen, seeking to set an example through their relatively socially conservative lives.[31]

Several primary influences and resources informed Gülen's political and social vision. These include the narrative stories of the Prophet Muhammad, the Nakşibendi Sheik Muhammet Lütfı Efendi, Said

---

the enacting of Islamic values see M. Hakan Yavuz and John L. Esposito, ed's., *Turkish Islam and the Secular State: The Gülen Movement* (New York, Syracuse University Press, 2003).

[30] The early Gülen was a devoted Nurcu, a follower of Nursi. Said Nursi (1876-1960) founded a movement of resistance to the ongoing Kemalist modernisation process. He redefined Islamic folk concepts to offer a modern Islamic political discourse that would constitute original ideas for addressing societal problems. Nurcu and neo-Nurcu groups have evolved into the most powerful and effective socio-political communities in contemporary Turkey. See M. Hakan Yavuz, *Islamic Political Identity in Turkey* (New York: Oxford University Press, 2003), 151-178. After the mid 1970's, a gradual differentiation of Gülen and his movement from the traditional Nur movement became apparent. Yavuz (2003, 304) suggests that this can be interpreted as a response to the secularist accusation that he was a Nurcu leader who possessing a subversive intention to Islamise public life. Rather than seek to change public perception of Nursi, the Gülen movement diluted its intellectual connections with Nursi and propagated itself as an educational movement.

[31] Peter Mandaville, "Sufi and Salafis: The Political Discourse of Transnational Islam" in *Remaking Muslim Politics: Pluralism, Contestation, Democratization*, ed. Robert W. Hefner (New Jersey: Princeton University Press, 2005), 316-317. The exact size of the Gülen movement is difficult to guess but it is estimated to have approximately six million followers within the boundaries of Turkey alone. With no formal membership it attracts a diverse constituency. Affiliations range from the devout and benefactors, who are unconditionally in service, to distant admirers and sympathizers.

Nursi, his family, certain Islamic intellectuals, and nationalistic and Sufi characteristics of his eastern Anatolian home.[32]

The neo-Nur movement seeks to improve Turkish society by using educational institutions, the market and informational media to raise a new generation with heightened patriotic and moral consciousness.

This religious consciousness is fostered, formed and perpetuated through engaging in social practices and educational institutions. To borrow a term from another, the aim is one of, "making objective religion subjective."[33] In the education of people then, subjects are not only brought to a greater place of personal identity and faith, but they are encouraged to externalize their Islamic consciousness for the greater good and uplifting of society as a whole.

Based on three coordinated tiers (businessmen, journalists and students), the movement has distinguished itself from other faith movements through its soft and conciliatory voice on hotly debated subjects such as secularism, the Kurdish question and the headscarf issue.[34] In the process it has reproduced a new vision of

---

[32] The movement is undoubtedly influenced by the concept of "Turkish" or "Anatolian Islam", the main premises of which are moderation and toleration. This has been formulated around the works of nationalist, Sufi and Turkish Islamist thinkers. Sufi-oriented Islamic movements have generally kept a healthy distance from the politics of their times in contrast to other Islamic movements. Sufi tradition has described itself as being based on the philosophy that all creatures should be loved as God's physical reflection and objects of the Creator's own love. In such a system, there is no place for the "enemy" or the "other." A more tolerant disposition would foster the multiculturalism of the Ottoman period and minimize conflict between Sunnis and Alevis, Turks and Kurds. See Bülent Aras and Ömer Caha, 2002, 142, 144.

[33] This phrase is borrowed from Hegel's notion of religion. When the universal truths of a religion are imbibed and personally appropriated it should motivate moral action and motivate communal interactions. See G. W. F. Hegel, *Three Essays*, translated by P. Fuss and J. Dobbins (Notre Dame, IN: Notre Dame University Press, 1984), 79. In this way the religio-economic practices of the Gülen movement are also associated to those in Max Weber's thesis of the Protestant work ethic; work inspired by religious belief produced the spirit of capitalism that affects rational capitalist action in Europe. See Max Weber, "The Protestant Sect and the Spirit of Capitalism", in *From Max Weber: Essays in Sociology*, ed's., H. H. Gerth and C. Wright Mills (New York:Oxford University Press, 1958), 302-322.

[34] M. Hakan Yavuz, 2003, 179. Yavuz (2003, 185) also highlights three main characteristics which differentiate Gülen from the traditional *ulema* (religious scholars). First, unlike the ulema, whose references are invariably the Qur'an and sunna, the reference points for Gülen and the new class of Muslim intellectuals include rational reasoning and Enlightenment thought. Second, Gülen maintains a remarkable mix between affirming the traditions yet encouraging independent thinking and critical thought. Third is his ability to interpret Islamic precepts within the context of modern social conditions, utilizing the ideas of world

"contemporary Islam" that offers a set of options for people to be both a good Muslim and actively modern.[35] Gülen is commonly seen to have succeeded in creating a middle path between the more overt political Islamism of the Refah Party (and its imitators) and the officially secular yet more accurately laic orientation of the Turkish state. This middle path is made possible primarily by means of knowledge, which serves as an intermediary space of sorts in which otherwise disparate communities are able to coexist.[36] Since the 1990's, the movement has presented its educational mission as a cure for identity conflicts, a bridge between local and global groups, and as a basis for interreligious dialogue.[37]

Whilst the Gülen movement and the AK Party have remained organisationally independent and disconnected in their activities, there is an organic continuity of sorts between them, and a shared cooperative and non-defiant attitude towards the laic Turkish Republic.[38] Where Refah, and before it the Democratic Party in the 1950's failed in communicating and negotiating with the state and military, both Gülen and AKP have successfully mobilised people

---

writers such as Kant, Shakespeare, Hugo, Dostoyevsky and Sartre to reinforce his interpretations of Islam to meet contemporary needs.

[35] Gülen invites Turks to render their collective service in the creation of a lasting work, namely the construction of a dynamic, powerful, yet morally grounded Turkey. It is to shape modern society (all the while stressing the importance of achieving excellence in modern science and technology) to the ideals of Islamic ethics, yet like the AKP, the mission is to realise, discuss and bring the message of Islam to everyday life.

[36] Peter Mandaville, 2005, 317-318. Mandeville notes that one of the most successful aspects of Gülen's approach has been the extent to which sharp divisions between Muslims and non-Muslims are absent from his discourse. Thus education becomes a global space of interfaith ecumenism, appealing to many beyond the faith of Islam. This is significantly different from comparably transnational *Salafi* approaches.

[37] See Bekim Agai, "The Gülen Movement's Islamic Ethic in Education", in *Turkish Islam and the Secular State: The Gülen Movement,* ed's., M. Hakan Yavuz and John L. Esposito (New York, Syracuse University Press, 2003), 48-68.

[38] For example, unofficial ethnographic survey conclusions from White (2002) and Turam (2007) would suggest that when the AKP declared its break from its more radical Islamist faction Refah, in 2002, many of Gülen's followers voted for AKP. Moreover, long held politically Kurdish south-eastern Turkey seats have also broken with tradition and supported AKP in recent elections. Members of the party and followers of the movement however, are generally not the same people. Although they have both attracted support across class boundaries, Gülen has mainly appealed to people with bourgeois aspirations for upward social mobility whereas the party relied heavily on votes from the more conservative urban poor and residents of the economically lower status and more traditionally minded rural areas.

from diverse backgrounds to engage the Republic. For instance, the AK Party has welcomed the school-building activities of Fethullah Gülen, largely because they support current state policy of combining laicism with a moderate Islam.

Comparable to the AK Party and its predecessors, Gülen redefines Turkish national identity as being essentially Ottoman and Islamic.[39] His vision in the Balkans and Central Asia is also akin to Ottoman imperial and contemporary AK Party vision, which would seek to integrate the Muslim populations of these regions into a coherent bloc.

Alternatively, Gülen's priority and loyalty to the state and the community over the individual has caused some to question whether the movement needs to better promote the formation of a sense of individuality. Furthermore the socially conservative nature of its adherents and rhetoric can lead to a lack of openness to robust critical thinking.[40] Ironically a fear-fuelled and state-guided anti-Gülen media campaign of 1997-2002 sought to criminalise his alternative thinking, ultimately forcing him to take refuge in the United States.

Gleanings from an Islamist's "marriage of convenience"

Few scholarly works have moved beyond the dichotomy between authoritarian and Islamic states.[41] Turam (2007) posits that, "The juxtaposition of Islam against the secular state has been historically reinforced by the representation of Atatürkism as an ideology of the Westernised elite that has either excluded or failed to appeal to Islamists." This has been the case for much of the Republican history of Turkey.

---

[39] Bülent Aras and Ömer Caha (2003, 143) claim that Gülen's goals are, "simultaneously to Islamicize the Turkish nationalist ideology and to Turkify Islam." He hopes to reestablish the link between religion and the state that existed in the Ottoman era, when leaders were expected to live their private lives based on Islamic regulations." Such an approach, they suggest, would strengthen and widen the state's legitimacy and enhance its ability to mobilise its population.

[40] M. Hakan Yavuz, 2003, 201.

[41] One such exception is that of Sami Zubaida, "Trajectories of Political Islam: Egypt, Iran and Turkey", *Political Quarterly* (2000), 60-78.

The history of modern Turkey, contends Yavuz (2003), is the story of conflict between a non-elected military-bureaucratic elite and all its perceived enemies, be they foreign or domestic. Believing in the primacy of the state over its citizens, this "security regime" has wielded Kemalism and its systems to ward off all Islamic actors.

Except in contemporary Turkey, because new Islamic movements have been neither anti-modern nor backward, a dramatic shift has occurred and continues to frame the political and social consciousness.[42]

The parameters for this short paper have focused on the two most influential of these Islamist movements. There are however, many other smaller Islamist groups within Turkey. Each has its own dynamic and history, yet notably all seem to be presently engaged in the process of modernisation based on a European model.[43]

As has been demonstrated then, with particular reference to the AK Party and Fethullah Gülen, present day Islamist political movements in Turkey are seeking to reposition themselves in the highly competitive relations of the national and global economy. To do this they have been willing to work alongside and sometimes in coalition with secular political elites. This effectively locates Turkish Islamist groups as participants in a culturally polycentric world.[44]

Shifting relations between recent Islamic actors and the Turkish state are significant in that they inform us about the demise in the gap between society and state. Interestingly, this transformation has preceded and even facilitated reform by creating alternative linkages and affinities between the state and Islamic actors. It is crucially not a process of fusion or unification between state and Islam, whether in the form of Islamisation of the state or the defeat of Islamism by secularism. Rather it illustrates how contemporary

---

[42] M. Hakan Yavuz, 2003, 266.
[43] Yılıdız Atasoy, 2005, 190.
[44] Yılıdız Atasoy, 2005, 4.

patterns of social change have allowed Islamic actors and the state to interact, reshape and even transform each other.[45]

In an effort to dispel several myths of clashes between the state and society Turam (2007) bravely suggests that closer relationships tell "the story of a rising agreement, cooperation, and a growing sense of belonging between secular state and Islamic actors."[46] However, while compromise on the part of Islamic groups can be well documented, concessions in kind seem less so on the part of the state and hard-core secularists. An ongoing court case in Turkey of unprecedented proportions has unveiled an elitist "hidden state" organization termed *Ergenekon*.[47]

These present day realities and results in the recent national referendum[48] would suggest Turam's optimism is, for the time being, somewhat misplaced.

Notwithstanding the importance of healthy realism, the continuation of positive interplay between the aforementioned socio-political forces and actors is still to be evidenced. Turam (2007) rightly identifies the locus of this interaction and contestation as being particularly in the realms of education, and also in the negotiation of boundaries between morally public and private lives. Further cooperation with the state can be witnessed in the

---

[45] Berna Turam, 2007, 9. Other ethnographic studies also point to the emerging convergence between Islamists and secularists in Turkey. See also Jenny B. White, Islamist Mobilization in Turkey: A Study in Vernacular Politics, Seattle: University of Washington Press, 2002. Likewise Şerif Mardin (2006, 6), in an historical approach, refers to the background as "the setting where secularism and Islam interpenetrate."

[46] Berna Turam (2007, 7).

[47] Over 100 highly influential and powerful people have been detained and questioned since mid-2008 as to their part in a clandestine network called *Ergenekon*. Alleged members have been indicted on charges of plotting to destabilize the country and to derail EU accession talks. Allegations range from assassinating intellectuals, politicians, judges, military staff, and religious leaders to the ultimate goal of toppling the government in a coup that was planned to take place in 2009. The non-compromising attitude, distrust and intolerant antagonism of some hard-core nationalists and secularists have been unceasing. Some, including a minority of state officials, even object to all institutional reform and EU membership. Their objections however, are motivated not by principles and ideology so much as reforms should not be undertaken under the political leadership of a pro-Islamic party.

[48] On September 12, 2010, Turkish people voted on the largest constitutional amendment since 1982. With a 58 percent 'yes vote,' the 26-article amendment package will usher in a number of progressive changes into the Turkish political and judicial system, including the curbing of various military powers of political intervention. While being a victory for the process of democratisation in Turkey, the stark provincial polarisation of the vote also confirms the deeper political battle that continues to rage between the reformists and the military-state defenders of the status quo.

promotion of Turkic ethnic politics and initiatives in Central Asia,[49] as well as promoting institutional reform and Turkey's membership in the European Union. Alliances can even be seen with the secular male elite in the sphere of gender politics.[50]

The AKP and Gülen movements capture the emergence of less confrontational and non-defiant Islamic agencies at a particular historical season of transition, one in which they reach out to, engage, negotiate and even associate with the most secular state of the Muslim world.

Like any nation-building however, this shift took place along the junctures of several if not numerous historical and sociopolitical realities. Çınar (2005) for example illustrates how these contextual interventions frequently relate to the everyday, that is people, places and notions of time. In keeping the state and social forces separate and autonomous yet in touch with each other, both spontaneous encounters and scheduled interactions between them can create a degree of elective affinity and cooperation between Islam and the state. Many of the pathways of interaction are temporary and spawn from everyday meeting points and scenarios (discussions pertaining to national loyalties, education, morality, and ethnic, gender and international politics) rather than formal political channels. Nonetheless they collectively contribute to a "marriage of convenience" of sorts between religion and politics.

The key to the flourishing of these patterns, says Turam (2007), is the non-confrontational attitude of actors, reinforced by their faith in submission to the collective good.

---

[49] Berna Turam (2007, 14) highlights how the homogenizing tendency of Turkic ethnic politics contradicts claims of developing a pluralist society as it promotes ethnic unity latent in both Islamic and secular nationalism in Turkey.

[50] Again Turam reveals the curious overlap between a seemingly progressive gender discourse, which aims to incorporate women into the public sphere, yet effectively fails to empower them. While female emancipation is a path that many women embark upon, the male bond between the Islamic and secular elites merely facilitates further cooperation and ultimately a sustaining of the patriarchal status (2007, 14-15).

As change agents they have illustrated how Islamist actors have the potential to make sporadic changes in authoritarianism without threatening the system per se.[51]

Çınar's thesis on the other hand (2005), contends that Islamic interventions in the public sphere have subversive effects upon secularist modes of power and control. But once these subversive acts are incorporated into an Islamist political ideology and project that they become equally totalizing and nationalist, reproducing the same binary oppositions around gender, class and nationhood, yet constituting an alternative modernisation project that seeks to transform the nation toward an alternative future.[52]

In either sense, liberal democracy cannot just be transplanted from one time or context to another. To some extent the Turkish example is a product of its own culturally specific Islam, the so-called "Turkish Islam." Following Yavuz's line of thinking then, Turkish Islam, unlike any other, had ethnic inclinations to be more liberal, tolerant, inherently pluralist and pro-democratic.[53] The distinction of Turkey does not lie in the specific merit of Turkish Islam or in Atatürk's legacy of a staunchly secular state. As Zubaida correctly asserts, political Islam is "integrated into national histories and cultures."[54]

This paper has challenged the premise that political Islam and Islamist political ideology can fully be understood as national political phenomena apart from the cultural beliefs, and local communalistic practices. White's "vernacular politics" (2002) and Özyürek's "everyday politics" (2006) helps to position the Islamist movement in Turkey since the 1990s as a grass-roots community

---

[51] Berna Turam, 2007, 156, 162. Some shared goals include Turkey's membership in the EU, economic liberalism and liberal democracy. Cooperation is generally in proportion to the extent with which each group feels it benefits that nation and advances the national interest.

[52] Alev Çınar, 2005, 30.

[53] M. Hakan Yavuz, 2003, 273. Yavuz argues "Turkish Islam is a Sufi Islam with dense Sufi networks that transmit the flow of ideas, practices and leaders, helping to link local and universal versions of Islam." He goes on to state that Turkey's Muslim intellectuals, unlike Egypt's Qutb or Pakistan's Mawdudi, were not didactic in their writings but as poets, philosophers and novelists drew upon Sufi foundries to bring a more narrative and eclectic style, in terms of sources and openness to divergent viewpoints. Moreover, due to a lack of colonial legacy or continued occupation, Europe never became the "other" in the construction of Turkish identity. See also Elizabeth Özdalga, "The Hidden Arab: A Critical Reading of the Notion of 'Turkish Islam,'" *Middle Eastern Studies*, 42/4 (2006), 546-566.

[54] Sami Zubaida, "Trajectories of Political Islam: Egypt, Iran and Turkey", *Political Quarterly* 71, 2000, 77.

and value-centred political process. Indeed, it has been able to incorporate and unify large numbers of people from diverse backgrounds around a shared ideology with Islam as the central idiom of interpretation. However it is their ability to remain embedded in local culture, praxis, and interpersonal relations which has forged a new sense of solidarity in the face of contemporary problems, and allowed a recreated and morally grounded community to become a vital political force.[55]

In other words, there is no unchanging "Islam" that exists as a single entity outside of history. To comprehend the nature of modern Islamism in Turkey and its place in a political democracy, it is necessary to go beyond how they are theorized to examine how Turkish Islam and politics are lived.[56]

In his earlier political days AK Party leader Erdoğan was convicted of making a seditious statement which suggested that Turks had to choose between God and Atatürk. The comment resulted in his temporary ban from politics. Indeed, even Turkey's illustrious

---

[55] Jenny White, 2002, 6-7, 261-262. To build on the existing community networks Islamic political parties in Turkey have had to become "intimate", interacting with constituents on an individual face-to-face level through known, trusted neighbours, and situated the political message within a local context of shared communal values and interest. Activists also worked through a variety of spheres from municipalities, charity foundations, marriage counselling, to mosque-instigated demonstrations. Consequently local politics becomes national, all the while carrying within it the coalitions and contradictions that reflect local and national diversity. See also Esra Özyürek's chapter entitled "Miniaturizing Atatürk: The Commodification of State Iconography", (2006, 93-124) and "The Islamist Subversion of the Republican Nostalgia", (2006, 157-177).

[56] Alexis Tocqueville's analysis of the United States in the early nineteenth century provides a compelling insight into the role that religion can play in linking and aligning the state with its populace. Contrasting America to France, which experienced an hostility and resentment between religion, polity, state and society, Tocqueville clearly illustrates that a certain level of synchrony between faith and political institutions can positively propel democracy and protect freedoms. American society has remained distinctly religious mainly because religion was perceived as a friend-not an enemy- of democratic institutions. Similarly, in the Muslim context, a limited yet fundamental consensus and understanding on the nature of national and political identity fosters harmony and is imperative for the partial accord between state and society. See Alexis Tocqueville, Democracy in America [1835-1840], Chicago: University of Chicago Press, 2000, 274-278. Interestingly, Turam contends (2006, 161) that the persistence of a strong alliance between religion and politics would seem to undermine democracy in the long run. Hence the continuing sporadic discontent between the Turkish state and Islamic actors is potentially valuable in that it limits the nature and scope of cooperation between them.

founder, Mustafa Kemal Atatürk (1881-1938), believed Islam was neither secularizable nor privatizable.[57]

It would seem however, that the more moderate, conciliatory approach of recent years is indeed the proper formula for maintaining the tenuous accord between the state and its increasingly faithful populace. Both the AK Party and the Gülen movement have demonstrated considerable commitment in attempting to bring harmony and integration to the historically diverse peoples of Anatolia. Reconciling religious values and tradition with the demands of modernity in a secular democracy is by no means an easy task.

Notwithstanding the trajectory of modern Turkey as being yet unclear, it would seem that the state, society and the new Islamists stand together at a crossroads, crucially closer than ever before. A Turkish proverb says, *"Bir elin sesi çıkmaz"*, meaning literally, "One hand does not clap."[58] In so far as Recep Tayyip Erdoğan and Fethullah Gülen continue to create a progressive, credible, substantive compromise between and in the everyday lives of heterogenous support groups, they will rely not on charismatic leadership but realise the proverbial truth – a person can do lasting work only in cooperation with others.[59]

Bibliography

Agai, Bekim. "The Gülen Movement's Islamic Ethic in Education." In *Turkish Islam and the Secular State: The Gülen Movement,* eds. M. Hakan Yavuz and John L. Esposito, 48-68. New York, Syracuse University Press, 2003.

Aras, Bülent and Ömer Caha, "Fethullah Gülen and his Liberal 'Turkish Islam' Movement." In *Revolutionaries and Reformers:*

---

[57] M. Hakan Yavuz and John L.Esposito, "Islam in Turkey: Retreat from the Secular Path?" in Turkish Islam and the Secular State: The Gülen Movement, New York: Syracuse University Press, 2002, xiii.

[58] Nejat Muallimoğlu, *Turkish Delights: A Treasury of Proverbs and Folk Sayings* (Istanbul: Milli Eğitim Bakanlığı Yayınları, 1998), 92.

[59] For a fuller explanation of the critical challenges facing the AKP leadership see Kumbaracıbaşı (2009, 178-188). The further development of institutional mechanisms will require the involvement of grassroots activists in policy formation. Failure to do so, says Kumbaracıbaşı, would in all likelihood ultimately render the AKP to a similar fate as that of previously dissolved parties.

Contemporary Islamist Movements in the Middle East, ed. Barry Rubin, 141-154. New York: State University of New York Press, 2002.

Atasoy, Yildiz. *Turkey, Islamists and Democracy: Transition and Globalization in a Muslim State.* New York: I.B. Tauris, 2005.

Çınar, Alev. *Modernity, Islam and Secularism in Turkey: Bodies, Places and Time.* Minneapolis: University of Minnesota Press, 2005.

Davison, Andrew. "Turkey, a 'Secular' State? The Challenge of Description." *South Atlantic Quarterly* 102 2/3 2003: 333-350.

Gözaydın, İştar. "Religion, Politics, and the Politics of Religion in Turkey." In *Religion, Politics and Turkey's EU Accession*, ed's. Dietrich Jung and Catharina Raudvere, 159-176. New York: Palgrave Macmillan, 2008.

Hegel, G. W. F. *Three Essays.* Translated by P. Fuss and J. Dobbins. Notre Dame, IN: Notre Dame University Press, 1984.

Hendrich, Béatrice. "Post-nationalist semiotics? The emblem of the Justice and Development Party AKP." In *Turkey Beyond Nationalism: Towards Post-Nationalist Identities*, ed. Hans-Lukas Kieser, 147-154. New York: I.B.Taurus,2006.

Kumbaracıbaşı, Arda Can. *Turkish Politics and the Riseof the AKP: Dilemmas of institutionalization and Leadership strategy.* New York: Routledge, 2009.

Mandaville, Peter. "Sufi and Salafis: The Political Discourse of Transnational Islam." In *Remaking Muslim Politics: Pluralism, Contestation, Democratization*, ed. Robert W. Hefner, 302-325. New Jersey: Princeton University Press, 2005.

Mardin, Şerif. "Center-Periphery Relations: A Key to Turkish Politics." *Daedalus* Vol. 102 No.1 (1973): 169-190.

Mardin, Şerif. "Religion and Politics in Modern Turkey." In *Islam in Political Process*, ed. James Piscatori, 138-159. Cambridge: Cambridge University Press, 1986.

Mardin, Şerif. "Turkish Islamic Exceptionalism Testerday and Today: Continuity, Rupture and Reconstruction in Operational Codes." In *Religion and Politics in Turkey*, ed's. Ali

Çarkoğlu and Rubin Barry, 3-25. London and New York: Routledge, 2006.

Muallimoğlu, Nejat. *Turkish Delights: A Treasury of Proverbs and Folk Sayings*. Istanbul: Milli Eğitim Bakanlığı Yayınları, 1998.

Narli, Nilufer. "The Rise of the Islamist Movement in Turkey." In *Revolutionaries and Reformers: Contemporary Islamist Movements in the Middle East*, ed. Barry Rubin, 125-140. New York: State University of New York Press, 2002.

Özdalga, Elizabeth. "The Hidden Arab: A Critical Reading of the Notion of 'Turkish Islam.'" *Middle Eastern Studies* 42/4 (2006): 546-566.

Özyürek, Esra. *Nostalgia for the Modern: State Secularism and Everyday Politics in Turkey*. London: Duke University Press, 2006.

Turam, Berna. *Between Islam and the State: The Politics of Engagement*. California: Stanford University Press, 2007.

Yavuz, M. Hakan. *Islamic Political Identity in Turkey*. New York: Oxford University Press, 2003.

Yavuz, M. Hakan and John L. Esposito, eds. *Turkish Islam and the Secular State: The Gülen Movement*. New York, Syracuse University Press, 2003.

White, Jenny B. *Islamist Mobilization in Turkey: A Study in Vernacular Politics*. Seattle: University of Washington Press, 2002.

Zengin, Ayşe. "Namus Kavramı ve Örtü" (The Notion of Honour and the Veil) *Milli Gazete* 17 June (1996).

Zubaida, Sami. "Trajectories of Political Islam: Egypt, Iran and Turkey." *Political Quarterly* 71 (2000): 60-78.

Issues affecting the relationship between Islam and the State in Australia

Richard Bath
Graduate student, Melbourne School of Theology

The first decade of the 21st century saw media and public discussion involving the topic of religion gain unprecedented attention. Since September 11, 2001, we've been introduced to terms such as *Al-Qaeda, The War on Terror, The Clash of Civilisations, Jihad, the Taliban* and many others which conjure up angst and debate across the globe. Australia has also been caught up in the politics of terror with several Islamists convicted of misdemeanours associated with terrorism. This paper examines some of the key developments relating to Islam in Australia and the issues which are consequently affecting its relationship with its governing authorities.

Immigration & Assimilation?

Of the immigrants that arrived in Australia prior to 2002 who are still living, 135900 stated their religion as Islam.[1] From 2002 to the time of the 2006 census, another 53,200 Muslims took up residence in Australia.[2] The main countries of origin for Muslim migrants prior to 2002 were Lebanon, Turkey, Afghanistan, Bosnia, Pakistan, and Indonesia.[3] Many of the Afghani, Lebanese and

---

[1] Australian Bureau of Statistics, 'Perspectives on Migrants, 2007'. http://www.abs.gov.au/ausstats/abs@.nsf/Lookup/3416.0Main%20Features22007?opendocument&tabname=Summary&prodno=3416.0&issue=2007&num=&view=_(2008).

[2] ABS, 'Perspectives on Migrants, 2007'.

[3] Abdullah Saeed, *Islam in Australia* (Sydney: Allen & Unwin, 2003), 12. Refer to table from 2001 ABS Census.

Bosnian migrants fled from violent civil conflicts and in more recent years there has been an influx of refugees from Iraq and Somalia. Many from these countries are not exclusively Muslim, with Maronite Catholics in Lebanon, Assyrian Christians Iraq, Bosnian Serbs, and ethnically Chinese Indonesians.

The total Muslim population in Australia at the 2006 census was 340,3894 and almost half were under the age of 25. This compares with 33% under 25 for Australia's non-Muslim population. Tellingly, the percentage under 5 years of age is nearly 11% compared with 6.3% of non-Muslims. Muslims tend to have large families as has been noted in other countries with newly arrived Muslims, although there are indications fertility rates do reduce over time. [5]

Public concern over Muslim immigration has generated vigorous public debate, although most of this has occurred in NSW, due possibly to 'Islamic Lebanese...[having] not adapted as well as the Turks'[6] as they settled predominantly in the South-western suburbs of Sydney.

Also taking prominent position in debate and government policy is acceptance of asylum seekers into Australia, many of whom have arrived as illegal boat people onto Australia's Northern shores. According to the UNHCR, of the 38,593 people seeking asylum in Australia between 2000 – 2004, 43.5% had originated from Muslim majority nations. Iraq and Afghanistan had the second and third highest number of refugees (after China) who entered Australia during this period.[7]

---

[4] Australian Bureau of Statistics, 'Religious Affiliation by Age by Sex' In *2006 Census Tables*. http://www.censusdata.abs.gov.au/ABSNavigation/download?format=xls&collection=Census&period=2006&productlabel=Religious%20Affiliation%20by%20Age%20by%20Sex&productype=Census%20Tables&method=Place%20of%20Usual%20Residence&areacode=0 (2007).

[5] Mary Kent, 'Do Muslims have more Children than other Women in Western Europe?' In *Population Reference Bureau*. http://www.prb.org/Articles/2008/muslimsineurope.aspx (2008). Moroccan born immigrants in the Netherlands have seen their fertility rates decline from 4.9 to 2.9 between 1990 & 2005. Local born Dutch women fertility rate remained at around 1.7.

[6] Gerald Henderson, *Islam in Australia: Democratic Bipartisanship in Action* (London UK: Policy Exchange, 2007), 9.

[7] Migration Policy Institute, 'Annual number of asylum applications by nationality, 1980 to 2004' In Country and Comparative Data. http://www.migrationinformation.org/datahub/countrydata/data.cfm (2005).

Responding to Terror

Islam became a major focus of attention in the Western mind on September 11, 2001. About 40 Australian citizens were killed in the attacks on the World Trade Centre and Pentagon but before this event there was 'considerable complacency about terrorism within Australia'.[8] An unprecedented re-alignment of national security ensued and 'federal and state police forces worked closely with intelligence agencies'[9] as a result. Australia also joined with the United States of America in its "War on Terror" against the Taliban regime in Afghanistan.

Thirteen months later Australians and other tourists and locals were targets in a series of suicide bombings on the Indonesian Island of Bali. Henderson argues this atrocity 'had an even more dramatic effect'[10] on the Australian psyche than the Al-Qaeda attacks on North America the previous year because of the 88 Australian who perished, many were stereotypical *Aussies*; for they were 'footballers on end-of-season tours or groups of women enjoying an overseas holiday'.[11] At the time, both attacks led to isolated acts of violent retribution against Muslims in Australia[12] and a flurry of polemical discourse from all quarters of society.

Local Muslim Professor Abdullah Saeed made a bold statement in 2003 claiming that 'Australian Muslims have no interest whatsoever in extremism, violence…suicide bombing and so on'[13] in an attempt to distance Islam from terrorism. But a series of raids on Muslim groups and individuals such as Jack Roche[14] in 2002 and Abdul

---

[8] Henderson, *Islam in Australia*, 12.

[9] Henderson, *Islam in Australia*, 13.

[10] Henderson, *Islam in Australia*, 13.

[11] Henderson, *Islam in Australia*, 13.

[12] Jasmin Lill & Jodie Munro O'Brien, 'Mosque Attacker Convicted,' *The Courier Mail*, 15 Jun 2007. Adam McMurray-Jones threw two molotov cocktails at the Holland Park mosque on 14/11/2001 which resulted in minor damage to its exterior facade.

[13] Saeed, *Islam in Australia*, 194.

[14] Henderson, *Islam in Australia*, 13. British born Muslim convert Jack Roche pleaded guilty to planning to attack the Israeli embassy in Canberra and was jailed until May 2007.

Naser Benbrika and his cohort[15] in 2005 with subsequent convictions challenged Saeed's assertion.

The reaction of the Muslim community to anti-terrorist legislation and subsequent monitoring by the Australian Security Intelligence Organisation (ASIO) and various policing agencies has generally been quite negative. A report by the Human Rights & Equal Opportunity Commission[16] found that many Muslim woman:

> ...believed they were victims of circumstance and felt lost within the country, the community and the system. Concern was expressed about antiterrorism legislation, such as fear of house being bugged or fire-bombed or fear of being deported.

Various Muslim lobby groups such as the Australian Muslim Civil Rights Advocacy Network (AMCRAN)[17] openly criticized the new anti-terror laws on the basis of limiting human rights and freedoms for practicing their religion in Australia. This particular group aligned itself with the Greens Party to lobby Federal Parliament regarding the new laws but in nearly every instance 'had little impact on the major parties – both...the Coalition and Labor- or within the broader community.'[18] Henderson posits the primary reason for such broad support of the laws is that 'most Australians believe that what appears to be a threat is, in fact, a threat...and they want government...to prevent further attacks'.[19]

The association of *Islam* with *Terrorism* has been vigorously debated in Australia. Muslim groups have been quick in attempting to convince Australians that terrorism doesn't have theological

---

[15] ABC News, 'Terrorist leader Benbrika sentenced to 15 yrs'.
http://www.abc.net.au/news/stories/2009/02/03/2481151.htm (2009). Benbrika from the Melbourne suburb of Dallas was sentenced to 15 years jail for his involvement in a terrorist cell which he led. Six other men in this group were also convicted and are currently serving shorter sentences.

[16] Human Rights & Equal Opportunity Commision (Aust), 'Living Spirit: Report on HREOC's Muslim Women's Project 2006'.
http://www.hreoc.gov.au/racial_discrimination/livingspirit/Living_Spirit_report.pdf (2006).

[17] Australian Muslim Civil Rights Advocacy Network, 'Be informed: Why every Muslim should be alarmed about the proposed anti-terror laws'.
http://amcran.org/index.php?option=com_content&task=view&id=62&Itemid=24 (2005). AMCRAN publish several booklets and information on the internet specifically for Muslims if they are ever subject to investigation or control orders etc.

[18] Henderson, *Islam in Australia*, 19.

[19] Henderson, *Islam in Australia*, 19.

underpinnings in Islam. The Islamic Council of Victoria in its media kit states that Muslims have committed acts of terror 'no more so than other groups of people'[20] and that terrorist acts are carried out by 'people who use Islam to justify political actions'.[21] But what of Qur'anic verses regularly cited by militants such as Sura 9.5 'which commands Muslims to fight anyone who refuses to convert to Islam'?[22]

Patrick Sookhdeo admits political and social injustices are often a source of unrest but the fact is that Islamists legitimise and justify violence and terrorism against non-Muslims from 'the Muslim source texts, classical Islamic theology, and paradigmatic early Muslim history'.[23] In response, many moderate scholars propose that these Jihadist verses should be confined to their original contexts claiming they 'were texts which were revealed to the prophet Muhammad in response to very specific conditions, and circumstances of his time'.[24]

The response of the State to this problem was most forcefully expressed at a conference of Imams in Australia in 2006 by then parliamentary secretary for immigration and multicultural affairs, Andrew Robb. He pushed responsibility of dealing with the problem into the Imams' hands, insisting that the Muslim community 'tackle the root cause, not the symptoms, of current difficulties... [and to] speak up and condemn terrorism'.[25] The same speech rejected terrorism as synonymous with 'orthodox Islam',[26] which some would see as forsaking history in an attempt to win the Imams' favor.

---

[20] Islamic Council of Victoria, 'Media Kit'.
http://www.icv.org.au/index.php?option=com_content&task=blogsection&id=9&Itemid=31 (2005).

[21] Islamic Council of Victoria, 'Media Kit'.

[22] Patrick Sookhdeo, *Global Jihad: The Future in the Face of Militant Islam* (McLean VA: Isaac Publishing, 2007), 64.

[23] Sookhdeo, *Global Jihad*, 43-44.

[24] Riaz Hassan, 'Islam: From Heretics to Believers' interview by Rachael Kohn (ABC Radio National *The Spirit of Things*, 16th March, 2008).
http://www.abc.net.au/rn/spiritofthings/stories/2008/2186299.htm (2008).

[25] Andrew Robb, 'Address to the Conference of Australian Imams'.
http://www.andrewrobb.com.au/news/default.asp?action=article&ID=166 (2006).

[26] Robb, 'Address to Imams' (2006).

Muslim Community Reference Group

An important development in relations between the Howard Federal Government (1996-2007) and Muslims in Australia was the formation of the Muslim Community Reference Group. Only 'those whom the government regarded as moderate'[27] were invited to this significant group which was given the mandate 'to create a more inclusive Australia in which people are less likely to be isolated and marginalised and possibly attracted to rigid and antisocial thinking that can lead to destructive activity'.[28] Radical groups and individuals such as 'Wassim Doureihi...of the radical Hizb Ut-Tahrir organization'[29] representing many excluded or isolated Muslims living in Australia were deliberated shunned in an effort to undermine their legitimacy. One contentious appointee on the group was former *Mufti of Australia:* Sheikh al-Hilali. However, his flirtation 'with Holocaust denial'[30] led to his prompt dismissal from the committee by the Government.

A major reason for the reference group's creation was due to the serious disquiet amongst Muslim Australians to the introduction of anti-terrorism legislation and its associated control orders and surveillance techniques. Islamic groups in Australia have tried to downplay the linkage between terrorism and Muslims[31] and instead blame the media for this perception and not themselves. However, included in the report submitted by the Reference Group is an outcome of research conducted by the University of Western Australia on Muslim identity which alludes to such a link:

> Militant forms of Islam are just one form of identity construction which just so happens to reaffirm an identity construction that is reminiscent of certain aspect of the medieval era and in its neo-fundamentalist form affirms the antagonistic construction of self and other at both the individual and civilization level.[32]

---

[27] Henderson, *Islam in Australia*, 25.

[28] Muslim Community Reference Group, *Building on Social Inclusion, Harmony and Security*, 6. http://www.immi.gov.au/living-in-australia/a-diverse-australia/mcrg_report.pdf (2007).

[29] Henderson, *Islam in Australia*, 24-25.

[30] Henderson, *Islam in Australia*, 25.

[31] Islamic Council of Victoria, 'Media Kit'.

[32] MCRG, *'Building on Social Inclusion'*, 35.

Whether such admissions become widespread within the Muslim community and lead to concrete progress in reforming its theology remains to be seen. But as Sookdheo comments, 'Western intervention in Muslim affairs, especially Muslim theology, would be seen by many Muslims as being itself justification for violent *jihad*'.[33]

Crime, Punishment & Cronulla

In the past ten years, a significant fracturing of social cohesion and deep community distrust became apparent in the light of several high profile criminal cases in the suburbs of Sydney. Before the Olympic games in 2000, a series of viscious 'gang rapes of young caucasian women... [committed by] Muslims of Pakistani and Lebanese background'[34] made headlines across the nation. Gang leader Bilal Skaf and his co-accused received substantial custodial sentences[35] which were later reduced in a series of appeals. A second series of gang rapes committed against teenage girls from late 2000 to 2002 further inflamed tensions with those convicted of the crimes receiving 'minimum sentences of between five and 16½ years'.[36]

Not long after the jailing of those involved in the above crimes, Sheikh Al-Hilali generated a storm of protest with his infamous *uncovered meat* Ramadan sermon in October 2006:

> If you take out uncovered meat and place it outside on the street, or in the garden or in the park, or in the backyard without a cover, and the cats come and eat it... whose fault is it, the cats' or the uncovered meat? The uncovered meat is the problem.[37]

---

[33] Sookdheo, *Global Jihad*, 419.

[34] Henderson, *Islam in Australia*, 18.

[35] Daily Telegraph, 'Gang rape brothers Bilal and Mohammed Skaf get jail cut', *The Daily Telegraph*, 17 Dec 2008. Bilal Skaf's initial sentence of 55 years in 2002 was reduced to 36 years and a non-parole period of 20 years in 2008.

[36] Natasha Wallace, 'Tegan tells her rapists: Go to hell', *The Sydney Morning Herald*, 6 April 2006.

[37] Richard Kerbaj, 'Muslim leader blames women for sex attacks', *The Australian*, 26 Oct 2006.

An outpouring of remonstration towards al-Hilali from virtually all sectors of Australian society followed, including the Prime Minister John Howard who described the sermon as 'appalling and reprehensible' and remarked:

> I totally reject the notion that the way in which women dress, the way in which women deport themselves can in any way be used as a semblance of a justification for rape.[38]

Many Muslims were equally incensed and publically bemoaned the fact that 'chauvinistic teachings and attitudes are common among many Muslims'[39] and called for al-Hilali's removal as *Mufti of Australia,* which came to pass in June 2007.

Public debate regarding the role of ethnicity in criminality still dominates radio talkback and print journalism. Former NSW detective Tim Priest was forthright in his article in the January 2004 issue of *Quadrant* with the explosive allegation that certain Lebanese gangs in Sydney 'were ruthless, extremely violent, and...intimidated not only innocent witnesses, but even the police that attempted to arrest them'.[40] The article openly criticized the hierarchy of the NSW police for going soft on such gangs and predicted the emergence of 'no go areas in south western Sydney, just like Paris'.[41] His anecdotal criticism, although tainted by embellishment, is both vindicated by the higher rates of imprisonment[42] of those born in Lebanon and challenged by the fact that criminals of such ethnicity are finding themselves behind bars.

---

[38] John Howard, 'PM Condemns Hilali rape comments', *ABC Radio PM*, Oct 26, 2006. http://www.abc.net.au/pm/content/2006/s1774556.htm (2006).

[39] Anne Henderson, 'Islam and Australia – the Next Phase', *The Sydney Institute Quarterly* Issue 30 (Feb 2007), 9. Henderson noted that the debate was significant in that it promoted vigorous debate and self-examination in the Muslim community in Australia.

[40] Tim Priest, 'The Rise of Middle Eastern Crime in Australia', *Quadrant* 68/1 (2004). It must be noted that many of his accounts have since been exposed as embellishments as they did not exactly correlate with actual police records.

[41] Priest, 'The Rise of Middle Eastern Crime in Australia', *Quadrant* 68/1.

[42] Australian Bureau of Statistics, '4517.0 Prisoners in Australia 2008'. http://www.abs.gov.au/ausstats/abs@.nsf/mf/4517.0 (2008). In the section 'Prisoners – country of birth', Lebanese-born Australians have a 73% higher rate of incarceration than Australian-born residents. This rate is comparable to those from PNG but about half that of Samoan and Vietnamese-born Australians. Ethnicity and religion is not taken into consideration so these statistics should not been seen as exhaustive.

The reasons for the problem of crime are connected by Riaz Hassan with a 'relative economic disadvantage'[43] which he attributes to high unemployment rates compared with non-Muslim Australians. He is not certain as to the exact reasons for this high unemployment situation but suggests 'lower levels of proficiency in the English language and prejudice and systemic discrimination'[44] may be to blame. However, at North Cronulla Beach in December 2005 several events conspired which still reverberate in the Australian psyche today.

It began when a group of 'Lebanese Muslims from the Western suburbs clashed with some young lifesavers'.[45] In the lead-up to this altercation tensions had arisen previously due to accounts of these gangs 'verbally abusing young, non-Muslim females for their (alleged) immodesty on the beach'.[46] The next weekend descended into rioting and chaos on the streets of Cronulla when around 5,000 mostly intoxicated 'young Australians of caucasian background...inflicted extreme violence on those they deemed to be of Muslim background'.[47] In response, bands of men from Sydney's western suburbs[48] went on a largely unimpeded rampage destroying property and assaulting people 'in the southern beach suburbs'[49], and firebombing the Auburn Uniting Church.

Much soul-searching and ink-spilling continued after these tumultous days, and fortunately efforts have been made to heal relations. Examples include the design, manufacture and marketing of female swimwear compatible with traditional Islamic values[50], and the involvement of 'members of the local Muslim

---

[43] Riaz Hassan, 'Social and Economic Conditions of Australian Muslims: Implications for Social Inclusion', *NCEIS Research Papers* 2/4 (2009), 10.

[44] Hassan, 'Social & Econ Cond.' *NCEIS* 2/4, 11.

[45] Henderson, *Islam in Australia*, 19.

[46] Henderson, *Islam in Australia*, 19.

[47] Henderson, *Islam in Australia*, 19.

[48] Or change this to "Sydney's heavily Muslim populated western suburbs"

[49] Henderson, *Islam in Australia*, 19.

[50] Laura Fitzpatrick, 'The New Swimsuit Issue', *Time Magazine,* 19 Jul 2007. http://www.time.com/time/magazine/article/0,9171,1645145,00.html (2007). Aheda Zanetti designed the 'Burqini' which has enabled Muslim women to join the North Cronulla Surf Life Saving Club.

community...who donated $500 that they had raised to help rebuild the church hall'[51] in Auburn.

Islamic Education: In my backyard?

Since 1983, Islamic independent schools offering regular education up to year 12 have been established across the nation.[52] Like other schools run along religious or denominational lines, these schools teach subjects particular to that faith. In the case of Islamic schools 'religious education, and...Arabic as well'[53] are taught and controversially for some, 'students are expected to follow Islamic rules...regarding dress and food while they are at school'.[54] It's an almost paradoxical situation when the Muslim Community Reference Group report itself calls for 'Islamic education that clarifies the differences between religion and culture'.[55]

Heavy reliance on Government funding, while not atypical for independent schools, provides 'around 80 percent'[56] of required revenue to ensure ongoing operation. But these subsidies haven't been provided without drama, as evidenced by the criminal case involving the Australian Islamic College in Perth where the director and principals were accused of having 'fraudulently gained $3.16 million from the state and federal governments'[57] by requesting finance for students who were not enrolled there, with two subsequently found guilty of these charges.

However, the main public dispute with respect to Islamic schools has centered around locating new schools in areas where few Muslims actually live. The NSW community of Camden has attracted significant media and public attention after the Qur'anic Society Dar Tahfez El-Quran applied to build a school on almost 6

---

[51] Lyndal Irons, 'Violence will not prevail in Auburn', *Insights* http://insights.uca.org.au/2006/april/auburn-uc.htm (2006).

[52] Saeed, *Islam in Australia*, 150.

[53] Abdullah Saeed, *Muslim Australians: Their Practices & Institutions* (Canberra: DCITA, 2004), 56.

[54] Saeed, *Muslim Australians*, 56.

[55] MCRG, *'Building on Social Inclusion'*, 37.

[56] Saeed, *Islam in Australia*, 150.

[57] Alana Buckley-Carr, 'Islamic School on Fraud Charges', *The Australian*, 28 Jun 2008.

hectares of farmland for up to 1200 students[58] in an area 'whose own Muslim population numbers fewer than 400'.[59] The group that applied to build the school is associated 'with an Islamic missionary group known as Tablighi Jamaat'[60], an 'extremely large,...influential and obtensibly peaceful'[61] movement which unfortunately has been influenced in some quarters by violent elements in recent decades.

The reaction to this organisation's plans were hostile to say the least. In late 2007, a public meeting attended 'by up to 800 people'[62], some of whom allegedly displayed 'signs and banners bearing racist slogans'[63] descended on the Camden Civic Centre opposed to the school. Ultimately the application to build the school failed in the courts due to incompatibility 'with Camden's rural zoning'[64] rather than ideological concerns expressed by local residents and churches.[65]

The Islamic influence on secular universities in Australia is seen by some as leading to a new clash of ideologies in higher education. Two very recent events highlight these tensions. Firstly, a significant initiative supported by the Muslim Community Reference Group and the Conference of Australian Imams is the 'National Centre of Excellence for Islamic Studies that could guide the development of university courses for religious leaders'.[66] With centres at the University of Melbourne, the University of Western Sydney and Griffith University in Brisbane, the National Centre

---

[58] Sally Neighbour, 'No Lessons Here', *The Australian*, 3 Jun 2009.

[59] Neighbour, 'No Lessons Here', *The Australian*.

[60] Neighbour, 'No Lessons Here', *The Australian*.

[61] Sookdheo, *Global Jihad,* 279. The CIA and Pakistani secret service infiltrated this organisation in the 1980s to recruit fighters for *Jihad* against the USSR military in Afghanistan.

[62] Paul Bibby, '800 protest against proposed Islamic school', *The Sydney Morning Herald,* 20 Dec 2007.

[63] Bibby, '800 protest' *SMH.*

[64] Neighbour, 'No Lessons Here' *The Australian.*

[65] Camden Ministers Fraternal, 'Submission to Camden Council Dec 22, 2008 – Re: DA 895/2007 Proposed Islamic School'. http://www.camdenpres.org.au/uploads/7a94b312-7ea0-876c.pdf (2008). Major concerns were the formation of religious ghettos and political and ideological views incompatible with the Australian way of life in the local area.

[66] MCRG, *'Building on Social Inclusion'*, 20.

offers several undergraduate, graduate and post-graduate courses in Islamic studies.[67] However, Griffith University has come under the spotlight for seeking additional funds from Saudi Arabia which according to critics are central to 'part of a Wahhabist "hearts and minds" campaign'.[68] The Rudd Labor Government (2007-2010) showed an awareness of this issue and of the view almost all Islamic student associations in Sydney Universities are run by Wahhabis:

> I certainly believe that we should try to restrict the degree to which Australian-Islamic institutions depend on outside funding, particularly Wahabi, Saudi Arabian.[69]

But whether the Australian Government has the fortitude to cut off the flow of funds and risk offending the Saudis remains to be seen. American expert Steven Emerson suggests a level of reciprocity should apply: 'There should be laws passed by Western governments prohibiting Saudi donations to universities until and unless Saudi Arabia operates a pluralistic religious environment'.[70]

Fostering and maintaining multicultural harmony in our secular universities has come under threat from aspects of Islamic theology and practice in relation to onsite facilities such as prayer rooms. At RMIT University in Melbourne a dispute went public when the 'Islamic student association... [campaigned] to have the multi-faith rooms declared Muslim-only'.[71] A major reason for such exclusive demands may stem from the fact that Australia has seen a massive influx of Saudi students in the past six or so years, many of whom are sponsored by Saudi Government scholarships.[72]

---

[67] National Centre of Excellence for Islamic Studies Australia, 'About us', http://www.nceis.unimelb.edu.au/about-us/about-centre (2008).

[68] Richard Kerbaj & Stuart Rintoul, 'Saudi's Secret Agenda', *The Australian*, 3 May 2008.

[69] Laurie Ferguson (Parliamentary Secretary for Multicultural Affairs),'A New Muslim Community Reference Group', interview by Stephen Crittenden (ABC Radio National, 26th March 2008). http://www.abc.net.au/rn/religionreport/stories/2008/2199156.htm (2008).

[70] Kerbaj & Rintoul, 'Saudi's Secret Agenda', *The Australian*, 3 May 2008.

[71] Milanda Rout, 'Uni rejects demand for Muslims prayer room', *The Australian*, 23 Mar 2009.

[72] Bernand Lane, 'English bar on Saudi market', *The Australian*, 12 Jul 2008. This report says higher education enrolments of Saudi students grew from 46 in 2002 to 1097 in 2007. A major reason was that the USA which traditionally accepted Saudi students had made it much harder for them to obtain visas since 9/11.

Anti-Vilification Laws

In early 2002, a seminar conducted by *Catch the Fire Ministries* in Surrey Hills, Melbourne became the litmus test for the newly-enacted *Racial and Religious Tolerance Act 2001* in the State of Victoria.[73] Three Muslim converts attended the seminar and made a complaint to the Victorian Civil & Administrative Tribunal (VCAT) which in 2004 ruled that Pastor Daniel Scot's seminar presentation was 'hostile, demeaning and derogatory of all Muslim people, their God, their prophet Mohammed and in general Muslim beliefs and practices'[74] and that Pastor Danny Nalliah, of Catch the Fire Ministries, had made statements 'likely to incite hatred towards Muslims'.[75] The decision was challenged by an appeal to the Supreme Court of Victoria which was upheld and mediation between the parties in June 2007 saw the Islamic Council of Victoria withdraw their complaint.[76]

Section 8 of the legislation was deemed to have been breached. It states:

> A person must not, on the ground of the religious belief or activity of another person or class of persons, engage in conduct that incites hatred against, serious contempt for, or revulsion or severe ridicule of, that other person or class of persons.[77]

There are exemptions in the law in Section 11 if a person 'in good faith...[is] conveying or teaching a religion or proselytising'.[78] But in the initial VCAT judgment Justice Higgins concluded that Pastor

---

[73] Victorian Civil & Administrative Tribunal Decisions, 'Islamic Council of Victoria v Catch the Fire Ministries Inc (Final) [2004] VCAT 2510 (22 December 2004). http://www.austlii.edu.au/au/cases/vic/VCAT/2004/2510.html (2004).

[74] VCAT, 'ICV vs CTF (2004)'.

[75] VCAT, 'ICV vs CTF (2004)'.

[76] Jenny Stokes, 'Religious Vilification complaint - finally resolved', *Salt Shakers*. http://www.saltshakers.org.au/html/P/265/B/404/ (2007).

[77] Victorian Government, 'Racial and Religious Tolerance Act 2001 – Sect 8.1' in Victorian Consolidated Legislation website.

http://www.austlii.edu.au/au/legis/vic/consol_act/rarta2001265/s8.html

[78] Victorian Government, 'Racial and Religious Tolerance Act 2001 – Sect 11' in Victorian Consolidated Legislation website.

http://www.austlii.edu.au/au/legis/vic/consol_act/rarta2001265/s11.html

Nalliah 'did not act reasonably and in good faith'.[79] The case received attention from around the world, particularly in Evangelical Christian circles, as it challenged the notion that one could freely criticize or voice concerns about a religion in the public square. It will be interesting to see if any cases are brought before VCAT in future years if Islamic polemicists make critical or derogatory statements regarding the Christian and Jewish faiths in the public arena.

Political Power?

Political organisations with Islamic roots and agendas are a very recent development in Australia, the most controversial being *Hizb ut-Tahrir (Party of Liberation)*. It is an organisation which according to its own website explicitly:

> ...aims at the correct revival of the Ummah through enlightened thought. It also strives to bring her back to her previous might and glory such that she wrests the reins of initiative away from other states and nations, and returns to her rightful place as the first state in the world, as she was in the past, when she governs [sic] the world according to the laws of Islam.[80]

It rejects western ideologies of 'nationalism and democracy'[81] and has been 'involved in attempted *coup d'etats*' in the past which has resulted in it being 'banned in Egypt, Jordan, Germany and several other countries of the Muslim world and the West'.[82] In Australia this organisation is still allowed to operate despite calls for its banning. In 2007 the Federal Attorney-General at the time, Philip Ruddock, said '"The threshold test for banning an organisation is that it has to be involved in terrorism or advocacy of terrorism"'[83], and to this day it remains a legal but highly scrutinised group which

---

[79] VCAT, 'ICV vs CTF (2004)'.

[80] Hizb ut-Tahrir Australia, 'About Hizb ut-Tahrir'.
http://www.hizb-australia.org/hizbut-tahrir/about-hizb-ut-tahrir (2009).

[81] Sookdheo, *Global Jihad*, 288.

[82] Sookdheo, *Global Jihad*, 288.

[83] Natalie O'Brien, 'Call to ban Islamic hardliners', *The Australian*, 17 Aug 2007.

has even launched a glossy magazine aimed at students in universities.[84]

Less extreme but certainly still courting controversy is the *Islamic Friendship Association of Australia* headed by Keysar Trad of the Lakemba Mosque in Sydney. This association prefers to take a more concilitary approach and involves itself in interfaith dialogue[85] and lobbying of Governments on behalf of many in the Muslim community. However, it generated deep public antipathy when it pushed for the legal recognition of 'polygamous unions... [to] help protect the rights of women in the relationship'.[86] Several Western countries (ie. Britain & Canada) are considering or allowing aspects of Shar'ia to operate parallel to existing law, but in Australia such an idea is not gaining traction at the current time; '"The [Labour] government is not considering and will not consider the introduction of any part of Sharia law into the Australian legal system", Mr McClelland said'.[87]

Citizens of Australia?

Differences between many Muslims in Australia and its non-Muslim people and institutions, as has been discussed, raises questions regarding citizenship and associated expectations and responsibilities. Tariq Ramadan, in a 2008 address at Griffith University, talked about the citizenship of Muslims living in the West and made this intriguing comment:

---

[84] Natalie O'Brien, 'Islamist hardliners launching magazine', *The Australian* 7 Apr 2008. The Australian Security Intelligence Organisation had investigated the group twice with the co-operation of Hizb ut-Tahrir.

[85] Islamic Friendship Association of Australia, 'About the Islamic Friendship Association of Australia'. http://www.speednet.com.au/~keysar/aboutifaa.htm.

[86] Australian Associated Press, 'Polygamous marriages should be recognised: sheikh', *The Sydney Morning Herald,* 24 Jun 2008.

[87] Australian Associated Press, 'Govt rules out Sharia law for Australia', *The West Australian,* 8 Feb 2008.

> You have to be loyal to the country, and loyalty to the country means that the country is respecting two fundamental rights; freedom of conscience and freedom of worship.[88]

Whether that freedom of worship extends to Muslims converting to another religion is not stated. However a 2007 survey in Britain revealed that for many it is not a two-way street. Thirty-one percent of British Muslims agreed 'that Muslim conversion to another religion is forbidden and punishable by death'[89] with a higher percentage of younger Muslims taking this hard-line view than their elders.

One response of the Australian Federal Government to the perceived problem of some Muslims expressing values and loyalties inconsistent with the Australian majority has been to change the rules relating to obtaining Australian citizenship. The new *Australian Citizenship Test* introduced in 2007 was primarily designed to ensure applicants gained 'an adequate knowledge of Australia and of the responsibilities and privileges of Australian citizenship'.[90] A report issued in April 2009 found that among the top 10 countries, Iraqi applicants had the lowest pass rate (84%)[91] which can be explained in part by the strict English language requirements on the test.

Conclusion: The Way Forward

Immigration and population growth has put pressure on social cohesion and resulted in revised citizenship requirements. The threat of terrorism has alerted security organisations and placed groups who espouse *Jihad* under the spotlight from both within and outside the Australian Muslim community. Selective consultation by high levels of Government has deliberately attempted to heal its

---

[88] Tariq Ramadan, 'Edited Transcript of the Keynote Address of Professor Tariq Ramadan', *ABC Radio National: Encounter,* 9 Mar 2008.
http://www.abc.net.au/rn/encounter/doc/Tariq_Ramadan_full_lecture.pdf (2008)

[89] Munira Mirza, Abi Senthilkumaran, & Zein Ja'far, *Living Apart Together: British Muslims and the Paradox of Multiculturalism* (London UK: Policy Exchange, 2007), 47.

[90] Dept of Immigration & Citizenship, 'Moving Forward...Improving Pathways to Citizenship'. http://www.citizenshiptestreview.gov.au/_pdf/moving-forward-report.pdf (2008), 8.

[91] Dept of Immigration & Citizenship, 'Australian Citizenship Test: Snapshot Report' http://www.citizenship.gov.au/_pdf/cit-test-snapshot-apr-09.pdf (2009), 9.

relationship with more moderate Muslims, but potentially inflamed and radicalised fundamentalist groups even further.

Culturally motivated crime has provoked violence, but quickened interaction and dialogue to heal the wounds. Islamic education has forced the Muslim community to examine pluralism but paradoxically opened the door to vehemently anti-pluralist forces from outside of Australia. Laws designed to enforce social cohesion and pluralistic thought have threatened Western givens of free-speech and only added fuel to the debate. Political involvement by Muslims has exposed faultlines within the *Ummah*, yet at the same time exposed the agenda of those intending to undermine the Judeo-Christian basis for most of our legal system and way-of-life. We live in interesting times.

It remains to be seen whether these events will ultimately bring about a deepened self-examination and reformation of Muslim theology and culture, or whether a re-assertion of a classical Muslim identity to win over Australia by stealth will prevail. However, Government policy to keep the peace and a democratic process which ensures all citizens can voice their concerns and debate the issues, without fear, must be protected. To do otherwise risks appeasing those who wish to transform Australia into a land of inequity, oppression and possibly even terror.

Postscript (2016)

Since this essay was originally written in 2009, there have been many significant events on the Australian political stage.

However, the main issues raised remain at the forefront of public debate (and regular outbursts of outrage and spilt ink!). The threat of Islamic terrorist attacks have become all-too-real on Australian soil in the past two years with the Lindt Café siege, shooting at Parramatta police headquarters, attempted murder of police at Endeavour Hills, the problem of local ISIS sympathizers, and ongoing arrests and court cases of those seeking to commit acts of terror. My concern that radical fundamentalist groups would be inflamed with antagonism towards Governments seems to have escalated.

Fortunately we have not seen a repeat of riots of the scale of Cronulla in 2005, however public disquiet with Islam continues to bubble away and emerged with the return of Pauline Hanson and her One Nation Party into Federal Parliament at the 2016 Election on a platform of halting Muslim immigration, banning Halal certification, and pushing for a 'Royal Commission to determine if Islam is a religion or political ideology'. On a smaller scale, governments and police have had to manage very public clashes between ultra-right wing agitators such as the United Patriots Front (UPF), and anarchist movements such as ANTIFA. Such clashes have sometimes developed as a consequence of local government planning approvals of the construction of new mosques and subsequent court challenges as was seen in 2014-15 in Bendigo and elsewhere.

On the education front, Muslim schools have grown rapidly, albeit with significant issues relating to Government funding. But given the increasingly aggressive secularism of public schooling, independent Muslim schools will undoubtedly become even more attractive to Muslim families despite funding pressures.

Many Australians and politicians have embraced more cosmopolitan Muslims such as Waleed Aly, yet remain troubled with more fundamentalist leaders within the Muslim community, even if they've shared dinner with each other. It's all too common for social media to become the battleground of public discourse and outrage, but genuine attempts to unpack Islamic theology occur outside of the mass-media spotlight – perhaps because of the fear of being castigated and ostracised, along with a general agnosticism of theology and paranoia of creating division.

Governments have largely held firm on not having parallel legal structures, particularly in comparison with the United Kingdom, but have resisted attempts to remove religious vilification laws. Despite these attempts to maintain the peace, negative attitudes and a fear of Muslims in Australia has not diminished. Rather a dialogue that is civil, honest, respectful, generous, and willing to engage with the theological aspects of Islamic belief and practice is required more than ever in the public square and halls of all levels of Government within this country.

Bibliography

ABC News, 'Terrorist leader Benbrika sentenced to 15 yrs'. http://www.abc.net.au/news/stories/2009/02/03/2481151.htm (2009).

Australian Associated Press, 'Govt rules out Sharia law for Australia', *The West Australian,* 8 February 2008.

Australian Associated Press, 'Polygamous marriages should be recognised: sheikh', *The Sydney Morning Herald,* 24 June 2008.

Australian Bureau of Statistics, 'Perspectives on Migrants, 2007'. http://www.abs.gov.au/ausstats/abs@.nsf/Lookup/3416.0 Main%20Features22007?opendocument&tabname=Summary&prodno=3416.0&issue=2007&num=&view= (2008).

Australian Bureau of Statistics, '4517.0 Prisoners in Australia 2008'. http://www.abs.gov.au/ausstats/abs@.nsf/mf/4517.0 (2008).

Australian Bureau of Statistics, 'Religious Affiliation by Age by Sex' In 2006 Census Tables. http://www.censusdata.abs.gov.au/ABSNavigation/download?format=xls&collection=Census&period=2006&productlabel=Religious%20Affiliation%20by%20Age%20by%20Sex&producttype=Census%20Tables&method=Place%20of%20Usual%20Residence&areacode=0 (2007).

Australian Muslim Civil Rights Advocacy Network, 'Be informed: Why every Muslim should be alarmed about the proposed anti-terror laws'. http://amcran.org/index.php?option=com_content&task=view&id=62&Itemid=24 (2005).

Bibby, Paul. '800 protest against proposed Islamic school', *The Sydney Morning Herald,* 20 December 2007.

Buckley-Carr, Alana. 'Islamic School on Fraud Charges', *The Australian,* 28 June 2008.

Camden Ministers Fraternal, 'Submission to Camden Council Dec 22, 2008 – Re: DA 895/2007 Proposed Islamic School'. http://www.camdenpres.org.au/uploads/7a94b312-7ea0-876c.pdf (2008).

Daily Telegraph, 'Gang rape brothers Bilal and Mohammed Skaf get jail cut', *The Daily Telegraph*, 17 December 2008.

Dept of Immigration & Citizenship, 'Australian Citizenship Test: Snapshot Report' http://www.citizenship.gov.au/_pdf/cit-test-snapshot-apr-09.pdf (2009).

Dept of Immigration & Citizenship, 'Moving Forward...Improving Pathways to Citizenship'. http://www.citizenshiptestreview.gov.au/_pdf/moving-forward-report.pdf (2008).

Ferguson, Laurie. (Parliamentary Secretary for Multicultural Affairs), 'A New Muslim Community Reference Group', interview by Stephen Crittenden (ABC Radio National, 26th March 2008). http://www.abc.net.au/rn/religionreport/stories/2008/2199156.htm (2008).

Fitzpatrick, Laura. 'The New Swimsuit Issue' in *Time Magazine*, 19 July 2007. http://www.time.com/time/magazine/article/0,9171,1645145,00.html (2007).

Hassan, Riaz. 'Islam: From Heretics to Believers' interview by Rachael Kohn (ABC Radio National *The Spirit of Things*, 16th March, 2008). http://www.abc.net.au/rn/spiritofthings/stories/2008/2186299.htm (2008).

Hassan, Riaz. 'Social and Economic Conditions of Australian Muslims: Implications for Social Inclusion', NCEIS Research Papers 2/4 (2009), 1-13.

Henderson, Anne. 'Islam and Australia – the Next Phase', *The Sydney Institute Quarterly* (Issue 30), February 2007, 9-12.

Henderson, Gerald. *Islam in Australia: Democratic Bipartisanship in Action* (London UK: Policy Exchange, 2007).

Hizb ut-Tahrir Australia, 'About Hizb ut-Tahrir'. http://www.hizb-australia.org/hizbut-tahrir/about-hizb-ut-tahrir (2009).

Howard, John. 'PM Condemns Hilali rape comments', ABC Radio PM, October 26, 2006. http://www.abc.net.au/pm/content/2006/s1774556.htm (2006).

Human Rights & Equal Opportunity Commision (Aust), 'Living Spirit: Report on HREOC's Muslim Women's Project 2006'. http://www.hreoc.gov.au/racial_discrimination/livingspirit/Living_Spirit_report.pdf (2006).

Irons, Lyndal. 'Violence will not prevail in Auburn', *Insights* http://insights.uca.org.au/2006/april/auburn-uc.htm (2006).

Islamic Council of Victoria, 'Media Kit'. http://www.icv.org.au/index.php?option=com_content&task=blogsection&id=9&Itemid=31 (2005).

Islamic Friendship Association of Australia, 'About the Islamic Friendship Association of Australia'. http://www.speednet.com.au/~keysar/aboutifaa.htm.

Kent, Mary. 'Do Muslims have more Children than other Women in Western Europe?' In Population Reference Bureau. http://www.prb.org/Articles/2008/muslimsineurope.aspx (2008).

Kerbaj, Richard. 'Muslim leader blames women for sex attacks', *The Australian,* 26 October 2006.

Kerbaj, Richard. & Rintoul, Stuart. 'Saudi's Secret Agenda', *The Australian,* 3 May 2008.

Lane, Bernand. 'English bar on Saudi market', *The Australian,* 12 July 2008.

Lill, Jasmin. & Munro-O'Brien, Jodie. 'Mosque Attacker Convicted', *The Courier Mail,* 15 June 2007.

Migration Policy Institute, 'Annual number of asylum applications by nationality, 1980 to 2004' In Country and Comparative Data. http://www.migrationinformation.org/datahub/countrydata/data.cfm (2005).

Mirza, Munira., Senthilkumaran, Abi. & Ja'far, Zein. *Living Apart Together: British Muslims and the Paradox of Multiculturalism* (London UK: Policy Exchange, 2007).

Muslim Community Reference Group, *Building on Social Inclusion, Harmony and Security*, 6. http://www.immi.gov.au/living-in-australia/a-diverse-australia/mcrg_report.pdf (2007).

National Centre of Excellence for Islamic Studies Australia, 'About us', http://www.nceis.unimelb.edu.au/about-us/about-centre (2008).

Neighbour, Sally. 'No Lessons Here', *The Australian*, 3 June 2009.

O'Brien, Natalie. 'Call to ban Islamic hardliners', *The Australian*, 17 August 2007.

O'Brien, Natalie. 'Islamist hardliners launching magazine', *The Australian* 7 April 2008.

Priest, Tim. 'The Rise of Middle Eastern Crime in Australia', *Quadrant* 68/1 (2004).

Ramadan, Tariq. 'Edited Transcript of the Keynote Address of Professor Tariq Ramadan', *ABC Radio National: Encounter*, 9 March 2008.

Robb, Andrew. 'Address to the Conference of Australian Imams'. http://www.andrewrobb.com.au/news/default.asp?action=article&ID=166 (2006).

Rout, Milanda. 'Uni rejects demand for Muslims prayer room', *The Australian*, 23 Mar 2009.

Saeed, Abdullah. *Islam in Australia* (Sydney: Allen & Unwin, 2003).

Saeed, Abdullah. *Muslim Australians: Their Practices & Institutions* (Canberra: DCITA, 2004).

Sookhdeo, Patrick. *Global Jihad: The Future in the Face of Militant Islam* (McLean VA: Isaac Publishing, 2007).

Stokes, Jenny. 'Religious Vilification complaint - finally resolved', Salt Shakers. http://www.saltshakers.org.au/html/P/265/B/404/ (2007).

Victorian Civil & Administrative Tribunal Decisions, 'Islamic Council of Victoria v Catch the Fire Ministries Inc (Final) [2004] VCAT 2510 (22 December 2004). http://www.austlii.edu.au/au/cases/vic/VCAT/2004/2510.html (2004).

Victorian Government, 'Racial and Religious Tolerance Act 2001 – Sect 8.1' in Victorian Consolidated Legislation website. http://www.austlii.edu.au/au/legis/vic/consol_act/rarta2001265/s8.html

Victorian Government, 'Racial and Religious Tolerance Act 2001 – Sect 11' in Victorian Consolidated Legislation website. http://www.austlii.edu.au/au/legis/vic/consol_act/rarta2001265/s11.html

Wallace, Natasha. 'Tegan tells her rapists: Go to hell', *The Sydney Morning Herald,* 6 April 2006.

Is Islam compatible with 21st century Western values and ideals?

Theo Kalmbach

Melbourne School of Theology

"America and Islam are not exclusive and need not be in competition. Instead, they overlap, and share common principles of justice and progress, tolerance and the dignity of all human beings" - Barack Obama (Cairo Speech, 2009)

The 'True Face' of Islam

September 11, 2001 opened the eyes of the world to the reality of 'fundamentalist' Islam. From the tyranny of Afghanistan's Taliban, to the violent vision of Al-Qaeda, for the past decade militant Islamism has gripped the imagination of the West, inspiring both fear and fascination. Ayatollah Khomeini's condemnation of America as the "Great Satan", the denunciation against Salman Rushdie and his *Satanic Verses,* the Danish cartoon riots, the calls of Osama bin Laden for *jihad* against the West. All of these dramatic and terrible memories reinforce the notion of Islam as a threat: a foreign, militant, expansionist religion; viciously anti-West, bend on world domination; anachronistic, medieval, irrational, and ultimately irrelevant.

Yet the designation 'Islam' transcends such a monolithic stereotype: it is tremendously diverse. Islam encompasses over a billion people, all belonging to different traditions and denominations: each containing their own distinct theological confessions, interpretive methods and practices and rituals. Islam speaks with many voices.

However, to engage in meaningful discussion, 'types' must be assigned. For the purposes of this discussion, three broad categories will be used, although these are by no means definitive:

The first major Islamic ideology is *traditionalism*. This encompasses the broad majority of Muslims, who see Islam as a distinct paradigm, encompassing not just religion but an entire culture. Mostly riding on the decrees of past generations, and trusting the religious leaders (*ulama*) for guidance, for these people, membership of the institution of Islam forms an important social badge. As for the West, "the traditionalist masses wish to take their place as equal partners in the modern world".[1]

The second stream of thought is that of the *modernisers*, who seek to "modernise Islam and re-present Mohammad in terms that could be appreciated and accepted by the non-Muslim world".[2] These Muslims, most often with Western ties, seek to follow a method of interpretation that re-contextualizes Islam, fitting it within a modern context, an endeavour that can generally lead to Westernization (assimilation) and secularization.[3]

The third stream is *Islamism*, popularly termed radical or fundamentalist Islam.[4] Political Islam "seeks to recreate in today's world the Islam of the seventh century. The destiny of Islam is to overcome all other religions and be installed as the world religion, and its victory is to be hastened, if necessary, by violence and terrorism".[5] It espouses that Islam is not just a different system, but a system fundamentally at odds with all others, and must dominate over or destroy all rivals. Unsurprisingly, Islamism is consciously opposed to Western ideas and institutions: particularly that of secularism.[6]

---

[1] P Riddell & P. Cotterell, *Islam in Context* (2nd ed.; Grand Rapids: Baker Books, 2003), 213.
[2] Riddell & Cotterell, *Islam in Context*, 213.
[3] Peter Riddell, *Christians and Muslims: Pressures and Potential in a Post-9/11 World* (Leicester: IVP, 2004), 19.
[4] John Esposito, *The Islamic Threat: Myth or Reality?* (3rd ed.; Oxford: Oxford University Press, 1999), 6.
[5] Riddell & Cotterell, *Islam in Context*, 213.
[6] William Shepard, 'Islamism: Concepts and Debates' in *Oxford Encyclopedia of the Islamic World* (ed. J. Esposito; Oxford: Oxford University Press, 2009, vol 3), 191.

What is 'The West'?

The term 'Western', although used as a geographic term, does not so much relate to an area – 'west' - but rather refers to a conglomeration of societies which share fundamental philosophical, social and political principles. These principles are derived from the concept of a liberal democracy, historically founded by the ancient Greeks and developed primarily by Christians. Pertaining to values, "the defining characteristics of a liberal democracy include a commitment to fundamental freedoms, within a framework of laws to prevent their abuse, such as freedom to practice one's own religion; freedom of speech; freedom of association; freedom to publish; and equality before the law".[7] Personal freedom, equality and respect are basic virtues that people intrinsically deserve, irrespective of status or background. Out of these values emerge "principles of justice and progress; tolerance and the dignity of all human beings".[8] Consequently, populations of western countries tend to be extraordinarily diverse: comprising a wide range of ethnicities, religions, cultures and life-styles, though Western societies expect a common commitment to the established legal system and unspoken value scheme.

Models of Islamic-Western Relations

The Assimilationist Model

Within Western academic circles, there are two broad models for describing Islam-Western relations: the assimilationist model, or the Clash of Civilizations approach.

The first of these, the assimilationist model holds that the tensions between Muslims and the West, both in the West and in the Muslim world, are the product of the incomplete assimilation of

---

[7] C. Cox & J. Marks, *The West, Islam and Islamism: A Comparison Between the Philosophy, Epistemology and Political Principles of 'Western' and 'Islamic' Societies* (Civitas – Institute for the Study of Civil Society: London, 2nd ed 2006).
[8] Barack Obama, 'Text: A New Beginning' in *The New York Times*. http://www.nytimes.com/2009/06/04/us/politics/04obama.text.html?_r=1 (June 4, 2009).

both sides into a global society. Resultantly, clashes in Europe or terrorism in America result from a failure by their host countries to properly assimilate Muslims within their borders. This 'failure to assimilate' results primarily from geo-politics, social inequality or ignorance. The identification of these causes is exemplified in the words of Edward Said,

> These are tense times, but it is better to think in terms of powerful and powerless communities, the secular politics of reason and ignorance, and universal principles of justice and injustice.[9]

Firstly, assimilationists attribute problems between Muslims and the west to socio-political factors, as geo-political conflict inevitably leads to racial tension. Secondly, social and economic injustice is a contributing factor, claimed to marginalize progressive Muslim leaders and strengthen support for radical Islamists. Lastly, and most fundamentally, assimilationists attribute conflict between Islam and the West to ignorance. Usually the blame is leveled at Western nations, for failing to respect and adapt to Islamic culture. If only all parties genuinely attempted to understand 'the other', assimilationists assert, all conflict will disappear, as both parties realise they want the same things.

Unsurprisingly, the answer presented is as either religious dialogue or political appeasement. Religious dialogue, initially serves as a vehicle to empower Muslims/ westerners to move beyond their differences and realise their commonalities. This is an approach most conspicuously advocated by the 'Dialogue of Civilisations' initiative, founded by Seyed Mohammad Khatami, former president of Iran (1997-2005) and backed by the UN.

The other solution is political appeasement. The posited solution is for affected countries to learn the values and beliefs of those opposing them. This takes the form of striving to accommodate and respect them by promoting and normalizing Islam, paying financial incentives and taking affirmative measures to neutralize socio-political grievances, as exemplified in the 2009 proposal to pay Taliban members to switch sides.[10] Assimilationists claim that these

---

[9] Edward Said, 'The Clash of Ignorance' in *The Nation*. http://www.thenation.com/doc/20011022/said (October 4, 2001).

[10] Ed Hornick, 'US Set to Pay Taliban Members to Switch Sides' in *CNN Politics*. http://www.cnn.com/2009/POLITICS/10/28/afghanistan.taliban.pay/index.html (October 29, 2009).

kinds of practical (and expedient) measures should harmonize and integrate the West with the rest, into an emerging global community.

The Clash of Civilizations Model

The 'Clash of Civilisations', the second model, first formally espoused by Samuel Huntingdon in his *Foreign Affairs* article 'The Clash of Civilizations?' (1993), and then later his book *The Clash of Civilizations and the Remaking of World Order* (1996), maintains that we are expressing a clash of civilisations between Islamic and Western societies, resulting from the aspiration of Muslims to create a global civilisation by displacing all competing societies. As Huntingdon asserts,

> The great divisions among humankind and the dominating source of conflict will be cultural. Nation states will remain the most powerful actors in world affairs, but the principal conflicts of global politics will occur between nations and groups of different civilizations...The fault lines between civilizations will be the battle lines of the future.[11]

Thus, under this model Islam is intrinsically opposed to the West, or at least, a completely different paradigm. It holds radically different values and esteems different ideals. As Huntingdon asserts,

> Western concepts differ fundamentally from those prevalent in other civilizations. Western ideas of individualism, liberalism, constitutionalism, human rights, equality, liberty, the rule of law, democracy, free markets, the separation of church and state, often have little resonance in Islamic, Confucian, Japanese, Hindu, Buddhist or Orthodox cultures... Indeed, the author of a review of 100 comparative studies of values in different societies concluded that "the values that are most important in the West are least important worldwide".[12]

---

[11] Samuel Huntingdon, 'The Clash of Civilizations?', *Foreign Affairs* 72/3 (1993), 22.
[12] Huntingdon, 'The Clash of Civilizations?', 23.

It is clear that, if Huntingdon is right, Western nations will lose predominance if they fail to recognize the irreconcilable nature of cultural tensions. As the eminent historian Bernard Lewis dramatically argues, what is happening "is no less than a clash of civilisations—the perhaps irrational but surely historic reaction of an ancient rival against our Judeo-Christian heritage, our secular present, and the worldwide expansion of both".[13]

Consequently, the events of September 11, 2001 saw Huntingdon's model catapulted into popularity, confirmed in the eyes of much of the world. However, despite recent historical events, Huntingdon's model has been widely criticised as too monolithic; too simplistic, failing to represent the diversity within Islam and indeed all cultures. Said, loaded with sarcasm, lambasts Huntingdon for his presumption to speak for an entire religion.

> In both articles, the personification of enormous entities called "the West" and "Islam" is recklessly affirmed, as if hugely complicated matters like identity and culture existed in a cartoonlike world... Certainly neither Huntington nor Lewis has much time to spare for the internal dynamics and plurality of every civilization... or for the unattractive possibility that a great deal of demagogy and downright ignorance is involved in presuming to speak for a whole religion or civilization. No, the West is the West, and Islam Islam.[14]

However, Said reacts too harshly, moving to an opposite extreme. Islam, though it is complex, is not as divided as he assumes. Firstly Islam is united theologically. Internally, there is a clear stress on unity: the oneness of God (*tawhid*), one *ummah*, one Book – the Qur'an- and one Caliphate. Whereas generally there is a promotion of diversity in Western societies, in Muslim societies the focus can tend towards promoting unity and sameness.

However, the ultimate reason for the veracity of Huntingdon's thesis lies in the fact that Islam functions as a *holistic system*. Islam is not simply a religion- despite the attempts of modernizers such as Tariq Ramadan who wish to cleave a distinction between Islamic 'religion' and Islamic 'civilization'.[15] Rather Islam encompasses all facets of existence: at the religious level, the political and economic

---

[13] Bernard Lewis, 'Roots of Muslim Rage', *Policy* 17/4 (2001-2), 26.
[14] Edward Said, 'The Clash of Ignorance', *The Nation*, October 22, 2001.
[15] Tariq Ramadan, *Western Muslims and the Future of Islam* (Oxford: Oxford University Press, 2004), 214.

realms, even the social level. As a *complete* system, Islam struggles to be secularized, to adopt foreign values. In everything it seeks submission. And as Cox and Marks controversially remark,

> The comprehensive control by religion of virtually every aspect of human life, individual and collective, enshrines the essence of totalitarianism and totalitarian control which is *inherently incompatible* with the concept of individual freedom which lies at the heart of liberal democracy.[16]

Fundamental tensions *do* occur at the ideological and cultural level. These drive political and social tensions across the globe. Consequently, our attention should turn to these 'flashpoints', these civilizational fault lines. And as we look at these tensions, the question must be posed: must Islam and the West perpetually be locked in a struggle for supremacy or can they peacefully co-exist?

Flashpoints Between Islam and the West

Political Faultlines

The Israeli-Palestinian Conflict

A fairly obvious fissure between Islamic nations and the US is the Israeli-Palestinian conflict. Currently America perilously and expediently juggles its interests on both sides, both acknowledging its "strong bonds" with Israel, and disgust at the "intolerable" situation of the Palestinians, suffering in pursuit of a homeland.[17]

Yet despite Obama's fervent claims that America "will not turn our backs on the legitimate Palestinian aspiration for dignity, opportunity, and a state of their own", many remain unconvinced, embittered by past history.[18] Ali Abunimah of *The Guardian* writes:

> Fair enough, but did Obama really imagine that such words would impress an Arab public that watched in horror as Israel slaughtered 1,400 people in Gaza last winter, including hundreds

---

[16] Cox & Marks, *The West, Islam and Islamism*, 12. [emphasis added]
[17] Obama, 'A New Beginning'.
[18] Obama, 'A New Beginning'.

of sleeping, fleeing or terrified children, with American-supplied weapons?[19]

It is clear that the emotion and enmity simply runs too deep. This is so pronounced that "the cause most frequently adduced for anti-American feeling among Muslims today is American support for Israel".[20] Such feelings form a great chasm between Islamic and Western nations.

However, it was not simply the deaths and the suffering that caused resentment. The Israeli occupation deeply struck at the pride, identity and history of the Muslim world.[21] And this was not painful simply because it deflated any notions of political supremacy, but also because of underlying religious dissonance. Most of the expelled Arabs were Muslims (with some Christians). While both Jews and Christians consider Jerusalem as their Holy Land, promised to them by God (Gen 13:14-15), the land holds special religious significance for Muslims: firstly because, from Jerusalem, Mohammad ascended to heaven (Q. 17:1). Secondly, and more fundamentally, it had for centuries been a part of *dar al-Islam*, the 'house of Islam', the geographical expanse in which sacred Islam dwells.[22] For non-Muslims to occupy that area is a shock and an insult, violating fundamental Islamic tradition.

And this sense of religious entitlement is further compounded by the overall negative portrayal of Christians and Jews in the Qur'an, creating a sense of racial supremacy. The Qur'an claims that the Jews are "cursed for their disbelief" (Q. 4:46), and have "wretchedness stamped upon them" as a result of their transgressions and killing of the prophets (Q. 2:61; 3:211). Muslims are commanded not to take them as friends/ allies (Q. 5:51), and the Jewish peoples made objects of ridicule, transformed into apes and pigs (Q. 2:65; 7:116; 5:60). Yet paradoxically Jews are also regarded as a legitimate community of believers, the "people of the book" (Q. 4:47), although they are accused of deliberately perverting their revelation (Q. 2:75). Regular exposure to this teaching clearly has a negative influence; the 2005 Pew Global

---

[19] Ali Abunimah, 'A Bush in sheep's clothing' in *The Guardian*. http://www.guardian.co.uk/commentisfree/2009/jun/04/barack-obama-middleeast (June 4, 2009).
[20] Lewis, 'Roots of Muslim Rage', 21.
[21] Esposito, *The Islamic Threat*, 11.
[22] Rollin Armour, *Islam Christianity and the West* (Maryknoll: Orbis Books, 2002), 164-165.

Attitudes Project commented on the fairly self-evident observation that "throughout the Muslim world, opinions of Jews are highly unfavourable".[23] Such teaching clearly contributes to this anti-Jewish sentiment. Obviously, to an extent, these passages need to be tempered by their historical context; however such "vile stereotypes"[24] clearly defy the Western ideals of the fundamental equality of, and need to respect, all races and religious groups.

Terrorism and *Jihad*

Another large point of tension is the issue of *jihad*, an institution responsible for the destruction of the Twin Towers and countless deaths subsequently. However, contrary to the assimilationist position, Islamic terrorism is not simply political. Those who commit such atrocities can find their justification in Islamic sacred scripture: over a hundred Qur'anic 'sword passages', even more Hadith. The prophetic *sunnah*, is even read by some Islamists as a manual for war. Martyrs are promised immediate access to heaven – "Paradise is under the shades of swords" (Al-Bukhari 4:63 cf. Q. 4:74; 61:10-12; 9:111). Not only that, but the underlying psychology of such Islamists is often 'apocalyptic' – containing the belief that societal change can only be wrought through a violent purgation – again finding support in many of the Qur'an's monochromatic images (i.e. Q. 8:39).[25] It is one thing for President Obama to say that "violence is a dead end", and for politicians to claim that 'Islam is a religion of peace', but it is another to read the Qur'anic injunction to " kill the polytheists wherever you find them, capture them, besiege them and sit in wait for them at every place of ambush" (Q. 9:5).[26] One cannot ignore the weight these passages can bring to bear on a devout Muslim wanting to obey God's will. So, as elements of the Qur'an challenge Obama's vacuous slogan that Islam is a religion of peace, we find ourselves confronted with a

---

[23] Pew Research Centre. 'Islamic Extremism: Common Concern for Muslim and Western Publics' in *The Pew Global Attitudes Project*.
http://pewglobal.org/reports/display.php?ReportID=248 (August 14, 2005).

[24] Obama, 'A New Beginning'.

[25] Armour, *Islam Christianity and the West*, 181.

[26] Obama, 'A New Beginning'.

book that, in part, contains the great potential within it to justify violence against the majority non-Muslim West.

Cultural Faultlines

Negative Stereotypes

Another factor that divides Muslims from Westerners is culture. Traditionally this has been geographic: distance has maintained pronounced cultural divisions. However, the historically recent emergence of new forms of electronic media (television; internet; MP3 technology) has given Muslim populations unprecedented access to Western culture and entertainment. Yet although it has bridged many divides, 'westernizing' many of its users, particularly youth, it has also created the opposite outcome: producing the negative perception among Muslims of the West being decadent and debased. Just as Westerners are saturated by the typical media images of active Islamic militants, launching rockets and firing AK-47's at US troops, so Arabs are bombarded with the television accounts of American bombs, and assault teams wielding M16s storming insurgent hotspots. Everything they see on screen – sexual promiscuity, religious indifference, the wanton violence of US troops – all of it is unconsciously assumed as representative of all members of the West.

In part this is a true picture. As a general trend, Western civilisations are increasingly becoming post-Christian and more permissive. But this is not the full picture: the Islamic media often exaggerates this decay. Such stereotyping ignores this, often leads to conspiracy theorising, as all problems - political, social and moral - are linked with the West.[27] This is often called *Westophobia*, which "refers to entrenched and endemically hostile attitudes to the West, and to perceived cultural traits of the West".[28] It is these widespread feelings of antipathy that hold the potential for exploitation by Islamists.

---

[27] Riddell & Cotterell, *Islam in Context*, 160-161.

[28] Riddell & Cotterell, *Islam in Context*, 160. Parallels *Islamophobia:* the fear or hatred of Muslims.

> By portraying the West as atheistic and morally decadent, Islamic radicals can effectively recruit followers by appealing to a shared Muslim antipathy for permissive values.[29]

As this happens, Islam and the West find themselves being forced into opposition.

It also leads to a culture of fear, as Islamists begin to find success advancing the argument that the blind imitation of the West threatens the loss of Islamic culture and identity, the so called effect of *westoxification*. Film, Television, Books and theme parks: all of it is seen as the march of the West through the world. As Hossein Nasr bemoans: "Tapes of the Qur'an are not about to invade the airwaves of Europe and the United states as the crudest products of Western pop culture are invading the East, while Western secularism is seeking in a virulently aggressive manner to impose not only its half-dying worldview, through that technology, upon the non-Western world, especially the Islamic".[30]

However, such sentiments, although influential and widespread, are no match against the cultural force of the West. Western culture is becoming very common throughout the Islamic world, subversively changing values from within and forming bonds of commonality that transcend mere geography. In fact, it could be argued that a youth in America may have more in common with their Pakistani counterparts than even their own parents.[31] Such a force irrevocably brings Western values and ideals into the Islamic world, mixing them together, culturally distant as they are.

Social Faultlines

Legal Flashpoints: The Thorny Issue of Shari'a and Personal Liberty

---

[29] Dinesh D'Souza, 'The Clash of Stereotypes: a Recent Survey Reveals What Muslims Detest Most about the West', *Christianity Today* 53/7 (2009), 54.
[30] Hossein Nasr, quoted in, Colin Chapman, *Islam and the West: Conflict, Co-Existence or Conversion?* (Carlisle: Paternoster Press, 1998), 15.
[31] For an interesting study of this, *see:* Benjamin Barber, *Jihad vs. McWorld* (New York: Ballantine Books, 2001).

Behind the fear of Islamism lies an enormous fear: that Islam will take away the freedoms and liberty Westerners enjoy. Islam means 'submission' and Islam, being a holistic system, seeks to influence all spheres of life. At minimal it restricts sexual freedoms (Q. 24:2; 27:54-55), forbids gambling (Q. 5:90), it even restricts diet: forbidding the consumption of pork (Q. 5:3) and alcohol (Q. 2:219). And in many Islamic countries these are matters of civil law (*shari'a*). Of course *shari'a* varies in its pervasiveness, from the partial application of Bangladesh and England, to the extreme applications of the Taliban of Afghanistan, where television, movies and music were banned, women were refused schooling, even forbidden to leave the house, all instituted brutally, with public executions and amputation of limbs. Thus Islamic law is perceived as cutting at the heart of personal liberty.

Even more worrying is the perception that Islamic law undermines the equality of all human beings. Despite Obama's assertion that "Islam has a proud tradition of tolerance", religious minorities are routinely treated like second class citizens: denied rights and freedoms afforded to their Muslim counterparts.[32] For example, Christians in Saudi Arabia and North Yemen are heavily discriminated against, forbidden to construct churches; even in Egypt, until 2005, church repairs required a presidential decree.[33] In most Islamic nations the evangelism of Muslims is banned and in some nations *dhimmis* (non-Muslims subjects of an Islamic state) are uniquely required to pay a *jizya* tax, in accordance with the Qur'an (Q. 9:28). Worst of all is the penalty for apostasy (*ridda*); the punishment stipulated for converting to another religion is death (Al-Bukhari 4:260; 9:271). Secularism may be criticised, but it offers unparalleled freedoms: equal status under the law, the freedom to follow *any* religion - even offering special benefits, such as exception from taxation. These are freedoms unavailable to many minorities in many Muslim lands, sitting in uncomfortable contrast with the West.

---

[32] Obama, 'A New Beginning'.

[33] Ethan Cole, 'Egypt Police Use Violence to Block Church Repair' in *The Christian Post*. http://www.christianpost.com/article/20080825/egypt-police-use-violence-to-block-church-repair/index.html (25 August, 2008).

Clash of civilisations or co-existence of cultures?

In summary, as the previous section has shown, although there are overlaps between Western and Islamic worldviews, the differences are marked: they are significantly different paradigms. However, the question remains, can Islam and the West peacefully co-exist? The hope of most is that they can; however before the realization of that hope lies several bridges and barriers to progress.

Academic Barriers

The first factor compounding the current conflict between Islam and the West is the almost totalitarian restriction of academic freedom by Islamic institutions. Partially it is a politico-cultural problem: Islam does not separate academic work from politics – the academy is not autonomous. This puts pressure on scholars to conform to expected norms as "freedom of expression and of access to information are frequently limited *since conformity with the dominant ideology is the central value*".[34]

Consequently, in such a culture "facts and data are selected and repressed according to whether or not they fit to the ideological framework".[35] This can be a great barrier to progress, discouraging dialogue and enquiry. Scholars who criticize Islam, or deviate from the orthodox position, can quickly find themselves subject to censoring, even facing threats and assassination. Even Bassam Tibi, a committed Muslim scholar admits that "my life has been repeatedly threatened, because of my commitment to the ideas of civil society, secular democracy and human rights against political Islam".[36] As Cox and Marks summarise,

> Those who oppose it [the Ideological mode] are not reasoned with but attacked unceasingly with annihilating language and even threats to their lives. The aim and often the result is an intellectual

---

[34] Cox & Marks, *The West, Islam and Islamism*, 15.

[35] Cox & Marks, *The West, Islam and Islamism*, 8.

[36] Bassam Tibi, *Political Islam, World Politics and Europe* (Routledge: London, 2000), 34.

conformity which destroys the inherent curiosity and open debate of the Academic mode.[37]

Scholars, both Islamic and Western, *must* be given the access to freely investigate and publish. Islamic communities cannot continue to boast of their vast scientific achievements, and yet persist to refuse Western scholars access to the early Qur'anic documents necessary to practice higher-criticism.[38] If Muslims are serious about pursuing truth, they must take the risk that they could be shown to be wrong, and be prepared to challenge their own traditions and assumptions.

The Characterization of Islam by Political Leaders

The second major threat posed to peaceful co-existence is the facile characterisation of Islam by political leaders, who ignore the differences between the two worldviews, treating them as the same. President Obama, for example, on the basis of personal experience, considers it "part of my responsibility as President of the United States to fight against negative stereotypes of Islam". He defines Islam around the stream that best embodies his modernizing values, before disconnecting radical Islamism from the 'true Islam' as he perceives it, like many politicians, labelling the Islamists as a minority on the fringes, their teaching as a distortion of Islam and their struggle as little more than self-interest. The modernizing political scientist Bassam Tibi provides a brilliant example of this thought-process,

> For me as a Muslim, Islam itself, being a tolerant religion, is not and cannot be a threat, and it is a disservice to world peace to speak of Islam, one of the world's major religions, in terms of "threat" and "confrontation." My religion is an open-minded faith, neither an intolerant political ideology nor a concept of world order, as Islamic fundamentalists- and some in the West- so fiercely contend.[39]

Although this is a claim based on personal experience, both Tibi and Obama betray their hidden presuppositions. Any Islam that

---

[37] Cox & Marks, *The West, Islam and Islamism*, 8.

[38] Cox & Marks, *The West, Islam and Islamism*, 10.

[39] Bassam Tibi, *The Challenge of Fundamentalism* (Berkeley: University of California Press, 2002), xxv.

accords with their preconceived (Western) values are painted as 'the true Islam', and any version of Islam that does not accord is portrayed as 'the deviant minority'. It is a shallow characterization, and one that ironically flies in the face of Obama's assertion that "Muslims do not fit a crude stereotype".[40] Surely if we are going to be truly honest and open, as Obama implores us to be, we need to acknowledge the fundamental differences between us, a notion that Obama seems to thoroughly oppose. Instead he simply chooses to recast Islam in his own image. At the end of the day, this is simply wishful thinking, and stifles real, useful dialogue, as the perceived deviant Islamic groups are disowned and marginalised, halting any hope of resolving tensions through dialogue. It is also highly arrogant and offensive, as *Obama* defines Islam, rather than giving Muslims the opportunity to define themselves. Currently all three types (modernists, traditionalists and radicals) come validly under the umbrella of 'Islam'. Some may have a greater affinity with Western values but Westerners need to stop romanticizing Islam and recognize the 'dark side' of Islamic history, and the brands of Islam that emerged: elements that do not necessarily align themselves with the West.

An Inconsistent Hermeneutic

Thirdly, a persistent barrier to peace is the fact there is no consistent hermeneutical approach to reading the Qur'an. Liberal readings that read the Koran in the light of Islam as a religion of peace *do not prevent* the radicals from using the same verses to justify violence.[41] As Patrick Sookhdeo observes, the Qur'an, on the whole, seems to be used "like a pick-and-mix selection", used to justify whatever the reader's presuppositions. There are laws such as the law of abrogation (Q. 2:106, 16:101), but even still, the Qur'an is dangerously plagued by ambivalence and ambiguity – which simply feed the confusion: puzzling non-Muslims and giving Islamists legitimate Qur'anic justifications for perpetrating violence. Thus, as Riddell and Cotterell rightly remark, "The way forward for Islam

---

[40] Obama, 'A New Beginning'.
[41] Riddell, *Christians and Muslims*, 200-201.

seems to lie in accepting for the Qur'an and the Hadith a hermeneutic, a system of interpretation, that will allow their *meaning*, intended by Mohammad for specific situations in the seventh century and not for unimaginable situations thirteen hundred years later, to be interpreted for the modern world by identifying the present *significance*".[42] To do so may take the edge off Islam-Western conflict, as people would know where they stand and militaristic interpretations of the Qur'an could be invalidated. Furthermore, there is hope for this. Although the door of *ijtihad* has, on the whole, remained officially closed, Reuven Firestone optimistically reminds us that "independent reasoning in Qur'an interpretation has continued at one level or another to this day and is currently very active".[43] Discussions in the West, Firestone asserts, *are* having an impact on the Islamic world, and there is a growing appreciation within the global Muslim community that there is a need to review traditional methods of interpretation.[44]

Conclusion

Islam and the West are historically and currently two different paradigms, connected although separate. These two institutions are undergirded by two radically different worldviews. Colliding, their differences, cultural and religious, result in the socio-political conflict evident today. However peaceful co-existence is possible. If Muslims can bring themselves to begin to appreciate the good in other cultures, and normalize an approach to Qur'anic interpretation that precludes the Islamists, then the faultlines between the two civilizations will begin to diminish. Likewise, if Western leaders stop characterizing Islam, and engage with it as it really is, both civilizations can begin to engage in honest discussion about the problems between them. Though Islam and the West are

---

[42] Riddell & Cotterell, *Islam in Context*, 214.
Also see: Andrew Rippin, *Muslims: Their Religious Beliefs and Practices* (London: Routledge, 2006), 305.

[43] Reuven Firestone, 'Jihād' in *The Blackwell Companion to the Qur'ān* (ed. A Rippin; Oxford: Blackwell, 2006), 318.

[44] Firestone, 'Jihād', 318.

currently in conflict, the potential and hope *is* there for peace and positive change.

Bibliography

Abunimah, Ali. 'A bush in sheep's clothing' in *The Guardian*. http://www.guardian.co.uk/commentisfree/2009/jun/04/barack-obama-iddleeast (June 4, 2009).

Armour, Rollin. *Islam Christianity* and *the West* (Maryknoll: Orbis Books, 2002).

Barber, Benjamin. *Jihad vs. McWorld* (New York: Ballantine Books, 2001).

Chapman, Colin. *Islam and the West: Conflict, Co-Existence or Conversion?* (Carlisle: Paternoster Press, 1998).

Cole, Ethan. 'Egypt Police Use Violence to Block Church Repair' in *The Christian Post*. http://www.christianpost.com/article/20080825/egypt-police-use-violence-to-block-church-repair/index.html (25 August, 2008).

Cox, C. & Marks, J. *The West, Islam and Islamism: A Comparison Between the Philosophy, Epistemology and Political Principles of 'Western' and 'Islamic' Societies* (CIS Occasional Paper No. 4; London: London School of Theology, 2003).

D'Souza, Dinesh. 'The Clash of Stereotypes: a Recent Survey Reveals What Muslims Detest Most about the West', Christianity Today 53/7 (2009), 54.

Esposito, John. *The Islamic Threat: Myth or Reality?* (3rd ed., Oxford: Oxford University Press, 1999).

Firestone, Reuven. 'Jihād' in *The Blackwell Companion to the Qur'ān* (ed. A Rippin; Oxford: Blackwell, 2006), 308-320.

Hornick, Ed. 'US Set to Pay Taliban Members to Switch Sides' in *CNN Politics*. http://www.cnn.com/2009/POLITICS/10/28/afghanistan.taliban.pay/index.html (October 29, 2009).

Huntingdon, Samuel. 'The Clash of Civilizations?', *Foreign Affairs* 72/3 (1993), 22-49.

Huntingdon, Samuel. *The Clash of Civilizations and the Remaking of World Order* (New York: Simon & Schuster, 1996).

Lewis, Bernard. 'Roots of Muslim Rage', *Policy* 17/4 (2001-2), 17-26.

Obama, Barack. 'Text: A New Beginning' in *The New York Times*. http://www.nytimes.com/2009/06/04/us/politics/04obama.text.html?_r=1 (June 4, 2009).

Pew Research Centre. 'Islamic Extremism: Common Concern for Muslim and Western Publics' in *The Pew Global Attitudes Project*. http://pewglobal.org/reports/display.php?ReportID=248 (August 14, 2005).

Said, Edward. 'The Clash of Ignorance' in *The Nation*. http://www.thenation.com/doc/20011022/said (October 4, 2001).

Ramadan, Tariq. *Western Muslims and the Future of Islam* (Oxford: Oxford University Press, 2004).

Riddell, Peter. *Christians and Muslims: Pressures and Potential in a Post-9/11 World* (Leicester: IVP, 2004).

Riddell, P & Cotterell P. *Islam in Context* (2nd ed.; Grand Rapids: Baker Books, 2003).

Rippin, Andrew. *Muslims: Their Religious Beliefs and Practices* (London: Routledge, 2006).

Said, Edward. 'The Clash of Ignorance', *The Nation*, October 22, 2001.

Shepard, William. 'Islamism: Concepts and Debates' in *Oxford Encyclopedia of the Islamic World* (ed. J. Esposito; Oxford: Oxford University Press, 2009, vol 3), 191-192.

Tibi, Bassam. *Political Islam, World Politics and Europe* (Routledge: London, 2000).

Tibi, Bassam. *The Challenge of Fundamentalism* (Berkeley: University of California Press, 2002).

Islamic Finance: A Poisoned Chalice?[1]

Prof Peter G Riddell
Melbourne School of Theology

Islamic financial operations have witnessed a huge and rapid expansion around the world, including the West, in recent years. Described by one commentator as "a cottage industry restricted to a handful of Arab countries only 30 years ago",[2] the Islamic finance industry currently holds assets worth around $1000 billion, registering growth of some 30% in 2009 and 2010, and witnessing the launch of 20 new Islamic banks across the world in 2009.[3]

There are several key factors supporting this growth. First, the huge windfall of revenue due to increase in oil prices from the 1970s onwards provided ample funds for developing this sector. The combined revenue from oil sales of the six member nations of the Arab Gulf Cooperation Council increased tenfold during the first decade of the twenty-first century.[4] The second factor stimulating this boom was the 2008 international financial crisis which threatened a meltdown of the world economy. In this climate, the availability of ready cash in large amounts from Islamic sources has proven to be a lure that many in the West cannot resist.

---

[1] This article first appeared in the *CSIOF Bulletin*, no. 4, 2011.

[2] Kevin Brown, "Wider appeal battles with signs of inefficiency", *The Future of Islamic Finance (Financial Times* Special Report), December 8, 2009, http://media.ft.com/cms/ac6257de-e2de-11de-b028-00144feab49a.pdf

[3] David Oakley, "Dubai debacle overshadows growth", *The Future of Islamic Finance (Financial Times* Special Report), December 8, 2009, http://media.ft.com/cms/ac6257de-e2de-11de-b028-00144feab49a.pdf

[4] http://www.ansamed.info/en/news/ME02.YAM19005.html (accessed: 7.10.08)

Furthermore, some Muslims have seen this as providing a historic opportunity to expand the Islamic faith. In the words of prominent Islamist scholar Yusuf al-Qaradawi:

> The Western system has collapsed and we [Muslims] have a complete economic philosophy as well as spiritual strength... All riches are ours... the Islamic nation has all or nearly all the oil and we have an economic philosophy that no one else has... [Muslims should] profit from the crisis to bring about the triumph of the (Islamic) nation, which holds the spiritual and material resources for victory.[5]

Principles and Methods

The over-riding consideration driving Islamic finance is that financial operations should be consistent with the dictates of Islamic Sharia Law. This legal framework is considered by most Muslim scholars to be from Allah, and therefore not subject to human critique or reproach. Sharia Law encompasses financial matters but goes far beyond them, also covering matters of the family, civil law, codes of punishment which can be quite draconian, and a host of other areas which address the minutiae of people's lives.

Reconciling the dictates of Sharia Law with the detail of international and domestic finances is no easy matter. There are several principles that underpin Islamic finance. First, interest (*riba*) on loans is banned; this inevitably means that Islamic economic operations tend to establish a kind of financial apartheid, given how fundamental the concept of loan interest is to western economics. Second, speculation (*gharar*) is also banned, and transactions must be based on an underlying existing asset or service; "if you are going to trade in an asset you have to own it first".[6]

Third, Islamic finance presents itself as placing special emphasis on seemingly ethical investments. Islamic financial institutions, be they banks, insurance agencies or other Shariah-compliant bodies, avoid all links with institutions dealing in weapons, gambling, pornography, pork or alcohol. Nevertheless, such an approach is equally possible with non-

---

[5] "Replace capitalism with Islamic financial system: cleric", *Qatar Morning Post*, 12 October 2008, http://www.qatarmorningpost.com/news/newsfull.php?newid=281538

[6] Saleh Ibrahim, "Islamic regulations can help economies in crisis", *Al Huda* No 34 (May-July 2009), http://www.alhudacibe.com/AlhudaMagazine/Issue-034/article04.php

Islamic financial operations and, indeed, there are many Christian financial institutions that prioritize ethical considerations in their operations.

Fourth, Islamic finance commonly operates on a risk-sharing model, whereby a financier will contribute cash and a borrower will contribute expertise in what is portrayed as a partner venture. But David Clark points out the flaw in this seemingly appealing concept: "Upon borrower default the financier will have the right to demand its interest in the *Musharaka* [joint venture] (or the assets forming the interest in the *Musharaka*) be purchased by the borrower at the price of the outstanding debt..."[7]

Finally, Islamic finance disapproves of companies that depend too heavily on borrowing, with a threshold seen as 33% of a firm's stockmarket value.[8] Again, this is normal practice for many member organisations of the vast non-Islamic financial sector as well.

In order to ensure that Sharia-based financial organisations are compliant with the above principles, Islamic scholars are engaged by companies to monitor and advise on appropriate policies and procedures. This highly specialised field is being driven by a finite number of scholars who wield enormous power and influence. One particular survey of this scholarly community concluded that "[t]he top six scholars hold 31.7 percent of all surveyed board positions in research by Funds@Work."[9]

Islamic Finance on the March

Although there are presently no global Islamic banks to rival HSBC, Lloyds TSB and such mammoth institutions, this situation is likely to change in the not-too-distant future. Dubai Bank, set up in 2002 before converting to an Islamic bank five years later, set its sights on becoming

---

[7] David Clark, "The Islamic Finance myth", http://www.shariahfinancewatch.org/blog/2010/04/23/the-shariah-compliant-finance-myth/

[8] http://www.ansamed.info/en/news/ME02.YAM19005.html (accessed: 7.10.08)

[9] "Factbox: How to take a bank Islamic", *Reuters*, April 25, 2010

a major global Islamic lender through acquisitions,[10] though the Dubai economic crisis of 2009 has slowed down such plans.

The rapid emergence of Sharia-banking windows in western financial institutions is noteworthy. The giant HSBC now offers Sharia-compliant services through its Amanah unit.[11] At the end of August 2008 the Swedish Avanza Bank offered its customers a new Islamic investment option, *Selector World Shariah Value*, a global fund of some 110 companies.[12] In Britain, high street banks are also responding, offering a small range of Sharia-compliant products, including bank accounts,[13] and drawing in Muslim scholars to advise on developing new services. These trends are encouraged by governments; for example, in March 2008 the British Chancellor of the Exchequer announced measures to promote Islamic finance,[14] reflecting the fact that at that time Britain was already the 10th largest holder of Sharia-compliant assets, leading other Western nations.

Furthermore, Britain's first Islamic bank, the Birmingham-headquartered Islamic Bank of Britain, reported significant growth in non-Muslim customers since the onset of turbulence on financial markets in 2008, with Islamic banks claiming to be insulated from the credit crisis,[15] though events in subsequent years cast significant doubts on this claim.

Problems with Islamic Finance

The appeal of Islamic financial institutions and their ways to influence both Western governments and individuals may well be a poisoned chalice. There are three main areas of difficulty that Western policy makers need consider.

---

[10] http://www.forbes.com/afxnewslimited/feeds/afx/2008/08/31/afx5374418.html

[11] http://www.forbes.com/afxnewslimited/feeds/afx/2008/08/31/afx5374418.html

[12] http://www.shariahfinancewatch.org/blog/2008/08/28/swedens-first-sharia-fund-is-being-launched-today/

[13] For example, see http://www.lloydstsb.com/current_accounts/islamic_account.asp (accessed: 04.10.08)

[14] HM Treasury, *Budget Report 2008*, London: The Stationary Office, 2008, 46. Available at http://www.hm-treasury.gov.uk/media/9/9/bud08_completereport.pdf (accessed: 04.10.08)

[15] http://www.birminghampost.net/birmingham-business/birmingham-business-news/other-uk-business/2008/10/03/non-muslims-turn-to-islamic-bank-as-a-safe-option-65233-21962049/

First is the level of debate within the Muslim community worldwide. Sharia finance encounters vigorous opposition from some Muslims due to debate about details of interpretation. In some cases, Islamic scholars understand the term *riba* to mean usury rather than simple interest on a loan. These scholars are more at ease with the concept of interest as understood in the Western capitalist context. On the other hand, those scholars who reject all interest tend to be from the more militant, Islamist end of the Islamic spectrum, the very kinds of Muslims that Western governments should not be encouraging.[16]

Further on the question of debate among Muslim scholars, even those who are closely involved with the sector can at times disagree about the forms that Sharia financing should take. An example of this was the ruling by the International Islamic Fiqh Academy in April 2009 that criticised the widely used *Tawarruq* instrument, suggesting that it too closely resembled conventional loans.[17] This debate highlighted the fact that the instruments of Islamic finance can sometimes be simply replicating non-Islamic financial policies and procedures but dressing them up in an Islamic guise.

The second main area of difficulty in Islamic financing is the myth that this sector is insulated from world economic downturns. In fact, since the world financial crisis took hold in late 2008, there have been some very significant crises within the Islamic finance sector as well. Chief among these was the Dubai debt collapse in 2009 associated with a $3.5 billion bond deal involving Nakheel, the United Arab Emirates' property developer. Uncertainty over payments to bond-holders of the world's biggest *sukuk*, or Islamic bond, caused the march of Islamic finance to falter for a time. The *Financial Times* reports that the Islamic finance industry "has been hit by the economic downturn, which caused several high-profile Islamic investment banks to default and restructure their operations and debt."[18]

---

[16] Patrick Sookhdeo, *Understanding Islamic Finance*, MacLean VA: Isaac Publishing, 2008, 17ff.

[17] Robin Wigglesworth, "Tawarruq loans split scholars", *The Future of Islamic Finance (Financial Times* Special Report), December 8, 2009, http://media.ft.com/cms/ac6257de-e2de-11de-b028-00144feab49a.pdf

[18] Robin Wigglesworth, "Islamic banks caught between two worlds", *The Financial Times*, 30 April 2010

The third area of difficulty is perhaps the most concerning. Sharia finance is potentially a vehicle for the spread of Sharia Law in its many other manifestations. In the words of Allyson Rowan Taylor of ShariahFinanceWatch.org,

> The dictates about Shariah Law are not just the simple things about the ethical investments interest-free. It also is the same Shariah Law that we saw during 9/11. It's the same Shariah Law that allows beheadings ... that goes against all the rights that we adhere to and love in the West.[19]

Even more compellingly, Frank Gaffney, President of the Center for Security Policy, issues a shrill warning:

> we should be especially wary of the purported silver-lining to the current Wall Street crisis: the infusion of vast quantities of petro-dollars, primarily from OPEC's Saudi Arabia and other Islamist nations in the Persian Gulf. It is bad enough that these putative rescuers of our subprime-fueled liquidity debacle are buying up engines of our capital markets for pennies on the dollar. Worse yet, they are, in the process, putting themselves in a position to promote Shariah-Compliant Finance and the seditious theo-political agenda it serves.[20]

Lest one think that such concerns are merely the statements of Islamophobes, it is worth taking note of Muslim voices opposed to Sharia, such as the group of activists who gather under the name of Muslims Against Sharia. Their website does not mince its words: "Sharia Law must be abolished, because it is incompatible with norms of modern society."[21]

These statements state overtly what is rarely mentioned by those promoting Islamic finance; namely, that this sector is merely the tip of the Sharia Law iceberg.

Further Reading

---

[19] Interview with Allyson Rowan Taylor on FoxBusiness.com, August 26, 2008, http://www.foxbusiness.com/video/index.html?playerId=videolandingpage&streamingFormat=FLASH&referralObject=3051056&referralPlaylistId=1292d14d0e3afdcf0b31500afefb92724c08f046&maven_referrer=staf

[20] "Into the Fire", September 15, 2008, http://www.centerforsecuritypolicy.org/Modules/NewsManager/ShowSectionNews.aspx?CategoryID=140&SubCategoryID=141&NewsID=17572

[21] http://www.reformislam.org/ (accessed: 7.10.08)

Ali, Jawad I. and Salah, Omar. "Pyrrhic Victory for Islamic Finance: The Further Growth of the Islamic Finance Industry", *White Paper: Taking Stock And Moving Forward: The State Of Islamic Finance And Prospects For The Future*, Dubai: Dubai International Financial Centre, 2010

Brown, Kevin. "Wider appeal battles with signs of inefficiency", *The Future of Islamic Finance (Financial Times* Special Report), December 8, 2009

Clark, David. "The Islamic Finance myth", http://www.shariahfinancewatch.org/blog/2010/04/23/the-shariah-compliant-finance-myth/

"Factbox: How to take a bank Islamic", *Reuters*, April 25, 2010

Ghoul, W.A. "The Dilemma facing Islamic Finance and Lessons Learnt form the Global Financial Crisis", *Journal of Islamic Economics, Banking and Finance*, vol. 7 no. 1 (Jan-Mar 2011), 57-76

HM Treasury, *Budget Report 2008*, London: The Stationary Office, 2008

Ibrahim, Saleh. "Islamic regulations can help economies in crisis", *Al Huda* No 34 (May-July 2009)

Interview with Allyson Rowan Taylor on FoxBusiness.com, August 26, 2008

"Into the Fire", September 15, 2008, http://www.centerforsecuritypolicy.org/Modules/NewsManager/ShowSectionNews.aspx?CategoryID=140&SubCategoryID=141&NewsID=17572

Khan, Bilal & Crowne-Mohammed, Emir Aly, "The value of Islamic banking in the current financial crisis", *Review of Banking & Financial Law* vol. 29 (2009-2010), 441-64

Krasicka, Olga and Nowak, Sylwia. "What's in It for Me? A Primer on Differences between Islamic and Conventional Finance in Malaysia", *IMF Working Paper* WP/12/151, 2012

Oakley, David. "Dubai debacle overshadows growth", *The Future of Islamic Finance (Financial Times* Special Report), December 8, 2009

"Replace capitalism with Islamic financial system: cleric", *Qatar Morning Post*, 12 October 2008

Sherry, Nick, MP. "The Future of Islamic Finance in Australia", Keynote Address, 2010 Islamic Finance Conference, Rendezvous Hotel, Melbourne, 8 June 2010

Sookhdeo, Patrick. *Understanding Islamic Finance*, MacLean VA: Isaac Publishing, 2008

The Future of Islamic Finance (Financial Times Special Report), December 14, 2010

Wigglesworth, Robin. "Islamic banks caught between two worlds", *The Financial Times*, 30 April 2010

Wigglesworth, Robin. "Tawarruq loans split scholars", *The Future of Islamic Finance (Financial Times* Special Report), December 8, 2009

Muslim Women in Prayer[1]

Dr Moyra Dale
Melbourne School of Theology

صلاة - Salat : Formal Prayer

In the upstairs hall of the mosque comes the sound of a youthful male voice with the call to prayer. Women in the hall rise and walk through to the balcony, form quickly into ranks and wait silently. Numbers of women appear now from inside rooms - the last few pass through the hall almost at a run. There's no curtain between the balcony and below - just the railing.

الله أكبر (God is great) - and they bend at the waist.

Rise, kneel and bow their head to the ground, rise.

Bend, stand, kneel and bow, sit up, bow, sit up.

Stand, bend, stand, kneel and bow, sit up, bow, sit up.

The voice croons the سلام عليكم ورحمة الله (Peace and the mercy of God be with you) and the kneeling women look to their left and right shoulders.

Salat is the basis of Muslim worship. Ordained by Muhammad, Prophet of Islam, even most westerners are now familiar with the picture of Muslims standing, bowing, prostrating, either together in rhythmic lines, or the solitary worshipper making office or sidewalk into a place of prayer. The times of *salat* divide the daylight hours, stretching and contracting with the seasons, marking the passage of daylight with the muezzin call in Muslim countries. Creation rather than clock defines times of *salat;* defined by the position of

---

[1] This paper was first given in an extended form at the 5th Lausanne Researchers Conference, Geelong, April 2008.

the sun, *salat* times move with diurnal rhythm through the more settled hours of the clock face. M. Eman, founder-teacher of a women's programme in a Middle Eastern mosque, explained them to me:[2]

Dawn prayer (الفجر) - starts when the sun begins to rise, about an hour and a half before the sun is risen, when the time of dawn prayer finishes.

Midday prayer (الظهر) – takes place at midday.

Mid-afternoon prayer (العصر) – is about 2 ½ hours after midday prayers, when a shadow is about twice the length of the object, and it lasts until sunset.

Sunset prayer (المغرب) – extends from the going down of the sun, and lasts as long as there is still a red glow or red line in the sky

Evening prayer (العشاء) – is when the sun has completely gone.

However poetic descriptions of nature have now turned into "electronic devices and special clocks ... which can tell the prayer times of many of the major cities in the world" (Mujahid, 2000:6).

Women performing salat (صلاة)

I knocked on my Muslim neighbour's door one day and she opened it, dressed as she so often was in the all-covering prayer skirt and top – they were always convenient to hand so that we could be properly covered if any man was at the door. As we sat and drank sweet Arabic coffee together, and talked over the affairs of the building and the day, her two-year old son pulled out her prayer mat and tried to don the skirt and top himself, in a play imitation of what he saw his mother do so often.

One of the five pillars of Islam, *salat* is incumbent on every believer – but gender influences its performance. In *The Muslim Woman's HandBook*, Khattab notes:

> In Islam, religious duties are to be performed by men and women alike. All Muslims, whether male or female, are required to pray five times daily, to fast in Ramadan, ... Having said that, however, there are some differences in the ways in which men and

---

[2] Words taken directly (and translated) from notes on lectures or from an interview with Madam Eman.

women are to go about performing these acts of worship, which sisters need to be aware of. (Khattab, 1994:1)

Places of Prayer

The activity of *salat* can consecrate almost any place for worship, but worship offered in the mosque gains more merit. Saqib assures us, "wherever a Muslim might be he can offer his *(sic) salat* (prayer) but the reward of a *salat* (prayer) offered in a mosque is far greater than that offered in an ordinary place", (1997:17): Emerick quotes it as twenty-five times better (1997:122). Cragg comments:

> ...everyone's prayer mat is a portable mosque and wherever they choose to spread it they can find their *Qiblah*[3] and worship God. ... Nevertheless the noon prayer on Fridays is to be said as far as possible in the place of corporate prayer. When so said its four *raka'at*[4] are reduced to two." (Cragg, 1985:99)

But here Cragg writes of men. Women cannot turn public places into prayer sites as men can. I have met women in sheltered places, even in old and ruined mosques, putting their handbag in front as a *sutra* (barrier) and prostrating on the bare and dusty stone floor; but they do not pray in public spaces with the same freedom as men. Cultural and religious requirements of modesty constrain their freedom to turn outside space into spaces of worship – their place of worship is the home.

Similarly, although in countries like Egypt and Syria more women are going to the mosque now for teaching, memorising the Qur'an and joining in *salat* and *dhikr* prayers, and have their own space in the upper rooms: when the time for Friday prayers comes and men arrive in their numbers, the women do not attend. The mosque space belongs *a priori* to men, no matter how much the women use it.

---

[3] Towards the direction of Mecca.

[4] Each round of standing, bowing, prostrating and standing again in *salat*.

Purity

While required of all Muslims, the performance of *salat* is constrained by rules of purity and covering. *Salat* prayer is preceded by ablutions.

> The intention of the heart: Say: "I intend purity from this pure water." Then say, *"In the Name of God the Compassionate the Merciful."*
>
> Wash your two palms up to the wrists three times.
>
> Rinse out your mouth three times with your right hand.
>
> Inhale water three times then clear your nose with your left hand.
>
> Wash your face completely three times, from your hair roots to the bottom of your chin and from ear to ear.
>
> Wash your hands to the elbows three times.
>
> Wipe your head with your hand.
>
> And with any water remaining in your hand from your head wipe, wipe your ears. Take care to clean the ridges of your ears inside and out with your fingers.
>
> Wash your feet and soles three times.
>
> And after washing, say: *I testify that there is no god but God and I testify that Mohammad is the Messenger of God.*

(Translated from a Ramadan poster prayer guide for children in the Middle East)

The simple rules of washing described above have been codified into booklets of complicated rules describing degrees of permitted purity of water, according to who has touched it, if it is running or still, until M. Eman commented tartly:

> A convert (to Islam) after four months wanted to return *(and leave Islam because people taught them a lot about purification forgetting about the things which are more important[5])*, because for months they'd been learning how to purify, how to pray. Does anyone have a shower without washing everything, without being purified. It takes one lesson!

When the body becomes impure, through fluids, solids or gas emerging from the body's boundaries, the worshipper needs to do

---

[5] Clarifying note in italics was added by Ebtisam, a disciple of M. Eman, when she checked the notes I took from the latter's lectures.

ablutions again to be able to pray *salat* (or fast, or hold and read the Qur'an). So women during their monthly period are not able to pray, until the flow has ceased and they can wash or purify themselves again. Thus in a system which relies on accruing points of merit through performing *salat*, and where more merit is gained when praying in the mosque or with others, women are constantly behind on the point score[6].

Dhikr and Du'a' – Prayers of Recollection and Petition

Beyond the obligatory *salat*, the devout Muslim draws on a generous variety of pious practices[7]. These are centred around different forms of adoration and petition, recitation of the Qur'an, and the rich practices of devotion in Ramadan. In this paper I focus on the *dhikr* (recollection through meditation and recitation) and the *du'a'* (supplication or petition). Not part of the five pillars of Islam, these are not subject to the same restrictions. Reliant on the initiative of the worshipper and encouragement of the community, these forms of worship offer us a more extended appreciation of Muslim devotional theology – how the worshipper understands her access, through faith community and faith practice, to her Creator.

Recollection (*dhikr*) and supplication (*du'a'*) are distinct practices, but without distinct boundaries. In practice there is often movement back and forth, from *dhikr* on the names of God, to *du'a'* and back to *dhikr*. The three forms, including *salat*, are not independent of one another:

> M. Eman: It's not a condition if I do *dhikr*, to then supplicate (*du'a'*), nor if I supplicate to do *dhikr*, or if I pray (*salat*), to supplicate; but we need to complete the *dhikr* by supplication

---

[6] Some commentators suggest that this intrinsic impediment is part of the reason for the stinging *Hadith*, that women are lacking in brain and religion (النساء نقصات عقل ودين) (Sahih Bukhari, Arabic-English translation, Vol.1, Hadith No. 301. See also Vol.3, Hadith No. 826).

[7] The word English word 'prayer' covers many of these practices. However it is also often a source of confusion in conversation between Muslims and Christians. In Islam the word *salat* refers only to the prescribed liturgical form of set phrases and actions in prayer. This is how most Muslims understand the word 'prayer'. So I have chosen to similarly restrict its use for clarity here, and to draw on different synonyms in referring to other forms of Muslim devotion.

(*du'a'*).' When a person has asked God's forgiveness and has become clean within and pure before God, then the supplication, if God wills, will be answered more.

الذكر - *Dhikr : Recollection*

M. Eman: Any formula or expression in which a person glorifies his Lord or praises or thanks Him or asks forgiveness for his sins, you could say is *dhikr*, ... any expression in which we find reverence and calmness.

Women are sitting in silent concentration. It is quiet, just the sound of lips moving with the beads, and someone's periodic murmur. A few of the women are rocking, some passing the prayer beads through their fingers. There is a little movement as women adjust their position. One woman takes off her coat. The outside noises of cars, voices, come in from the road. Inside the women are quiet, still, concentrating. The girl beside me is crying. She swallows, continues to pass the prayer beads through her fingers. A low voice begins to recite something, and others join in quietly for a little while. Then there is silence again, with only the muted sound of voices whispering to themselves, lips moving. A woman in the front row begins to sing quietly, a song of worship. عرفتك يا رب بقلبي وفكري ("I knew you, O Lord, in my heart and my thoughts.") *She sings this a few times, and some other phrases. It is quiet, beautiful. Others sit quietly, some moving their lips, some rocking their bodies a little.*

Surah Al-Baqarah (2:152) has the promise: *Therefore remember me, I will remember you* (فاذكروني أذكركم). Padwick notes on this verse: "In all the devotional comments and prayers based on the promise, the meaning hovers between 'remembrance' and 'mention'" (1961:16). The *dhikr* prayers are drawn from the Qur'an, *Hadith* and other sources to centre the extended awareness of the worshipper on God. Recited or sung, accompanied by movement or quiet sitting, they draw the reciter to reflect on God's names and nature. So the popularly chosen chants may serve as an indication of how those praying them look to God, the aspects of God's nature that they focus on as most significant. They express the direction or longing of the pray-ers' hearts towards God. For many Muslims the *dhikr* occupies a major part in their religious life. M. Eman told me:

> The only thing that God has prescribed for us to do all the time is the *dhikr*.... 'Remember God with many remembrances' (أذكروا الله ذكرا كثيرا) (Surah Al-Ahzab, 33:41). ... *Salat* is five times and Pilgrimage once a year and Fasting once a year. But the *dhikr* is frequent and so the *dhikr* is very important in our lives.

The imperative to constant recollection is reminiscent of the Pauline enjoinder to "pray at all times."[8] While the worshipper is called to be constantly mindful of God, there are also set times recommended, both individually and corporately. M. Eman noted:

> It's required from people to do the *dhikr* at home on their own each day, every morning and evening. But the *dhikr* together, we do it on Thursday and Tuesday before the lesson and on Friday if we are together.

For the leaders in this mosque, *dhikr* was an important prelude to the lessons. M. Eman told the women: "The lesson without the *dhikr* is about a quarter of its usefulness. The *dhikr* is the spiritual preparation and gives us concentration, so we don't miss half the lecture" (P.53).

Outside the twice-weekly lecture programme, there were also set times for women to come for *dhikr* sessions in the mosque.

As a mystical practice outside the five pillars, *dhikr* has always had its critics within Islam. So M. Eman was careful to assure me, "There are many verses in the Noble Qur'an which emphasise the *dhikr*, perhaps hundreds of verses on *dhikr*."

Words of recollection

What is prayed in the *dhikr*? M. Eman is careful to ground the common expressions in the *Hadith* and example of Muhammad.

> M. Eman: For we are ordered to praise God, may He be praised, and to ask for God's forgiveness, and to say, 'There is no change or strength except in God and to say God be praised, and in His praise may (our) great God be extolled,' and these *adhkar* came from the sayings of the Prophet (pbuh),

---

[8] 1 Thess 5:17, Eph 6:18

and one saying of the Prophet (pbuh) said, 'Two light words on the tongue are weighty in the scales on the day of the Resurrection.'

Unlike the set *salat*, the individual has freedom of expression here. The act of recollection is important, rather than the specific words to achieve it.

> M. Eman: Perhaps all the *dhikr* could be, the Name of God, God only; if we say, O Patient One, O Generous One, O Forgiving One, O Merciful One, Praised be God, There is no god but God, God is greater, There is no changing or strength except in God - any formula is acceptable. What's important is that we remember God and his greatness and his creation and his characteristics.

Dhikr enacted

At the mosque I attended, the women sat quietly, eyes usually closed, often with prayer beads being passed through their right hand. There was a pattern of silence, quiet spoken invocations of the name of God, and chants. Depending on who led it, some, like M. Eman, gave more place to silence, others spent more time in chants. But this wasn't the only way.

> There are those who don't do the *dhikr* in this way; they do *dhikr* with their eyes open for example, or standing; we do it sitting. Really *dhikr* is required in every situation. God (to whom is Honour and Majesty) said of believers 'Who make mention of God standing and sitting and (reclining) on your sides' (فاذكروا الله قياما وقعودا وعلى جنوبكم) (Surat Al-Nisa', 4:103).

Prayer beads: misbaha - مسبحة

Prayer beads are a common part of *dhikr*, and draw further accusations of innovation (بدع) from its critics. M. Eman defends their use:

> Prayer beads are only to remind the person to do *dhikr*, because he could perhaps get distracted, and when he finds the *misbaha* in his hands he remembers. There are some Muslims who don't like the *misbaha* and say that it is forbidden and an innovation and wasn't around in the time of

the Prophet (pbuh). We don't praise with the *misbaha* because of it, but it just reminds us.

Women murmur the names of God as they pass the beads through their fingers, slowly or quickly. When I asked about the speed, M. Eman explained: "If we move quickly the whole body shakes in the recollection of God and this keeps one more alert." Ebtisam had a different explanation:

> Guiding the speed depends on what you say. If you say something short like *'God be praised'* (سبحان الله) you are quick, but if you say something long like *"There is no god but You, may you be praised. For I was one of the unjust, and you are the most Merciful of the merciful"*
> (لا إله إلا أنت سبحانك إني كنت من الظالمين وأنت أرحم الراحمين)
> you are slow.

دعاء – *Du'a' : Supplication*

The women have been involved in dhikr. *Now there is a slight shifting of position of women, leaning forward slightly, hands together, palms up. M. Eman leads in the* du'a'. *There are about five minutes of petition for Muslims throughout the world, for our sisters in Iraq, in Palestine. She asks God to heal us, our land, our society. Don't cut us off from your service. God, purify us from our sins and trespasses. The women join in with* 'Amin' *after each petition. M. Eman finishes by saying, "The* Fatiha",[9] *and the women murmur it quietly with her. At the end a number of them wipe their faces with their hands.*

The *du'a'* supplications[10] express the pray-er's desires for God's intervention in the happenings of the world, both individual and among the corporate Muslim *umma*. As *du'a'* is prayed in the community, it indicates something of the way these women see their place in the wider community, and how they hold onto the sovereignty of God and His purpose for his people alongside what is

---

[9] The first chapter of the Qur'an: its recitation seals or sanctifies occasions.

[10] While petition is for all, intercession is more restricted. "Intercession is not for all – it's among the most faithful people, who are outstanding." It can be done by people "who do lots of good works or who do a great work, they will intercede for us. ... As much as we do great works, we may be able to do more of the work of intercession." (M. Eman)

happening in the world.

In *du'a'* the hands are not busy with prayer beads, but most typically held together, palms up, in a supplicant position. Women may stand or sit, according to the position they have been in. *Du'a'* can take place anywhere, on any occasion, and everyone can do it. Women at the mosque, including M. Eman, would often ask me to petition for them, or say, "Supplicate for me, and I supplicate for you." However certain situations make the supplication more efficacious.

> Petition, when the person has done the ablutions and is sitting facing the direction of the *qibla*, of course is received more than from an inattentive person who is watching the television and says, 'O Lord, give me...'

One of my early visits to M. Eman was just after her husband and daughter had returned from making the lesser pilgrimage[11] to Mecca. She offered us water from the spring of Zamzam, served in small golden cups, and instructed us to say a petition when we drank it, because God would answer it. The Night of Vigil in Ramadan is also a time when petitions are believed to be answered. As I sat beside M. Eman at the mosque on that evening, she told me to petition for my family, petition for my children.

Content

ادعي لي (Petition for me!) is a common part of interaction among devout Muslim women, as it is among Christians, who say, "Pray for me (صليلي)", reflecting the wider use of the term *salat* among the Christian population. It can mean a general petition for well-being; or frequently among young women, for success in studies or family.

When I asked M. Eman if there were specific preferred intercessions, she told me:

> If you're in a tight situation, the best petition is, *O God, give us ease; O God, have mercy on us.* For example, when I'm longing for some specific knowledge, and I begin this learning I say, *O God, teach me, my Lord increase knowledge to me; O God, open to me the doors of learning.* And when I am upset about my manners and my

---

[11] The 'Umra (عمرة) – a pilgrimage to Mecca that doesn't take place at the time of the official Haj.

behaviour with those around me, *O God, make my manners better.* This is according to the situation of the person, as he likes specific petitions. For example, today I want a petition for forgiveness, and I always have to say it, but for example, if I am concerned about my livelihood I ask for income, and when I am at rest on my income, I ask for good health. For example (when) my daughter is studying, then my most frequent supplication is *O God, make her among the top and outstanding students, O God make best in her course.* Of course (it's) according to the situation and context.

Du'a' and Dhikr in the Mosque

Private petitions at home were more personal: in the mosque petitions were more of public concerns. 'Our sisters in Palestine and Iraq' were often mentioned in times of *du'a'*. Sometimes there was a clear connection to the content of the petitions. At other times more general invocations of praise or supplication were used, presumably said with intent for the women mentioned. Here again the boundaries between recollection and supplication were fairly fluid.

In the following example, general *dhikr* invocations are used with specific 'intent' or focus:

M. Eman says, "Sisters, we're going to have special prayer for our sisters in Palestine and Iraq.

She starts and the women join in:

O Living and Eternal One, in your mercy we seek your help

(يا حي ويا قيوم برحمتك نستغيث).

The phrase is repeated a number of times, followed by other phrases such as:

O God, help us, O Helper of those who call for help

(أغثنا يا غياث المستغيثين)

God has considered us, and blessed is the deputy

(حسبنا الله ونعم الوكيل)

This phrase is also repeated a number of times, and the last utterance is a lengthened final word, with a rise and then quick drop in pitch at the end of the word.

God

(الله)

There is no god but You, praise to You. For I was among the unjust, and You are the most merciful of the merciful.

(لا اله إلا أنت يا سبحانك أني كنت من الظالمين وأنت أرحم الرحمين)

O most Merciful of the merciful, have mercy on us.

(يا أرحم الرحمين أرحمنا)

O God, to you is our petition.

(اللهم إليك دعائنا)

For we have not depended (on anyone) other than You

(فلا تكلنا إلى سواك)

O God, requite for us our master Muhammad the Apostle of God

(اللهم أجزي عنا سيدنا محمد رسول الله)

Be pleased with us and purify our hearts

(يرضيك عنا وأطهر قلوبنا)

Your love, O God, purifies our hearts. Who is equal to you or makes beloved like you.

(حبك اللهم طهر قلوبنا من سواك ولا تجعل محبوباً سواك)

The Fatiha ...

And praise to God, Lord of all that exists

(والحمد لله رب العالمين)

In these petitions, God is named as *Living, Eternal, Merciful, to be Praised*. Sometimes His characteristics are doubly invoked, perhaps as if to add spiritual force even as the meaning is intensified grammatically by doubling: He is *Helper of those who call for help, Most Merciful of the merciful*; and appealed to: *If You don't give, who will give?*, and *No one pardons except You*.

He is asked to *purify* (us from our sins and trespasses, our hearts), to *reveal* (our concerns), to *heal* (our bodies, hearts from superstition, our land, our society), to *pardon*, to *have mercy* (on us, on Muhammad, on all Muslims), to *give relief* (to oppressed

Muslims), to *unite* (our ranks), to *keep others from having power* (over us in our sins) and to *keep* (evil and rebellious people) *from us*. The petitioners who *seek God's help* have *their strength weakened*, and were *among the unjust*; but God is Most Merciful. His revealed characteristics are the basis for petitioning for His intervention in the lives of the weak, sinful and needy.

The time of *dhikr* and *du'a'* is usually concluded by reciting the *Fatiha*. Some (often older) women may wipe their faces when they have murmured the *Fatiha* or another phrase of invocation into their open hands. M. Eman explained the practice:

> The wiping is blessing (*baraka*), it illuminates the face, and this also is not essential and so we don't wipe our faces in *salat* and this is not essential, it's for blessing, nothing more. ... In the recollection (*dhikr*) of God this could bring healing. Of course this healing is conditional on using *du'a'*."

The act of reciting the characteristics of God enables the pray-er both to face her context with confidence that God will act, and at the same time is seen as a means of bringing His blessing or power to bear on the situation through the act of invocation. "And the *dhikr* is accountability for the person, and forgiveness of sins." The blessing *(baraka)* released through *dhikr* is effective for healing, forgiveness of sins, success in business ventures. Thus the recollection (*dhikr*) enables the object of the supplication (*du'a'*).

Enactment of *salat* and the rest of five pillars entails punishment if they are neglected, and recompense, or merits received, if they are performed satisfactorily. Thus (while some of the pillars such as the pilgrimage can bestow forgiveness of sins) through the allocation of merits, they form a primary part of Divine accounting towards the afterlife and entry into paradise. But it is through popular devotion in *dhikr* and *du'a'* that people are able to access divine power now in their daily lives – both in gaining strength to cope through the affirmation of God's sovereignty and mercy, and also in more direct power for healing, blessing and success. Women, through these forms of devotion, can gain access to God at any time, untrammelled by the restrictions of purity and dress attached to the required forms of *salat*. For both recollection and supplication, while the conventions of purity and dress are preferable, they are not necessary. For *dhikr,* "the ablutions are preferred. It's not prescribed, but it's preferable to be clean, having done ablutions." But these forms of worship are possible for women at any time. "The menstruating woman can do *dhikr*, can make supplications (*du'a'*)." Similarly the rules of dress are less binding: a woman can remove her coat if the mosque room is hot, during the *dhikr*, but she dons it again to join in the *salat*. In *salat* set words are prescribed: in *dhikr* and *du'a'* at the mosque there are commonly-used phrases learned and repeated, but the worshipper's expression is not limited only to these. Someone doing *dhikr* at home "can feel more reverence by himself, and is able to say what he wants and supplicate (*du'a'*) as he pleases, if he wants to call out or cry out, or whatever is appropriate with God according to his situation, he can do so." So *dhikr* and *du'a'* enable women, whatever their context of ritual purity, to access God's power and blessing for their daily family needs.

> Wherever women are marginalized in the orthodox tradition and barred from the sacred precincts, their spiritual needs and their need for community are channelled into ritual performances they *can* do, and what they can do is often done in response to needs in their personal lives. (Doumato, 2000:38)

Women's needs - responsibilities in life and faith

In the Middle East generally, men occupy the official religious space. They have primacy of space in the mosque; they stand in the *minbars* of the mosques (and pulpits of churches); they officiate at religious and legal ceremonies, teach the meaning of the sacred writings, and pass on the official interpretations of faith and religious life. But Middle Eastern women are in a different place. They are immersed in all the grounded, messy parts of daily life, carrying out the duties that can make one unclean and not able to participate in the mandated religious activities, responsible to keep ordinary family life going at all the times of crisis or passage.

At the consummation of marriage, it is the mother of the bride who visits the couple next morning. At birth, women are in attendance. It is women who carry out the messy business of changing babies – men can't do it, because it would mean they would be unclean and have to purify themselves again in order to carry out the ritual prayer. Women fit in ritual prayer as they are able around their duties. It is through imitation of their mothers in the homes that toddlers learn the practices of prayer and piety. When Muslim women have their monthly period, the cyclical preparation of the body for new life, they are unable to participate in ritual prayer, fasting, or reading/holding the Qur'an. Similarly Christian Orthodox (and some Protestant) women will not take communion at that time, as they are unclean to approach the sacred elements. And at death, it is women who are there washing the body and preparing it for burial.

The Qur'an makes the witness of two women equal to the witness of one man (Surat Al-Baqarah, 2:282). But there are also situations when the word of one woman is equal to a man, enough for a verdict: and nearly all those cases relate to the rites of passage of life. M.Eman detailed them for me:

- One woman is sufficient to testify to a birth.
- If a woman breastfeeds a child, she stands in a mother relationship to it, and this will guide future decisions about marriage (in other words, the child of the wet nurse stands in a sibling relation to the breastfed child, and may not be eligible as marriage partner). The witness of one woman that she has seen the other woman breastfeeding the child is enough.
- If a man claims that his new wife has 'shame' in her when he takes her, the witness of one woman examining her is enough to verify his claim; and in examining for a girl's virginity, the witness of one woman is enough.
- The witness of four people, whether men or women, is necessary to prove adultery.[12]
- And in sighting the new moon for the beginning and end of the fasting month of Ramadan, the word of one man or one woman is sufficient.

It is women who are involved at all the rites of passage that ensure the continuation of life patterns from inception to end. So, beyond personal piety, they use *dhikr* and *du'a'* to bring blessing into the

---

[12] The Shi'ite reading is apparently different. Iranian law (Qisan Bill 1982, Article 91) specifies that adultery is proved through four just men, or three just men and two just women, ... and so on.

domains of life where as women they carry particular responsibility – family needs, daily health, rites of passage.

Emotions

However these practices are not only mechanical means of accessing Divine blessing for life. People can be deeply emotionally engaged. I commonly see people weeping quietly, or murmuring 'O Lord' with a choked voice, sniffing, during both *dhikr* and *du'a'*. This is especially but not exclusively, so during Ramadan; and television coverage of the Pilgrimage shows crowds, both men and women, in tears during the times of corporate worship. While M. Eman is careful to clarify that a show of emotion doesn't guarantee its veracity, she explains the importance of tears:

> A tradition of the Prophet (pbuh) says 'God will not torture the eyes that weep from awe of God'. For God will not make the person enter the fire who weeps from reverence of God. Therefore the person who, when he contemplates the greatness of God and his weakness, and contemplates the mercy of God and his sins and stubbornness, and so suffers because of his sins and his littleness with God, will weep.

Another friend explained the benefit of tears in terms of a cleansing or cathartic effect. She preferred to go to a particular mosque for the suhur (سحور) prayers (between midnight and the pre-dawn meal) during Ramadan, where the sheikh was especially popular because of his emotive voice.

A young woman told me about her experience in the Night of Vigil of Ramadan. She explained how people attend the *tarawih* prayers,

> and then there is 'staying up in the night' (قيام الليل). They end with prayers an hour before sunrise (الفجر) - about 3-4.30 a.m. It is about reverence and tears. God comes down to the first heaven and answers prayers. It's solitude (خلوة), you and God alone. You feel as if you're flying, pray until tears come, it's a strange feeling, tears come suddenly. You pray to God, feel with everyone, love everyone, feel soft, forget your worries; and what I feel at night, I try to follow in the day, as I am able.

Conclusion

Taken together, the analysis of these different forms of devotion, as practiced in the women's programme in a Middle Eastern Sunni mosque, give us a richer picture of the devotional life of Muslim women. As such it provides a more adequate base for engaging with Muslims. As we understand more of their prayer experience towards God, we may more adequately find the place of meeting, of shared longing or understanding, as we seek to understand more fully with them the nature of God and how we come to Him.

Bibliography

Qur'anic references taken from *Translation of the meanings of the Noble Qur'an*, by Dr. Muhammad Taqi-ud-Din al-Hilali, and Dr. Muhammad Muhsin Khan. King Fahd Complex for the Printing of the Holy Qur'an. Madinah, Kingdom of Saudi Arabia.

Bayoumy, Yara (2006) *Women Preachers.* Reuters: Cairo. Mon Jun 26, 11:38 PM ET

Cragg, Kenneth (1956, 2nd ed. 1985) *The Call of the Minaret.* Collins: London.

Doumato, Eleanor Abdella (2000) *Getting God's Ear. Women, Islam, and Healing in Saudi Arabia and the Gulf.* Columbia University Press: New York.

Khattab, Huda (1993, 1994) *The Muslim Woman's Handbook.* Ta-Ha Publishers: London.

Mujahid, Abdul Malik (ed) (2000) *Prayer for Beginners.* Darussalam Publishing House: Riyadh.

Padwick, Constance (1961) *Muslim Devotions.* SPCK: London

Philips, Abu Ameenah Bilal (1995) *Islamic Rules on Menstruation and Post-Natal Bleeding (Revised Ed.)* A.S.Noordeen: Kuala Lumpur

Saqib, Muhammad Abdul Karim (1997) *A Guide To Salat (Prayer).* Riyadh: Darussalam

http://www.islamonline.net/english/introducingislam/Worship/Heart/article03.shtml Accessed 25 March 2008

http://muslim-canada.org/salaat.html Accessed 27 March 2008

http://www.sunna.info/prayer/TheBasicsoftheMuslimsPrayer.php #Introduction Accessed 27 March 2008

http://www.sunnah.org/ibadaat/dhikrtable.htm Accessed 25 March 2008

Notes for Contributors

Submission requirements:

Manuscript

- Papers should not exceed 5000 words, although the Editor retains the discretion to publish papers beyond this length.
- It is preferable that submissions be prepared in Microsoft Word format.
- All papers are to be written in English, and an English transliteration given to any quotations or short phrases in original language.
- Authors are advised to use gender inclusive and non-discriminatory language.
- Any visuals should be integrated into the document, or sent separately as separate jpg or gif files with an explanation as to their position in the paper.
- Footnotes and bibliography should follow the style used in previous issues of this Occasional Paper series.

Submission

- Papers to be considered for inclusion are to be submitted directly to the Editor.
- Submissions are to be forwarded via electronic mail to csiof@mst.edu.au. If submitting within Australia, a hard copy must also be posted to the CSIOF, 5 Burwood Highway, Wantirna Vic 3152.
- A declaration that the submitted articles are your own work and that you've acknowledged the work/s of others used in the articles in the references, etc. must be included with any submission.
- A covering letter that includes the authors' names, titles, affiliations, with complete mailing addresses, including email,

telephone and facsimile numbers should be attached to the paper.

Review of submissions
- All submissions will be sent to referees for anonymous recommendation.
- The Editor holds the right to make editorial corrections to accepted submissions.

Copyright:

The CSIOF Occasional Papers series is published by the Melbourne School of Theology. The copyright for any published papers will remain with the author. MST publishes these papers on the following conditions:

- They do not appear elsewhere (including web pages) for 180 days from the date of publication in the CSIOF Occasional Papers series.
- Whenever they are printed elsewhere (including web pages), the following notice will be included: "This article first appeared in the __ issue of the CSIOF Occasional Papers series".
- We retain the right to use the paper in any CSIOF publications, reprints, or in electronic form (ie. Online, CD-Rom, etc.).
- We retain the right to use a portion or description of the paper with your name in our promotional material.
- Authors are themselves responsible for obtaining permission to reproduce copyright material from other sources.
- The author will be presented with two copies of the publication.

www.ingramcontent.com/pod-product-compliance
Lightning Source LLC
Chambersburg PA
CBHW050636300426
44112CB00012B/1815